THE POLITICS OF TRADE

CYNTHIA A. HODY

The Politics of Trade

AMERICAN POLITICAL
DEVELOPMENT AND FOREIGN
ECONOMIC POLICY

DARTMOUTH COLLEGE

Published by University Press of New England / Hanover and London

Dartmouth College
Published by University Press of New England, Hanover, NH 03755
© 1996 by the Trustees of Dartmouth College
Printed in the United States of America   5   4   3   2   1
CIP data appear at the end of the book

To

JOHN

And in memory of

ROBBY

CONTENTS

In the last decade of the twentieth century, as the global community faces a growing array of complex and interrelated social problems, public policymakers increasingly will turn to scholars and practitioners for guidance. To chronicle and disseminate the substance of the compelling discussions that will result, the Nelson A. Rockefeller Center for the Social Sciences at Dartmouth College, in collaboration with University Press of New England, has inaugurated this series of books.

Rockefeller Series books will be disparate in content but united in a common approach: presenting ways in which social scientific expertise is brought to bear on public policy issues of current or historic importance. The specific topics addressed will be as diverse as were the interests and work of U.S. Vice-President Nelson A. Rockefeller, which included state and local government, the environment, Third World economic development, publicly funded art, racism and intergroup conflict, and the functioning of communities. Authors will assess historical or existing policies, as well as the need for new or adjusted policies, in a search for viable solutions to pressing social, political, and economic problems.

The Rockefeller Series draws upon two sources for its books, the annual Nelson A. Rockefeller Monograph Competition, and works generated from Rockefeller Center research programs or Center-sponsored conferences. Included in the latter are scholarly works originating in one or more of the eight social science departments associated with the Center.

The overriding goal of the Nelson A. Rockefeller Series is to stimulate academics, policymakers, practitioners, and the public to think about and understand societal processes and the public policy implications associated with them. It is our fondest hope that these volumes will promulgate innovative and useful ideas, for as P. W. Bridgman notes, "There is no adequate defense, except stupidity, against the impact of a new idea."

George J. Demko, Director of the Rockefeller Center

This book examines how the institutional arrangements for American trade policy-making were changed during the first half of the twentieth century, and it considers the implications of these changes for international economic cooperation. By illuminating patterns of institutional development, it provides a context for understanding the range and limits of these arrangements as policymakers explore options for the next century.

The study begins with a puzzle. The United States became an industrial powerhouse and a dominant actor in the world economy during the late nineteenth and early twentieth centuries. Its economic transformation unquestionably altered the relationship between domestic interests and the world economy. However, the policy that mediated this relationship—U.S. foreign economic policy—remained essentially unchanged. Throughout the period, American policy was unalterably protectionist. In response to severe economic downturns and a persistent problem with revenue surpluses, American policymakers made repeated attempts to adjust U.S. policy in order to address these problems. These attempts failed because the policy problem was rooted in the political process. New policies demand new politics.

This study analyzes the process of institutional change that was the necessary precursor to policy change. Its analytic framework facilitates examination of the efforts of policymakers to recast policy processes (understood as longstanding patterns of interorganizational relations) in order to pursue previously elusive policy goals. It combines a substantive focus—international trade and U.S. trade policy—relevant to international political economy with a dynamic approach to the study of institutional change inspired by work on American political development. Thus by focusing on and examining the patterns of institutional relations that defined the American trade policy process over time, this analysis not only helps to explain the how and why of contemporary U.S. trade policy, but it also helps account for the nature of international economic cooperation in the postwar period.

I am grateful to a number of people who helped me tremendously in writing this book. I express my heartfelt thanks to Arthur Stein, John Munro, Stephen Krasner, Carol Barner-Barry, Stephen Skowronek, Ronald Rogowski, Mary Wharmby, and Mary Yeager, who commented generously and thoughtfully on the manuscript at various stages of its preparation. Susan Seitz, David Shetterly, and Mary Wharmby provided reliable research assistance. Maria Laude, Michael Romary, and Anna Soderberg of the reference staff at the Albin O. Kuhn Library at the University of Maryland, Baltimore County, amiably helped me chase down obscure sources.

Most important of all, I am grateful for the love and support of my family as I endeavored to complete this project. My husband, John Munro, read numerous drafts of the manuscript. He gave me excellent advice about revisions and was always there to push me forward when I grew discouraged or overwhelmed. My children, Joey and Amelia Munro, exhibited patience and understanding as they anticipated the day that "Mom finished her book" and could spend more time with them (at least until the next project).

Columbia, Maryland   C. A. H.
March 1995

PART I

INSTITUTIONAL CHANGE AND U.S. TRADE POLICY

It has been conclusively shown by experiments repeated again and again, that the methods of tariff making by Congress, which have now obtained for so many years, cannot, from the very nature of the case, bring really satisfactory results. . . . [The people] know that the system on which [the current tariff] was made, the same system on which its predecessors were made, encourages a scramble of selfish interests, to which the all-important general interest of the public is necessarily more or less subordinated. . . . Very little improvement, indeed, will follow any attempt to revise the tariff by methods hitherto used. The thing to do is to change the methods.
—THEODORE ROOSEVELT, *The New Nationalism*, 1910

CHAPTER ONE

Introduction:
Institutional Impediments to
Trade Liberalization

Today, as the twenty-first century approaches, the United States is at a crossroads. The era of cold war is over and, by most accounts, so too is the era of America's global economic hegemony. With its twin deficits (budget and trade), enormous debt, and dwindling manufacturing base, the United States presents almost a mirror image of itself a hundred years ago. Today, as it was then, the challenge is to rethink policy and retool government in order to advance American economic interests in a dynamic world economy. This study aims to place the contemporary policy-making challenges and policy choices into historical and analytical context by focusing on the earlier era. Understanding the policy-making transformation that marked the early decades of this century can serve to inform the efforts of those now embarking on a similar quest of transformation.

The United States became an industrial giant and the dominant power in the world economy during the last decades of the nineteenth century. This economic metamorphosis necessarily altered the relationship between domestic interests and the world economy. Yet the policy that mediated this relationship—U.S. commercial policy—remained fundamentally unchanged. Throughout the nineteenth century, tariffs (taxes on imports) were the primary instrument of both commercial and fiscal policy in the United States, and the most salient characteristic of the policy process that produced tariffs was Congressional logrolling. As a result, American commercial policy of the post–Civil War period was highly protectionist (sometimes by design but, with increasing frequency, by default).

Beginning in the late nineteenth century, people in and out of government started to recognize the incongruity between commercial policy and economic reality. How could a policy, perhaps defensible for a nation-state entering industrialization, remain appropriate for a state with the largest and most developed economy in the world? In response to severe cyclical downturns in the economy and a persistent problem with revenue surplus, American policymakers made repeated attempts to adjust tariff policy in order to promote overseas trade expansion and eliminate the troublesome revenue surpluses. These attempts failed. By the first decades of the twentieth century, a growing number of prominent Americans began to realize that the policy problem was rooted in the policy process—that is, the process had to change before the policy could. Still, the resolution of the commercial/trade policy problem took years, and tremendous consequences, including the collapse of world trade in the 1930s, resulted from this lag.

New policies demand new politics. This is a point that has renewed salience as leaders and analysts debate policy options for the twenty-first century, but it is one that contemporary critics of the policy status quo habitually miss. Political institutions have to change, and new patterns of institutional relations have to be established, in order for alternative policies to emerge. This study examines how the institutional arrangements for trade policy were changed during the first half of the twentieth century. It then considers the implications for policy and, consequently, for international relations that followed from these changes. Finally, it provides a context for understanding the range and limits of these institutional arrangements as policymakers explore options for the next century.

Institutions, Public Policy, and the Commercial Policy-Making Dilemma in the United States

Institutions are established norms, practices, relationships, or organizations that pattern behavior and delimit options. They embody and perpetuate fundamental social values. Governmental institutions facilitate collective action by providing a mode for reaching agreement on allocative decisions. Thus, institutions mediate interests, but the impact on policy outcomes of this mediation is never value-neutral. Institutional arrangements are not simply conduits of societal interests, and policy is not simply a reflection of the stated preferences of a dominant coalition. Institutions and the policy processes they engender set a range of possible policy options through which societal interests are inevitably filtered.

Over time, new economic and demographic realities can make the policy repertoire of existing institutional arrangements inappropriate and obsolete. Changing the repertoire necessitates changing the institutions. However, institutional change is situational, driven by changing conditions and constrained by existing institutional arrangements as well as by policymakers' conceptions of the problems they confront and their cognitive frameworks for dealing with them. In the American case, the difficulties of achieving institutional change are compounded by a written Constitution that defines the limits of institutional reform and, thereby, the universe of possible policy options.

The Founders' intent was to structure a government based on the principles of majority rule and the protection of minority rights. The sovereign people and their interests were to be represented in government by individuals selected from territorially based districts and states. Elected officials would represent the majority interests of their districts, but these interests could not predominate over interests represented by other officials (Madison, [1788] 1981, pp. 320–25). The Founders designed a government largely incapable of choosing among interests. They wanted a government that would act (when it acted) in the interest of all, that would, in other words, generate the public good: "In the extended republic of the United States, and among the great variety of interests, parties, and states which it embraces, a coalition of a majority of the whole society could seldom take place on any other principles than those of justice and the public good" (Madison, [1788] 1981, p. 325). In practice, however, because it was next to impossible for policymakers to choose among interests, logrolling became the norm.

Logrolling is bargaining between legislators, who exchange promises of support. Logrolling permits all interests to win and is the best one can expect from a government that has difficulty choosing among interests (i.e., either everyone wins or everyone loses). Logrolling produces a policy that provides specific and immediate benefits to numerous discrete interests. The costs of such a policy are diffuse and remote (Lowi, 1964).[1]

During the late nineteenth century, Congress enacted numerous tariffs, because in most cases there was no opposition to them. Interestingly, where groups did oppose certain tariffs, tariff rates showed some flexibility (Tarbell, 1911; Ratner, 1972). Opposition groups, however, generally failed to emerge. The different rewards offered by higher and lower tariffs explain this phenomenon. A low tariff (i.e., freer trade) is like a collective good. As consumers, everyone would benefit from the reduced prices freer trade offers. But because the collective good of free trade cannot be denied to those who fail to lobby on its behalf (and because the costs of protection—i.e., higher prices on protected products—are dispersed), no groups materialize to pursue it. (Importers of intermediate goods are notable exceptions. For them, lower tariffs offer selective benefits, i.e., lower production costs.) In contrast, tariffs offer selective benefits to discrete groups of producers. They may, for example, allow higher profit

---

1. Theodore J. Lowi calls this distributive policy.

margins to the producers who succeed in securing a tariff. Therefore, numerous small and geographically concentrated groups emerge to pressure for higher tariffs, while few groups are likely to push for lower ones (Olson, 1965).[2] The structural predisposition of Congress to logroll, coupled with the nature of the issue and the resultant interest group pressure, inevitably produced a policy consisting of numerous specific and ad valorem tariffs—tariffs high enough to choke off any significant foreign competition.

Dissatisfaction with American commercial policy grew in response to a succession of economic downturns that marked the last quarter of the nineteenth century. Surplus productive capacity, first in agriculture (1870s) and later in manufacturing (1890s), was the popular explanation for America's economic woes, and the expansion of foreign trade was widely accepted as the best way to eliminate the surpluses (Terrill, 1973). However, American political institutions could not accommodate a policy designed to promote overseas trade. Such a policy usually involved concluding agreements with trading partners that resulted in mutual tariff concessions. In other words, a trade policy where all interests obtain tariffs was no longer appropriate. The United States needed a policy of trade liberalization that would allow officials to choose among interests and determine who would get tariffs and who would not.[3] This goal eluded Congressional policymakers. In fact, by the late nineteenth century, "Congress demonstrated an inability to develop an economic perspective commensurate with the analytic task at hand" (Edwards, 1970, p. 837).

At the turn of the century it was clear to progressives of both political parties that America's existing institutional arrangements could not produce commercial policies appropriate for the United States. The range of commercial policy options afforded by the existing pattern of institutional relations was very narrow. It produced only indiscriminately protectionist policies because all groups shared equal access to the policy-making process, and they all wanted the same thing—high tariffs. The pattern of institutional relations that defined the American trade policy process made it impossible for officials to discriminate among interests and pursue a more liberal trade policy.

Madison's constitutional design of separate institutions sharing powers was intended to protect the sovereign people from arbitrary government. The purest possible expression of the public will was to result from its

2. Geographically dispersed producers are unlikely to organize to pursue protection for the same reasons that prevent consumers from organizing for trade liberalization. Under such circumstances protection can be viewed as a collective good (Pincus, 1977, pp. 143–57).
    3. Lowi (1964) calls this regulatory policy.

several forms of popular representation (Wood, 1969, pp. 519–64). Madison did not foresee the possibility that logrolling and pork barrel policies could come to characterize policy-making on certain issues. He also did not anticipate the need to control, restrict, or otherwise manage interest group access to the policy process because he did not foresee that such access would lend itself to logrolling. Everyone who wanted something (e.g., a tariff) got it.

Over the years, the United States achieved trade liberalization. This achievement was made possible by institutional change—change that altered the pattern of institutional relations in trade policy-making and thus muted the impact of pressure from particularistic interests.

Institutional Change: Necessary Component for the Transformation of American Foreign Economic Policy

The importance of institutional change to the adoption of liberal trade policies is best demonstrated by considering it in the context of other explanations for the switch from protectionism. These explanations include structural or neorealist approaches to the study of foreign economic policy and arguments about the relevance for policy of domestic interests and the political coalitions they form. The point is not to dismiss these explanations but to show that each offers an incomplete interpretation of American trade policy. In other words, without institutional change, neither the imperatives of global economic hegemony nor the impact of social interests and their societal coalitions could ever have been manifest in policy.

Scholars who subscribe to structural approaches maintain that a state's trade policy is determined by its power relative to other states in the international system. States with a preponderance of economic power relative to others pursue liberal trade policies and favor an open world economic order. Less powerful states tend to prefer protectionist over liberal trade policies (Krasner, 1976, Lake, 1988, Greco, 1990). According to what became known as hegemonic stability theory, the United States advocated liberalism and an open international economic order in the post–World War II period (as Great Britain had in the nineteenth century) because as global economic hegemon it was in its economic and security interests to do so (Keohane, 1980).

A noted weakness of the structural explanations for international trade is the lag between the achievement of hegemony and the establishment of an open (or liberal) trade structure. The American case demonstrates this point well. The United States emerged from World War I the preeminent economic power, yet its commercial policies did not begin to veer away from protectionism until 1934, and they were not truly "liberal" until the Trade Expansion Act of 1962.[4] Since an open trading structure is contingent in part upon the policies adopted by the hegemon, the lag phenomenon must to some extent be rooted in the domestic political situation of the hegemon: "[E]arlier policies in the United States beget social structures and institutional arrangements that trammelled state policy. After protecting import competing industries for a century, the United States was unable in the 1920's to opt for more open policies, even though state interests would have been furthered thereby" (Krasner, 1976, p. 342).

However, even if the economic hegemon unilaterally adopts a policy of free trade, a liberal economic order will not emerge without trade agreements between countries. In order to adopt the role of leader in the world economy and to promote the creation of a liberal economic order, the United States needed a trade policy process that could not only produce lower tariff rates but could also accommodate the negotiation and enactment of bilateral and/or multilateral trade agreements. Such agreements are central to the emergence of a liberal trade order, for, contrary to the contentions of some hegemonic stability theorists, the hegemon cannot force countries to lower their barriers to trade (Stein, 1984). The American trade policy of the late nineteenth and early twentieth centuries failed on both counts.

According to Alexander Gerschenkron (1943), James Kurth (1979), Peter Gourevitch (1984), and Helen Milner (1988), among others, coalition formation among societal actors who derive their interests from the world economy or from the international division of labor determines a country's foreign economic policies. Proponents of this explanation note that countries with different regime types have historically adopted similar policies when economic groups in those countries share similar interests and when their pattern of coalition formation is the same. Likewise, states with similar political structures will adopt different policies if societal actors in both states either do not share the same interests vis-à-vis the world economy or their configuration of coalition formation is not the same. The societal argument may include the institutional arrangements for policy-making as an intervening variable in the analysis, but the causal impact of these arrangements on policy outcomes is considered minimal.

---

4. Hegemonic stability theorists have used several types of measures to confirm a hegemonic distribution of power in the international system. Stephen Krasner (1976), for example, operationalizes political economic power in terms of the relative size and level of economic development of the state. David Lake (1988) considers productivity (also a measure of economic development) and proportion of world trade. By Lake's measures, the United States did not achieve hegemony until the post–World War II period.

For the American case, Gourevitch (1984) maintains that the societal coalitions formed by the two major political parties and the policy position advocated by the winning coalition in succeeding elections explain trade policy over time: "American history notes 'Gold Democrats,' free-trade-oriented merchants and bankers pushed toward the Democratic Party in opposition to their protectionist brethren in the Republican Party" (p. 97). Coalition formation, however, registered little impact on trade policy in nineteenth-century America. In fact, the politics of trade in the United States prevented the articulated policy goals of party coalitions from becoming law:

It has not . . . been a sudden conviction of sin in voting for a particular policy which has so often turned a repentant electorate against the party entrusted with the mandate to make that policy effective. Rather it has been the failure of the party, a failure repeated by both great national parties, to enact a tariff the duties in which conformed equitably and without glaring exceptions to the policy which the electorate had intended to establish. (Page, 1924, p. 2)

The motif of Republicans raising tariffs and Democrats lowering them is a chimera for the analyst seeking an explanation for the politics of American trade. The Republicans achieved higher duties by relying on logrolling. However, the weakness of the societal coalition argument is best demonstrated by the Republicans' poor record in the ratification of trade treaties negotiated under the provisions of the Dingly Act of 1897. Moreover, when the Republican party platform advocated a downward revision in tariff rates in 1908, the party could not deliver. The result was the much criticized Payne-Aldrich Act of 1909, which failed to lower tariff rates.

Likewise, the Democrats, with majorities in both houses of Congress and with one of their own in the White House, never really achieved their stated policy goals: "tariff for revenue only" and "free raw materials." The 1846 Tariff Act, lauded by the Democrats as an application of free-trade principles, was in reality a moderation in the application of protection. The same could be said about the Wilson-Gorman Act of 1894. Reform advocates in the Democratic party, including President Grover Cleveland, could not compel party support to secure their policy goals.

Societal interests formed party coalitions, and these coalitions articulated trade policy goals, but in the nineteenth and early twentieth centuries the institutional arrangements for trade policy-making largely determined policy outcomes. These arrangements had to be changed before the policy could be.

Some might argue that the triumph of free-trade principles in the United States during the 1930s and 1940s accounts for the subsequent adoption by the United States of liberal trade policies. This argument has also been made to account for the rise of free trade in nineteenth-century Europe (Kindleberger, 1975). According to this position, the flagrant use of protectionist policies during the Great Depression and the division of the world into trading blocs during this period worked to discredit protectionism. In the aftermath of World War II, free trade became associated with peace and freedom. A sizable majority of American policymakers jumped on the free-trade bandwagon and have remained there (more or less) ever since. This purportedly explains the initial emergence of liberal trade policies in the United States and America's long-standing commitment to liberal policies despite changes in the distribution of global economic power.

A fundamental transformation from support of protectionist principles to support of trade liberalization did occur, and the importance of this transformation should not be underestimated. Indeed, the gradual abandonment of protectionist policy is due in significant part to the vigilant efforts of avowed advocates of free trade among policymakers of the legislative and executive branches of government. However, this does not mean that analysts can assume an automatic translation of ideas into policy. The historical record precludes the acceptance of any such assumption. In the nineteenth century, Britain's retreat from highly protectionist policies took decades. A commitment to the principle of free trade was not reflected in policy until the British state developed the administrative capacity to secure its revenue from a source other than customs revenue (Stein, 1984, pp. 360–83).

In the American case, the triumph of free trade in principle during the 1930s and 1940s was neither complete nor absolute and was only slowly manifested in policy. It could not guarantee the establishment of the International Trade Organization (ITO) in 1947, and it could not prevent American-sponsored limitations to free trade from becoming part of the General Agreement on Tariffs and Trade (GATT) (viz., Article 19, the escape clause provision). In fact, the United States did not produce truly liberal trade legislation until 1962. (Between 1934 and 1962, all reductions in tariff rates were authorized as amendments to the Smoot-Hawley Act of 1930.) And even in 1962, the triumph of free-trade principles in policy was far from complete. In fact, trade policy continued to exhibit vestiges of protectionist ideas that had been popularized decades earlier (Goldstein, 1993).

Something about how political institutions operate informs (circumscribes and inhibits) the translation of ideas into policy. The nature and dynamics of the nineteenth-century trade policy process precluded the pursuit of policies based on free-trade principles. Political institutions in

the United States afford ready access to numerous interests. With regard
to nineteenth-century trade policy-making, this meant that any industry
that demanded protection from imports got protection. It was, in other
words, a policy process that could and did give full vent to a wide range
of protectionist ideas. Thus, in the context of the nineteenth-century trade
policy process, achieving policy in line with free-trade principles would
have necessitated a widespread, if not universal, practical commitment
to free trade. Such a commitment did not materialize. For advocates of
industries protected from import competition, support for free trade (to
the extent it existed at all) was support in theory only. In practice, they
defended protectionism. Without institutional change, policymakers who
endorsed free-trade principles could never have implemented a policy
reflecting their free-trade position.

Popular explanations for the emergence of liberal trade policy in the
United States (and the establishment of a liberal economic order) tend to
give insufficient weight to the impact that political institutions make on
policy. Without an institutional focus, they cannot explain the time lag
between the emergence of the United States as economic hegemon (or
the formation of societal coalitions advocating trade liberalization or the
increased salience of free-trade principles among policymakers) and the
enactment of liberal trade legislation.

Institutional change, therefore, is an essential component of any explanation of twentieth-century U.S. trade policy. However, organizational
procedures and patterned role relationships within or among institutions
generally do not change spontaneously; there must be some impetus (or
more likely, some combination of impetuses)—for example, a new distribution of economic power among states, the emergence of different
societal coalitions, innovative ideas reflecting awareness of altered situations—to spur such change. Nevertheless, new distributions of economic
power or new coalitions of societal interests will not result in a more liberal trade policy (and, by extension, will not result in a more open global
economy) if the existing institutional configuration cannot support such
a policy. But simply stating that an understanding of institutional change
is essential for explaining U.S. trade policy tends to belie the complexity
of the causal dynamic at work. This complexity stems from the nature of
institutional change itself.

It is a relatively straightforward causal proposition to assert that the
policy processes of institutions yield policy outcomes; if these processes
change, their policy products change. In this statement there is an independent variable and a dependent variable. The causal dynamic becomes more complex if we ask, "What induces institutional change, which
in turn produces new policy outcomes?" Viewed this way, institutional

change becomes an intervening variable. We can add further complexity by noting that sometimes, despite plenty of inducements, institutions do not change, so neither do their policy outcomes. Under these circumstances, institutional change (or more specifically the lack thereof) becomes a constraining variable. The fact of the matter is that, depending on the circumstance, institutional change can be viewed as an independent, an intervening, or a constraining variable in the analysis of American trade policy.

This analysis explores the various facets of the causal dynamic linking institutional change (as well as what induces and impedes it) to trade policy liberalization in the United States and the creation of a liberal world economic order in the post–World War II era. When the focus of analysis is on policymakers endorsing and pursuing an alternative policy-making process in order to achieve what they deem an appropriate policy response in the face of new economic or political realities, institutional change is treated much like an intervening variable. Viewed as intervening variable, institutional change shapes the policy responses brought on by the independent variable or variables, but that there will be a response is not seriously questioned. Thus, viewing institutional change exclusively as an intervening variable, it seems inevitable that such change will occur.

As the trade policy-making history of the United States demonstrates, any presumption about the inevitability of institutional change is both misguided and misleading. Because policymakers of the early twentieth century variously interpreted the trade policy-making challenges they confronted, they endorsed and pursued a variety of different policy-making solutions, sometimes simultaneously, in a setting of existing organizational interrelationships. In such a context, proposed alternatives to existing policy-making processes are seldom, if ever, adopted whole-cloth even under the most propitious circumstances. Not infrequently, detractors of policy-making reform co-opt the ideas of reform advocates for their own purposes. Sometimes, policy-making alternatives are discredited because of the way they are administered, and sometimes the institutionalized policy-making reform comes to reinforce rather than to replace the existing policy-making process. In each of these situations (all of which pertain, to one degree or another, to American trade policy-making history), the setting of organizational interrelationships and the process of institutional change serve to constrain policy outcomes, and therefore, for purposes of policy analysis under such circumstances, the process of institutional change should be viewed as a constraining variable.

Since the process of institutional change cannot be fit into a rigid causal framework without obscuring and distorting the process itself, in this study institutional change is treated both as intervening and constraining variable in the analysis of twentieth-century U.S. trade policy. It is also treated, where appropriate, as independent variable. To explain the nature of the post–World War II international trade regime, for example, one needs to look no further than the scope and limitations of the American trade policy process—the product of institutional change. For this aspect of the study, institutional change is most usefully viewed as independent variable to explain the emergence of the liberal trade order. Thus freed from the confines of a narrowly construed causal framework, the challenge of this study—to capture the role that institutional change plays in accounting for twentieth-century U.S. trade policy—can be more fully realized.

Institutional Change and American Political Development: Studying the Transformation of the Trade Policy Process

The chapters that follow analyze the patterns of institutional relations that defined the American trade policy process over time. They analyze the cumulative impact of succeeding attempts to reform the commercial policy process, which ultimately resulted in institutional change; a wholly new policy process emerged. They also analyze the impact that institutional change had on policy and consequently on international economic relations.

At the most general level, the chapters consider the extent to which reform attempts permitted the formulation of policy that increased the level of U.S. involvement in the world economy (liberalization).[5] The chapters discuss why certain reforms "worked" in the achievement of trade liberalization and why others did not. They also highlight the international ramifications of America's trade policy. Finally, the chapters contribute to a broader understanding of the relationship between institutions and their policy products.

Each substantive chapter first examines how American officials assessed the trade policy problem. The point is to analyze how widely American trade policy problems were recognized, how they were interpreted, and what proposals were made to correct them. Second, the results of each reform attempt are evaluated. Such evaluation facilitates an analysis of the way interests were mediated under the new policy pro-

---

5. Policy liberalization is gauged by (1) the level of tariff rates (falling rates indicating increased involvement) and (2) the number and kind of international trade agreements and treaties negotiated and implemented by the United States. Because of the pre-1945 focus of this study, the elimination of nontariff barriers (NTBs) is not considered part of the process of trade liberalization. It was the success of liberalization, defined by the above criteria, in the post-1945 period that has made NTBs a critical aspect of contemporary efforts to further trade liberalization.

cess. Such evaluation also highlights the characteristics of the policy and/ or policy process that were the objects of later attempts at reform. Third, the implications of the reform attempt are explored. How were tariff rates affected in the short and long term? Did the United States increase its involvement in the world economy as a result of the change? Finally, the various effects of alterations in the American trade policy process and the subsequent changes in policy for the world economy and international economic relations (and vice versa) are assessed. Although it is some- times difficult to isolate the causal relationship between American policy and the world economy, enough evidence exists to suggest that Ameri- can policy exerted a significant influence on the course of international economic development and on the world economy in general.

Chapter 2 explores the concept and process of institutional change. It also probes the institutional context of trade policy-making in the United States and within this context examines the range of possible alternative patterns of policy-making. Underlying this analysis of institutional change is an appreciation of the necessary historicity of institutional study. Every event has the potential for being both unique and repetitive. This is the case even if it occurs in the context of the repeating sequence of an estab- lished policy process. Thus, what may appear to be another instance of "politics as usual" may ultimately come to mark the emergence of a new pattern of institutional relations. Consequently, institutional change (or the lack thereof) cannot be predicted. Change, however, particularly social change, is not necessarily a random occurrence. It frequently in- volves learning. Accordingly, this study treats institutional change as a process of problem solving and social learning that can result in the cre- ation of new patterns of institutional relations. These new patterns make possible the enactment of policies and the attainment of goals that previ- ously eluded policymakers.

Institutional change, therefore, cannot be packaged into predictive or causal theory. It would be a mistake, however, to conclude from this that the process defies theoretical analysis. The application of causal theory may be inappropriate to the study of institutional change, but construct- ing an analytical framework for assessing probabilities relevant to institu- tional change most certainly is not. Chapter 2 details such a framework. It examines the basic dynamic underlying the patterned sequences that ultimately define institutions and institutional relations. It also considers the social conditions (viewed over time) that are more or less likely to lead to changes in these patterned sequences.

Chapter 3 is the first of the case study chapters. It considers tariff reform efforts of the post–Civil War period of the nineteenth century. The chapter reinforces what may be an obvious point: tariff and foreign economic policy problems in the United States predate the twentieth century. The third chapter also calls attention to the fact that alternatives to the trade policy process championed in the twentieth century had their antecedents in the nineteenth.

The focus of Chapter 4 is the Underwood Tariff Act of 1913, which saw Woodrow Wilson and leading Democrats in Congress use party to pass moderate tariff legislation. Chapter 5 considers the Tariff Commission and the effort to adjust tariff rates according to "scientific" criteria. These chapters analyze failed attempts to alter the trade policy process. As will be demonstrated, the attempts failed; but viewed over time, their impact on subsequent institutional change should not be overlooked or underestimated. Each experience helped shape the evolving perceptions of policymakers about the nature of the policy dilemma they confronted. Moreover, each experience led many to revise their views regarding how best to address the problem. Of these two episodes from the history of American trade policy, Woodrow Wilson and the Underwood Tariff Act of 1913 have been chronicled more extensively. However, it is the 1920s experiment with scientific tariff making that has had the more sustained impact on trade policy.

Chapter 6 examines the Trade Agreements Act of 1934. Significant institutional change ultimately resulted from this legislation. With it Congress delegated tariff rate–setting authority to the president by enabling him to negotiate trade agreements. With this act and its subsequent renewals, the United States altered course. The pattern of institutional relations in trade policy was transformed. This pattern, institutionalized after 1934, has remained the hallmark of American commercial policy-making.

In sum, chapters 3 through 6 reveal a process of trial and error that over time resulted in the transformation of the American trade policy process. Interestingly, vestiges of the failed attempts at reform did not disappear. They remained to inform succeeding attempts at policy-making reform.

In the final chapters, some of the broader implications of the transformation of the trade policy process are considered. Chapter 7 explores the impact of the transformed policy process on international economic cooperation during the post–World War II period. The concluding chapter places this examination of institutional change and the U.S. trade policy process in the broader context of scholarship in American politics and international relations. In sum, these chapters consider, in light of the study that precedes them, the prospects for the policy process and for international trade in the world economy of the 1990s. This is a point of considerable significance as we approach the end of the century.

An increasing number of policymakers and well-respected commentators have questioned continued American allegiance to liberalism in trade policy. Advocates of "managed" and "strategic" trade policies abound. Often, support for a new direction in trade policy is packaged as part of a broader vision of economic renewal and reform. Some, like Lester Thurow (1992) and Robert Kuttner (1991), offer a stinging critique of the policy status quo and its ideological moorings. They recommend fundamental reconceptualization of the business-government relationship. While their recommendations differ in some important ways, both endorse an unequivocal retreat from laissez-faire policies. Interestingly, and importantly from the standpoint of this study, neither author addresses the institutional setting from which all policy emanates. Other scholars, most notably Paul Krugman (1984, 1986), underscore in their work the benefits to be gained from astute application of strategic trade policy. In the final analysis, however, scholars like Krugman remain profoundly skeptical about whether there could ever be well-legislated and well-administered strategic trade policy in the United States. Their skepticism stems directly from disparaging assessments (implicit or explicit) of the institutional setting in which trade and industrial policy-making take place in the United States.

The focus of this inquiry is precisely the institutional setting for trade policy-making in the United States. It analyzes the forging of institutional arrangements that enabled American leaders to steer a steady course of trade policy liberalization in the post–World War II period. This examination has, therefore, considerable relevance for anyone interested in reassessing American foreign economic policy in light of a dramatically transformed world economy. An exploration of the origins, creation, and early development of the existing trade policy process underscores the relevance of institutional design to policy outcomes. This point is as salient today for those anticipating the policy requirements of the next century as it was for turn-of-the-century leaders grappling with policy choices for the twentieth century.

Contemporary critics and proponents of policy change need to appreciate the scope of the existing policy process. This does not mean they must necessarily "make do" with the policy status quo if they conclude that the desired alternative exceeds current institutional capacities. It does mean, however, that steering a new policy course may require institutional retooling. It is outside the scope of this study to provide a blueprint for such retooling. It does shed substantial light on the range and limits of institutional design options—the universe of possibilities informed by the U.S. Constitution and the institutional dynamics of the existing policy process.

Institutional Change and the American Trade Policy Process

Institutional change, as a concept, is somewhat of an oxymoron. While lacking the implicit humor associated with the now classic label "jumbo shrimp," its inherent paradox is only slightly less apparent. Change, on the one hand, is about transformation. We know it has occurred if something identified at one point in time is recognized as having transformed, either partially or totally, at a later point. Thus, integral to the concept of change are assumptions about time and about the relationship between reality[1] and time. Institutions, on the other hand, are popularly labeled as such because, in a world of change, they persist. They are enduring social structures that regularly perform important societal functions; they yield generally predictable outcomes. Accordingly, institutions are considered bulwarks of stability in a sea of change. Hence, the paradox of "institutional change."

At the same time, however, common sense tells us that institutions must change. Without the ability to change, they would rapidly become obsolete and unable to function effectively. This realization reinforces the paradox of institutional change while simultaneously justifying serious inquiry into its nature: How do institutions change without compromising their distinctive character as guardians of social stability? This chapter probes the various aspects of that question and aims to begin to unravel the paradox of institutional change. It also discusses the nature and process of such change in the American political context, with specific reference to the American trade policy process. The chapter thus specifies the analytical framework underlying the case studies of U.S. foreign economic policy-making in subsequent chapters.

---

1. Or more precisely, perceptions of reality.

Change, Institutions, and Institutional Change

The analysis in this section begins by separating the constituent elements of the "institutional change" concept. Before anything useful can be said about the particulars of institutional change, we must appreciate its component parts. Only then, equipped with greater understanding, can they be rejoined and their dynamics be examined.

Change

Change is associated with either the process of transformation or its manifestation. Therefore, it can be identified or measured only by reference to some index. "Time" is frequently used for this purpose. Physicists may ponder the attributes of time as a naturally occurring phenomenon. Recent work in the social sciences, however, questions the utility of assumptions about natural time for analyzing social structures and processes (e.g., Giddens, 1984; Elchardus, 1988). Far more useful for these purposes is an approach that views time as a *culturally contingent concept* (Elchardus, 1988, p. 44).

Acknowledging cultural contingency in no way diminishes the usefulness of time as a reference against which to measure change. Properties common to various cultural ideas about time can be used to measure and analyze social change. Two attributes, or properties, of time common to most cultures are *sequence* (linear time) and *repetition* (cyclical time). Sequence, or linear time, is the more familiar. It is easily captured by the simple act of sequential counting (1991, 1992, 1993, 1994, 1995). In contrast, cyclical time "produces (the possibility to recognize) repetition or equivalence and hence the distinction between alternating states" (Elchardus, 1988, p. 46). It is captured by the recognition of repetitive patterns (summer, fall, winter, spring, summer, fall, winter, spring . . .).

Time conceptualized in these analytically distinct but simultaneously operating ways facilitates the study of change. Most basically, this conceptualization permits the perception of change. Perceiving change is made possible by the ability to recognize its opposite—the repetition or recurrence of "the same old thing" (or its functional equivalent).[2] Moreover, time conceived as both linear and cyclical informs and nuances our understanding of change.

Change takes on meaning only if it is measured against constancy.[3] Thus, events measured against linear and cyclical time may simply repre-

2. According to Mark Elchardus (1988), "a change of state can only be observed when not everything is changing (at the same time and rate)" (p. 46).
3. What Elchardus (1988) calls *relative invariance*.

sent particular instances in basically unchanging patterns. However, every event also carries within it the potential to be truly unique, to shift the pattern. Because every event has the potential for *both* uniqueness and sameness, two alternative perspectives on change versus constancy can be identified.

The first approach distinguishes change from "variations on a theme" —unique incidents in a repetitive sequence that remains basically unaltered. To capture this difference, analogy is useful. The rules of a game (board, card, etc.), for example, specify a repetitive process. The actual play of the game varies from one instance to the next, but the basic nature of the game remains the same. If the rules change, however, the game itself becomes something else. According to this first approach, change would be identified only with the creation of a new sequence by altering the rules of the game; it would not be associated with the particulars of how the game is played on any given occasion.

The second approach would distinguish "degrees of change." This would involve differentiating minor changes in a familiar sequence from a major change that creates a wholly new pattern. For example, a teacher, given student performance during the course of a single semester, might choose to lower her usual grading standard and assign A's to students who score 85 and above instead of to those who score 90 and above. She varies an existing pattern for one semester and returns to the grading "norm" the next. According to this second alternative for assessing change, the particular incident that departed from the norm would be considered a minor, or small, change even if in subsequent semesters, the original pattern of assigning A's to students with scores of 90 and above were reasserted. Unquestionably, assessing change in this manner dilutes the concept of change and diminishes its significance. In addition, it creates uncertainty because the shift from minor to major change can happen very subtly over time, and reasonable people can disagree about the point at which minor changes become major.

The problems associated with this alternative approach to assessing change are underscored as we extend the above example. Let us assume that, over the course of a number of semesters, our teacher discovers that, for whatever reasons, her best students consistently perform around the 85 percent mark. At some point, she could establish a new grading standard, a new pattern against which to assess student performance. She may consciously mark the shift or she may not. In either case, the emergence of a new pattern would also constitute change. We might even label it major, or big, change. However, using the same basic label (i.e., change) to designate both variations on an existing pattern and the establishment of a wholly new one undercuts the salience of the change concept. For this reason, the label "change" will be used in this study only to identify the emergence or creation of new sequences or new patterns.

Yet identifying change according to this standard is not always simple or straightforward. Appearances can be deceiving. What first appears as a dramatic departure from the past may come to represent simply a peculiar variation on an existing theme. On the other hand, what appears initially as a relatively insignificant modification in a repeating sequence may, in retrospect, be seen as marking the emergence of a wholly new theme or pattern. Obviously, therefore, no event can be analyzed in isolation. Each event under scrutiny must be examined in the context of and with an appreciation for relevant repetitive sequences. In addition, events subsequent to the one(s) in question must also be examined to determine whether or not change has occurred.

Since the simultaneity of linear and cyclical time creates the potential for any event to be both unique and repetitive, developing a predictive theory about change is impossible. This does not, however, mean that change is necessarily random. Social change, for example, frequently involves learning. Learning is an enduring alteration in thought or behavior that results from an assessment of past experience. Social change, in other words, is often deliberately sought. And the improbability of predictive theory building notwithstanding, the analyst can identify the circumstances under which change is more or less likely to occur. With specific regard to institutional change, it is possible to gain knowledge about the nature of institutions and their procedural dynamics (i.e., their "relative invariance") and then to analyze both the institution's opportunities for change and the constraints mitigating against change.

Institutions

Institutions are social structures. Considered abstractly, structures "in one way or another create (the possibility of) relative invariance and sequential order" (Elchardus, 1988, p. 47). As pillars of order in society, institutions are relatively less likely to change than other types of social structure: "Institutions are distinguished primarily as mechanisms that (more or less successfully) lend the polity its integrity, that facilitate its routine operations, and that produce continuity in the face of potentially destabilizing forces" (Orren and Skowronek, 1991, p. 3).

Because of this relatively invariant quality, institutions serve to define the limits of change for society as a whole. This does not mean, however, that institutions cannot change or that they are uniform in their resistance to change. All institutions change or are subject to change at different times and at different rates. Moreover, institutions do not operate in isolation or in tandem. Thus, "coexisting institutions manifest a multiplicity of ordering principles and . . . these juxtapose various time-lines of order and change" (Orren and Skowronek, 1991, p. 18).

The sine qua non of political institutions is control. Political institutions aim to control the behavior of individuals and other institutions in order to achieve specified goals. Some of a society's most basic goals are manifested in the rules of its institutions. Officials occupying positions of authority within these institutions interpret these goals, as well as articulating other issue-specific aims and formulating policies to achieve them.

Policy articulation and formulation are seldom the purview of a single institution. The U.S. Constitution, for example, created a government in which institutions share powers. It is in interaction that the specialization associated with the process of institutionalization becomes evident. In other words, policy-making typically requires the establishment of agreed-upon procedures and assignment of roles both to and within institutions. These procedures and roles are sometimes generally applicable, but more frequently they are peculiar to an issue area. Issue-specific procedures and roles that develop within or between political institutions constitute a policy process. Every policy process, therefore, represents a sequence of institutional behaviors that limit the options available for the articulation and implementation of specific policies. However, no pattern of policy-making is frozen in time; it is not static. Rather, policy processes are dynamic; they evolve continuously.

These points require clarification. First, institutional relationships set the patterns of policy-making. These patterns are not rigidly fixed. There can be many variations on a theme; the theme or fundamental pattern, however, is always discernible. The nineteenth-century trade policy process in the United States featured tariff rate setting by Congress as its central theme, its basic pattern. In contrast, the fundamental pattern of the contemporary trade policy process has been the Congressional delegation of authority to the president to negotiate trade terms with other nation-states. Stasis did not characterize the nineteenth-century process. The historical record is replete with variations on the theme of rate setting by Congress. The point to emphasize is that these variations in their nineteenth-century applications did not undermine but rather safeguarded the integrity of the Congress-centered trade policy process.

Second, history unfolds seamlessly. Therefore, identifying a single moment when patterns of institutional relations transform is impossible. New patterns of institutional relations emerge or evolve out of old ones. Turning points—watersheds—can be identified only *after the fact*. In 1934, Congress gave the president authority to neogotiate trade agreements. This authority was limited to three years. If this authority had not been renewed or had Congress reasserted its traditional tariff-rate setting pre-rogatives, the Congressional delegation of authority to the president would be viewed today as a recycled variation (from the 1890s) of the "tried and true" Congressionally centered policy process. This did not happen. Instead, a new pattern supplanted the old, and a new policy process emerged.

Such institutional change occurs because policy processes that result from the patterns of institutional relations are not infinitely versatile. In a constantly changing political-economic system, new challenges, prob-lems, or contingencies arise and require the articulation of new goals. These, in turn, may fundamentally challenge an existing policy process.

Institutional Change

The repetitive sequences within and between institutions that consti-tute policy processes are not immutable. New goals may elicit responses that over time become established as new patterns of institutional be-havior. These responses are hardly ever wholly original. They frequently represent ideas adapted from other issue areas and policy contexts. Some-times they are repackaged responses adapted from past circumstances and applied to contemporary ones. Whether institutional change will re-sult from any particular set of responses to policy challenges cannot be predicted. However, when such change does occur, it is invariably the product of problem solving and becomes institutionalized through the process of social learning.

Seeing institutional change as a process of social or organizational learning facilitates its analysis. As mechanisms that pattern individual behavior, institutions provide a set of responses to various contingen-cies (Elster, 1979). The idea of learning, or more precisely, experiential learning—"a change of beliefs (or degree of confidence in beliefs) or development of new beliefs, skills, or procedures as a result of the ob-servation and interpretation of experience" (Levy, 1994, p. 283)—can be usefully applied to political institutions if we accept that learning has a collective dimension: "Social learning is created only by individuals, but alone and in interaction, these individuals acquire and produce changed patterns of collective action" (Heclo, 1974, p. 306). Thus, organizations "learn" but only because the people who serve in them do. Organiza-tional learning occurs when individually drawn "inferences from history [become encoded] into routines that guide behavior" within and among organizations (Levitt and March, 1988, p. 320).

Social learning applied to political institutions has three basic compo-nents. First, there are individual agents of change who identify problems and advocate solutions. These individuals can occupy positions in or out of government. The important thing is that they themselves have experienced cognitive change. They have come to believe that certain patterns of organizational behavior[4] within and between political institutions— patterns that constitute a policy process and from which policy is generated—are inappropriate in the face of new realities, and they come to advocate ways to address the new conditions. Again, the point to underscore is that the ideas or solutions these individuals champion reflect their own experiential learning, learning that takes place in a setting of organizational interrelationships.

The setting of organizational interrelationships is the second component of social learning applied to political institutions. Institutions as social structures are relatively impervious to change. They embody long-standing patterns of behavior and organizational interrelationships. Altering these patterns may require institutions and the officials in them to surrender cherished prerogatives, to redefine their roles and missions vis-à-vis other officials and organizations, and consequently, to relinquish some or all of the control they exercise over outcomes. Since the quality of relative invariance that characterizes institutions can be traced, at least in part, to their ability to control outcomes, institutional change inevitably involves the redefinition of control relationships and the establishment of new behavioral patterns within or between organizations.

The process of social learning involves people in a collective setting using past experience to reassess their personal and organizational interests in light of new contingencies. Such a reassessment frequently challenges the cognitive frameworks that indiviudals hold. A cognitive framework forms when an individual's ideas about how best to safeguard his or her interests fuse with a pragmatic appreciation of the interorganizational dynamics of the political process. Such a cognitive framework is called a schema (Anderson, 1980).

"A schema is an internal representation which organizes and guides information processing" (Peterson, 1985, p. 496). It works as a mental blueprint for problem articulation and solving. As applied here, a schema is distinct from an ideology. Based on moral principles, an ideology is an integrated set of beliefs about the world that offers a vision of the future that is rooted in these beliefs. In contrast, a schema is a practical guide to making sense of the world and thus shapes the thinking of the individuals involved in the problem-solving process. It defines, for each of them, the legitimate problems and legitimate solutions.

---

4. Levitt and March (1988) refer to these as "routines," a broad label that includes "the forms, rules, procedures, conventions, strategies, and technologies around which organizations are constructed and through which they operate" (p. 320).

Policy-making processes, products of established patterns of interorganizational relations, usually involve more than one participant, and these participants do not all have the same set of schemas. What matters, however, is not that they have an identical set of schemas but that there is a basic congruence between and among the schemas salient to the particular policy-making process in which they are engaged. Since policymakers work within the same institutional framework, they often do share similar basic schemas about that institutional framework, its policy-making processes, and the policy options available to them. Moreover, individuals try to preserve some reasonable consistency between their salient schemas and the salient schemas of the people with whom they work (Lewin, 1947). Policy, viewed through the conceptual lens of shared schemas is, therefore, neither random nor ad hoc. Policy outcomes tend to conform to widely shared aspects of the policymakers' schemas.

Circumstances are prone to change, and policy consensus can crumble as policymakers, broadly defined, reassess the nature of the problems they confront and reevaluate the prescribed solutions. Accordingly, the third component of institutional change viewed as a process of social learning is the impact of previous policy experience on the schemas of the policymakers, both individually and collectively. Widespread and repeated criticism of existing policies motivates individuals whose diagnosis of the problem and recommended solutions depart from the consensus framework. Repeated episodes of policy failure offer these agents of change otherwise unavailable opportunities to promote their solutions.

For the ordinary official, moreover, policy failure increases the costs of maintaining the status quo and decreases the risks of trying something new.[5] Perceptions of policy failure also engender dissonance in the minds of ordinary officials. This dissonance creates psychological discomfort and further motivates the individual or group to search for ways to reduce that discomfort (Festinger, 1957). This process leads to questions about how policymakers have traditionally defined both the policy problem and its solution. Not surprisingly, negative appraisals of existing policies and perceptions of policy failure increase during times of crisis. With regard to foreign economic policy, crisis periods are those of prolonged or rapidly recurring economic downturn and war. In contrast, policies that generate little or sporadic criticism reinforce the schemas that support them. They

---

5. Scholars have typically viewed cost-benefit calculations of elected officials in terms of an electoral imperative (see, for example, Downs, 1957; Mayhew, 1974). For non-elected officials, scholars see costs and benefits measured with reference to budget allocations (see, for example, Wildavsky, 1986).

are renewed with minor adjustments, and the institutional arrangements that produced them are strengthened.

Viewing institutional change as a process of social learning enables the analyst to identify the major components of the process of change and can serve useful purposes in policy studies, including this one. This conceptualization sheds light on why policymakers pursued the kinds of changes they did. It helps to demonstrate why the policy goals sought were seldom wholly realized (at least in the opinion of individual policymakers), and it helps the analyst recognize and understand the impact on policy of the successive and cumulative events that result in institutional change.

The components of social learning—the individual agents, organizational setting, and experience with previous policy outcomes—do not remain constant. As the manifestation of new thinking in an issue area (or isssue areas), institutional change permits the realization of previously elusive policy goals. Goal achievement, in turn, recasts the issue for other policymakers. They come to accept as routine policy-making what was once considered extraordinary. They adopt new cognitive frameworks, which inspire further innovative thinking. This, in turn, frequently transcends the narrow focus of a single issue area. Moreover, because it alters organizational interrelationships, the institutional change achieved in one period transforms the universe of policy options available in the next. New organizations and new prerogatives figure prominently in subsequent attempts at institutional change.[6] The process of institutional change is nuanced in yet another way. Old organizations seldom disappear. While their original patterns of intra- and interorganizational relations are eclipsed with institutional change, they frequently shift to other policy contexts or supplement the new policy process (the product of institutional change).[7]

Without a doubt, institutional change is a dynamic and nuanced process. This study attempts to impart an appreciation for and an understanding of these nuances by weaving together several distinct strains of

6. This may or may not occur depending on a variety of circumstances, including the policy options afforded by the now existing institutional arrangements.

7. Judith Goldstein (1993) argues that ideas institutionalized via legal procedures in one era persist in subsequent periods despite the fact that they represent outmoded thinking and tend to contradict contemporary ideas about economic policy. Instead of viewing these institutionalized ideas as so many ossified layers of legal sediment that produce outmoded policy, this study views these organizations and procedures in the context of the policy-making process in which they operate. Examined in terms of patterns of intra- and interorganizational relations, the analysis reveals that organizations and procedures that in their origin might have been the centerpiece of the policy-making process in subsequent eras come to support alternative policy-making processes.

scholarship in the social sciences. It integrates concepts drawn from the literature on the sociology of time (e.g., Giddens, 1984; Elchardus, 1988) with insights derived from the work of analysts of policy change who explore such change as manifestations of social learning (e.g., Heclo, 1974). It is also flavored by the insights of social and political psychologists who have explored the interrelationship of cognitive frameworks, experience, affect, and decision making (e.g. Festinger, 1957; Peterson, 1985). Finally, its focus on "institutions in time" is wholly consistent with those scholars of the "New Institutionalism" who argue persuasively for a historically grounded approach to the study of institutions (e.g., Skowronek, 1982, 1993; Orren, 1991; Orren and Skowronek, 1991).

Patterning Institutional Relationships in the Context of American Democracy

The structure of American government, particularly its form of legislative representation, predisposed the policy-making process to logrolling. For trade policy this meant a plethora of indiscriminate and inordinately high tariffs. Fundamental reform of trade policy required a fundamental change in the policy process. Policymakers in the legislative and executive branches of government had to find an effective way to alter the policy process without violating the existing constitutional order. They needed to transform the logrolling-driven approach to trade policy-making so that trade policy could discriminate among interests, determine who would get protection (and on what basis), and thereby further overseas trade expansion.[8] This would permit the dismantling of the elaborate schedule of protective tariffs that had been legislated since the mid-nineteenth century. Of course, the form that trade policy would take was inextricably linked to the outcomes possible under the new trade policy process.

The challenge was to recast the issue of tariff reform. Some broader vision of the policy context and/or of the policy-making process was necessary in order to identify solutions to the troublesome policy dilemma that tariff reform represented. *How* the issue was recast would, in turn, suggest a course of action—an alternative policy process. Given the contours of the policy dilemma, moreover, these alternatives were certain to incorporate a strategy or strategies for managing and regulating interest group access to the policy process. They also would have to identify an

---

8. In other words, they had to create "autonomy enhancing capacities." Eric Nordlinger (1981) explores the viability of a "state-centered" model of politics (as opposed to "society-centered") for democratic states. Nordlinger, however, does not specify what constitutes an "autonomy enhancing capacity or opportunity." Perhaps this is because his definition of the state does not include an organizational/procedural dimension.

appropriate means for implementing the strategy. Importantly, strategies and means had to respect the constitutionally mandated roles of the executive and legislative branches of government, even though these roles have never been rigidly fixed. They have always been subject to interpretation and reinterpretation by the Supreme Court. Because of changes in the makeup of the Supreme Court or new Court decisions, strategies and means that may have been deemed inapplicable at one time due to constitutional prohibition may subsequently become available. A new set of justices can overrule a past decision, or a Supreme Court decision relevant to one policy domain can serve as precedent for policy-making changes in another.

Some turn-of-the-century reformers came to view the tariff and the failure to achieve tariff reform as symptomatic of systemic problems plaguing the polity. They operated from cognitive frameworks that suggested a standard solution, tailored where necessary to suit the particulars of the tariff problem. The tariff and tariff reform, therefore, fit into the agenda of the Progressives of the late nineteenth and early twentieth centuries. Others recast the tariff issue itself. They ceased to consider it primarily a domestic policy concern and came to view it in the broader context of foreign economic policy. They began to think of the tariff as an instrument for promoting overseas trade expansion, downplaying its role in raising revenue or protecting domestic producers. From this cognitive framework, tariff reform would have to be accomplished through a strategy-means combination different from that advocated by the Progressives but derived from the same constitutional context.

This discussion raises an important question: How could reform-minded officials in the United States reconceptualize policy-making? What new approaches to policy-making could be tried and through what means? In other words, what was their universe of options?

Strategies

Government officials both mobilize popular preferences and react to them. They also use or diffuse them. These officials can manipulate the access of groups to the policy process in ways delimited by existing institutional arrangements. The object of manipulating group access is to somehow distance interest groups from the policy process so that the policy produced reflects a broader public interest rather than particularistic interests.

When narrow interests have too much influence on the policy-making process, government officials can choose between two strategies for altering the situation. One strategy is to minimize interest group access to the process. Alternatively, such groups can be given access. The strategy is to combine them in such a way that they can be played off against one another to reveal broadly based policy preferences. Then government officials can pursue policy free from pressure to respond to particular, narrow interests.

Whether politicians prefer to transform the policy process by allowing limited group access or by shielding the process from narrow interests largely depends on how they define the issue in question and its relationship to the public interest. On the one hand, those who accept the idea that the public interest can be discerned through group interaction seek limited and controlled group access. They believe that some insulation from group access is necessary to prevent too much influence by particularistic interests. But they also maintain that group interaction, properly channeled, will yield policy decisions that fairly reflect the public interest.

On the other hand, those who argue that the nature of the issue makes it impossible to define the public interest in a group context prefer to separate policy-making from group interaction. From their point of view, when policy-making involves technical problems or transcends national boundaries, the public interest cannot be served by the participation of particularistic groups. Policy-making in the public interest requires careful evaluation of complex data, and the policy-making process must reflect this need.

On issues pertaining to economic regulation, American reformers of the Progressive era tended to gravitate to the latter strategy. Witness the creation of a number of independent regulatory commissions during this period. However, some self-declared Progressives (e.g., Woodrow Wilson) remained unconvinced about the universal utility of policy-making by highly specialized regulators. Wilson, for one, advocated the infusion of disciplined political parties into the policy-making process and thus favored the former strategy.

Means

All governments are made up of both political and bureaucratic institutions. Both have specific organizations and procedures; both have officials occupying positions of authority. In a democracy, both bureaucratic and political institutions are accountable to the people. The fact that officials in a bureaucracy are only indirectly accountable to the electorate makes possible different degrees and different kinds of group access for bureaucratic and political institutions.

In the United States, the Constitution structures American political institutions so that they vary in their internal and external receptivity to change. Since the Constitution is vague regarding the internal organization and operation of the three branches of government, there are few

Table 2-1. Alternative Patterns for Trade Policy-making in the United States

Means	Strategies	
	Combine interests to control access to policy process	Separate interests from policy process
Bureaucratic	Corporatist alternatives	Commission alternatives
Political	Party alternatives	Power-sharing alternatives

impediments to changing procedures and rules—or even creating new organizations to guide such tasks as fact-finding and law-making.[9] Constitutionally unspecified rules, procedures, and organizations can be altered to change the nature of group access to the policy process.

Bureaucratic organizations can relieve the political ones of the burden of policy-making. The idea is to take the issue out of the political arena so that decisions can be made based on specified standards without reference to any particular interest. Although elected officials occupying political institutions remain ultimately accountable for the policy, they can use the bureaucracy to achieve policy goals while taking the heat off themselves. However, without an accompanying strategy for managing interest group participation in policy-making, this use of bureaucratic organizations can yield undesirable results. Government authority can expand in an unfocused way without established forms and procedures for using this authority.[10]

Alternatively, elected officials can change or create rules, procedures, and relationships within or among institutions that enable them to pursue new policies. For example, the Constitution did not provide for political parties. In fact, many of the Founders were concerned about the potential evils of "faction." As soon as the Constitution was written, however, the process of ratification gave rise to the Federalists and the Anti-Federalists. Thus, from the start, parties have been an institution in the American political system. And over time, they have performed many needed functions, including policy-making functions. Thus, they represent a potential resource for those seeking to transform a policy process. Parties can theoretically provide policymakers with a means to aggregate interests and thus effectively pursue policy goals.

9. An excellent example of this is the development of the Congressional committee system. The development of this system of committees and subcommittees has had important consequences for policy. (See Shepsle, 1988, and Shepsle and Weingast, 1984, 1985, and 1987.)

10. Theodore Lowi (1979) calls the philosophy undergirding this approach to government "interest-group liberalism," and he argues that it has become the predominant philosophy of government in the United States.

Linking the strategies to the possible means discussed above yields four alternative patterns available to policymakers in their efforts to transform the American trade policy process. These alternative patterns should be viewed as general categories or types under which specific reform proposals can be grouped (Table 2.1).

Corporatist Alternatives

This pattern of policy-making would have leaders of functional associations representing labor, business, and agricultural sectors regularly involved in the formulation, adoption, and administration of public policy. The traditional lines of group-state interaction (through Congress) would be bypassed, and a new "system of interest intermediation" would be created (Schmitter, 1977). The formation of large, sector-defined organizations would be encouraged by guaranteeing these organizations access to the policy process. Through a bureau, agency, or board, organization leaders would interact with one another as well as with state officials. Accommodation of various societal interests in terms of some broad conception of national policy goals could be achieved through such interaction.

Corporatist alternatives have not been systematically pursued in the United States. Americans have not been accustomed to viewing business and government as partners. Rather, observers have usually characterized their relationship as necessarily adversarial. Over the years, only a very few American reformers even began to conceptualize policy-making as a partnership endeavor. While there have been sporadic attempts to create such an arrangement, these have occurred during times of crisis. The War Industries Board's mobilization efforts for World War I offer one example of the application of corporatist principles (Cuff, 1973). Another is found in the early New Deal legislation designed to promote cooperation between government, industry, and labor through the National Recovery Act, as well as between government and agriculture through the Agricultural Adjustment Act (Schlesinger, 1958).

Policy-making through a kind of corporatism was briefly attempted in matters tangentially related to tariff policy. Between 1914 and 1917, for example, cooperative relations between government and industrialists selling overseas were encouraged by the National Foreign Trade Council. Organized by Secretary of Commerce William C. Redfield, it was made up of representatives of the largest corporations and banks interested in foreign business. The council worked to improve the merchant marine, to modify the antitrust laws that impinged on overseas trade expansion, and to build public and Congressional support for the idea that foreign trade was important to the nation's well-being. This cooperative effort between government and business did not last long. When the United States entered World War I, such cooperation ended (Becker, 1982, xii).

Proposals for an American industrial policy have surfaced during the past decade. These include proposals for the creation of economic cooperation councils or industrial development boards that would recommend industrial policy, sector by sector. Thus far, the economic councils that have been formed (e.g., the President's Council on Competitiveness) have served more as policy coordinators and defenders of the status quo than as agents of change. However, the calls for an American "industrial policy" continue to grow in number, and the adversarial mentality about business–government relations is waning in some quarters. Indeed, corporatist policy-making may suit some of the new thinking about promoting American competitiveness in a post–Cold war global economy.

Party Alternatives

Political parties in a democracy "organize, institutionalize, and channel conflict over control of the regime" (Lowi, 1967, p. 239). In the United States, they provide a means for orderly succession, a system of internal organization in the legislature, a way to coordinate relations between the executive and legislative branches, and a mechanism for linking the federal government to the states and localities. In other words, they perform functions essential to the operation of the American political system. American political parties, however, are not policy parties. They rarely aggregate interests around a platform that becomes the policy agenda if the party wins an election. American parties cannot compel their members in government to toe the party line on policy matters.

Throughout American history, parties did not insulate government officials from the pressures of narrow interests. Since members of Congress, in particular, were dependent on local party nominations and support, it behooved them to cater to the party organization back home. Thus, the growth of party politics in America could not prevent the use of logrolling to expedite the legislative process. On the contrary, elected officials embraced logrolling as a means of courting local interests (Lowi, 1967, p. 274).

Thus, party politics precluded tariff reform. The two major political parties represented different coalitions of interests, but these coalitions did not inhibit their participants from logrolling. In the nineteenth century this translated into a trade policy of oscillating tariff rates. The Republican coalition raised rates; the Democratic one slightly modified them. The overall trend was toward increasingly higher tariff rates.

Critics of the American political process have advocated responsible parties (i.e., parties that perform both constituent and policy functions) as the panacea. As large, heterogeneous organizations representing national constituencies, responsible parties could serve the public interest and see this interest enacted into policy by ensuring that their members vote the party line. The party could, thereby, help elected officials to resist the pressures of groups representing narrowly defined interests.

The history of American tariff policy is littered with attempts to forge responsible party coalitions as a means to secure tariff reform. The most successful of these attempts was made in 1913, when the Democrats, under the leadership of President Woodrow Wilson, passed the Underwood Tariff Act. The political and policy implications of this act are the subject of chapter 4.

Commission Alternatives

Policy-making via commission embraces the idea that social and economic problems cannot be solved through political maneuvering but by experts who would undertake scientific investigations and derive appropriate policies (Cushman, 1941). The essence of this alternative is the application of scientific or other knowledge by trained and disinterested professionals to issue areas ranging from resource management to the protective tariff. Freed from the political exigencies of satisfying a multitude of narrow interests, these professionals could determine policy according to established principles and the public interest. The most notable attempt to establish such an institution in the American system was the establishment of the independent regulatory agencies, starting with the Interstate Commerce Commission in 1887. Subsequently, many others were established, particularly during the New Deal period. These independent regulatory agencies, however, did not achieve the insulation from particularistic influence that their founders expected. Rather, over time, they tended to be "captured" to a greater or lesser extent by the sectors they were designed to regulate.

In most other government settings the regular bureaucracy performs these tasks. This was not possible, however, because the American bureaucracy was patronage-based until passage of the Civil Service Act of 1883. And even then, only 10 percent of the federal bureaucracy was covered. The United States did not achieve a predominantly merit-based civil service until well into the twentieth century. The nineteenth-century "state of courts and parties" did not have one (Skowronek, 1982). Moreover, in a government setting where separate institutions share powers, Congress was reluctant to empower the regular bureaucracy to assert the public interest in matters relating to the regulation of business and of the economy. Such a move would have strengthened the power of the executive and ultimately of the president (Shonfield, 1965, p. 320).

The Progressives of the early twentieth century advocated the commission idea as a means to circumvent partisan political influence on the economic policy process. Progressives envisioned a bipartisan tariff commission where appropriate tariffs could be determined scientifically. Theodore Roosevelt's Bull Moose platform of 1912 called for the establishment of such a commission. Originally opposed to the idea because he championed tariff reform through party government, Woodrow Wilson changed his mind in 1916 and endorsed it. Congress established the Tariff Commission in September 1916, and during the decade of the 1920s an unsuccessful attempt was made to insulate trade policy-making through this commission. The creation and subsequent mandates of the Tariff Commission are the subject of chapter 5.

Power-Sharing Alternatives

Power sharing aims to change the rules, procedures, and control relationships between the political institutions involved in the policy process. The object of the change is to improve the policy process by making it less malleable by particularistic interests. Congress can, for example, change its own rules and procedures to minimize the access of special interests to the policy process and achieve some degree of insulation. With regard to the tariff, changes of this sort were, in fact, proposed, and some were even implemented. In the late nineteenth century the House Ways and Means Committee reported tariff bills to the House floor under a closed rule to prevent crippling amendments. Unfortunately, the impact of this procedure was repeatedly undermined in the Senate. Proposals for supplanting hearings as the source of information for Congress also abounded. Some envisioned the Tariff Commission as an aid to Congress in its rate-setting task.[11]

Congress can also delegate authority in policy-making to the president. As a nationally elected official, the president can be more sensitive to the national interest than can members of Congress. This is particularly apropos if the issue can be defined as a foreign policy matter. In the 1934 Trade Agreements Act, Congress delegated to the president authority to set tariff rates in situations involving bilateral trade negotiations. Members of Congress avoided pressure from their constituents by placing the "tariff ball," so to speak, in the president's court. Sharing power with the president in tariff rate setting, however, did not represent an abdication of responsibility by Congress. Rather, the application of this alternative

11. This point is discussed in the chapter on the Tariff Commission.

required members of Congress to redefine their own role in the trade policy process. This alternative proved successful for American trade policy-making. Its success can be measured by the progressive lowering of American tariff levels and by the changed rules and procedures that governed the trade policy process after 1934. How it worked and why it worked will be discussed in chapter 6.

Conclusion

In the United States, the nineteenth-century pattern of institutional relations pertaining to commercial or trade policy featured Congress legislating tariff rates (subject to presidential approval or after a veto override) and the president negotiating commercial treaties (subject to Senate ratification). A nettlesome dilemma arose when the tariff evolved from being primarily an instrument of revenue generation to being an instrument of protection and of compensation for other indirect taxes that increased production costs. Members of Congress were compelled to defend the particularistic interests of their constituents, defined in terms of the tariff, at the expense of broader goals, such as overseas trade expansion and the elimination of revenue surpluses. The result was that during the late nineteenth and early twentieth centuries, there was no meaningful lowering of tariff rates, despite an often proclaimed desire to do so. There also was no effective government-sponsored program of trade expansion because the Senate consistently failed to ratify trade treaties that offered concessions in the form of tariff rate reductions.

Policymakers of the late nineteenth century made repeated attempts to change trade policy. Because of the institutional framework within which the policymakers were operating, these efforts were ineffective. They represented variations on the theme of tariff rate setting by Congress, and as such, they could not sufficiently mitigate the impact of Congressional logrolling. However, they did offer potential alternatives to the existing pattern of institutional relations when and if they became viewed as substitutes for, rather than supplements to, the existing policy process.

Late-nineteenth-century efforts at tariff reform marked the advent of new thinking about tariffs and commercial policy in the United States. These new ideas coalesced into coherent, albeit competing, cognitive frameworks during the early decades of the twentieth century. Each framework identified a context for the tariff-making problem in the United States. Each also envisioned a solution, the solutions reflecting the contexts into which the tariff issue was cast. To be realized, however, these solutions had to be embodied in an alternative policy process.

These alternative policy processes (outlined above) represented four possible routes to a desired end: a foreign economic policy deemed appropriate for the United States in the twentieth century. Between 1913 and 1945, policymakers applied three of the four to the trade policy process. But because of the nature of the American political system and the dynamics of the institutional change process, these changes only imperfectly reflected the envisioned policy-making alternative. The flawed and cumulative application of policy-making alternatives yielded a wide range of policy effects, the most significant of which was the liberalization of trade policy. Thus, the power-sharing alternative, an idea resurrected from the 1890s, was applied under the dire economic circumstances of the 1930s. And it was administered, in part, with vestigial organizations and procedures from the 1920s attempt to produce scientific tariffs. This became the vehicle for American trade policy liberalization.

PART II

FORGING A NEW AMERICAN TRADE POLICY PROCESS

The tariff has been one of the most colossal stems of deliberate patronage that has ever been conceived. And the main trouble with it is that the protection stops where the patronage begins; and that if you lop off the patronage, you would have taken away most of the objectionable features of the so-called protection.
—WOODROW WILSON, address at the National Press Club, September 9, 1912

That there is a vital defect in the method of making the tariff is revealed therefore by the failure of successive acts to conform in important particulars to the policy which the majority of voters thought they were endorsing at the polls. The cause of failure has been the influence of special interests which are not national in scope but are confined to industrial groups, geographical sections, or political blocs and factions. What has made it possible for the influence to overcome the national will has been the lack of trustworthy information showing what rates of duty would truly accord with the mandate of the people. The defect in method, therefore, consists in a tariff without knowing what the duties in it ought to be.
—THOMAS WALKER PAGE, *Making the Tariff in the United States*, 1924

We should not be discouraged if public officials move timidly under existing laws. The evils of politics in the tariff and of the tariff in politics cannot be disposed of in a day. Institutions grow slowly. The foundations have been laid and the edifice of sound policy is beginning to rise.
—WILLIAM S. CULBERTSON, *Reciprocity*, 1937

Understanding the Limits of Tariff Policy Reform in Nineteenth-Century America

The origin of the trade policy dilemma that confronted American officials in the twentieth century is found in the tariff policies of the late nineteenth century. During this period, American officials tried to respond to new domestic economic realities. The legacy of Civil War taxation (high protective tariffs), combined with rapid development of America's industrial base and the cyclical economic downturns and periodic revenue surpluses that marked the years 1875 to 1900, kept tariff reform on the legislative agenda.

Throughout the period, logrolling was the most salient feature of nineteenth-century American policy-making in trade. It would be a mistake, however, to characterize commercial policy-making of the era solely by reference to the logroll. In their efforts to tailor tariff policy to meet the challenge of new circumstances, officials innovatively applied ideas and modalities that would distinguish policy-making changes of the twentieth century. That none of these innovations supplanted tariff rate setting by Congress as the quintessence of nineteenth-century commercial policy-making does nothing to diminish their significance. In fact, the experience of the nineteenth century can be viewed as an integral part of a process of institutional change that came to fruition during the first half of the twentieth century.

Analyzing and evaluating the nineteenth-century trade policy process, with particular reference to evolving policy goals in a dynamic economy, will showcase both the resilience of established patterns of institutional relations and the limits of such resilience. The analysis will also demonstrate that the policy-making reforms that figured so prominently in the early twentieth century had their origins in the late nineteenth century.

Toward these ends, the sections that follow delineate the economic and political objectives that nineteenth-century policymakers sought when they levied taxes on imports and the problems they confronted (viz., persistent revenue surpluses and the need to promote overseas trade as a means to circumvent economic vicissitudes) when they succeeded too well at legislating tariffs. The following sections also consider how American policymakers tried to address these problems. Their resolution required a systematic reduction in tariff rates. This goal remained elusive even though innovative ideas about policy-making reform were championed and periodically adopted. Because these reform efforts had little impact on the existing pattern of institutional relations that prevailed in trade policy-making, institutional change did not result.

The Economic and Political Objectives of Commercial Policy, 1861–1900

Considered predominantly a domestic policy concern, the application of tariffs to imported goods served three purposes during the latter half of the nineteenth century. First, tariffs were used to generate revenue. Young governments often rely on this method of indirect taxation when they lack the administrative resources and/or legitimacy to extract taxes directly from the citizenry (Kindleberger and Lindert, [1953] 1978, p. 143). Second, tariffs on imports performed a protective function, protecting domestic producers from foreign competition. Third, tariffs were routinely used to compensate producers for other taxes that raised their costs of production so that imported goods would not have an advantage in the home market.

Revenue Tariffs

A tariff policy designed solely to generate public revenue will tax most imports at a uniform rate (ad valorem), assign high duties to luxury items, and/or tax commodities that are widely consumed but not widely produced in the domestic economy at specific rates. All of these features characterized the United States' first tariff act (1789), which levied a 5 percent duty on imports, higher duties on luxury items, and a few specific duties on articles like coffee, tea, and molasses (Taussig, 1888; Pincus, 1977).

During periods of revenue shortfall, Congress legislated higher taxes on imports. Secession and civil war precipitated an incredible escalation of tariff rates. Every session of Congress from 1861 through 1865 passed some increase of duties on imports. By 1864, average ad valorem rates had reached 49 percent, up from 19 percent in 1857 (Ratner, 1972, p. 30).

When the need for revenue decreased, the duties on strictly revenue items were lowered. Congress passed reductions on tea, coffee, wines, sugar, molasses, and spices in July 1870. By 1872, when Congress passed an across-the-board 10 percent reduction in tariff rates, coffee, tea, and raw sugar were admitted duty-free (Taussig, 1931, p. 184). (The 10 percent reduction was short-lived, however. When economic depression caused a drop in imports and a consequent drop in revenue, Congress repealed the reduction.)

By the end of the 1870s, the government faced more revenue difficulties in the form of repeated surpluses. Economic recovery and the upsurge in imports resulted in surpluses in excess of $100 million for 1880, 1881, and 1882. The fact that so-called revenue duties had already been largely eliminated complicated the resolution of the surplus problem. Protective duties filled the coffers of the U.S. Treasury.

Protective Tariffs

Although protective tariffs had long been a feature of American commercial policy (there was even a protective aspect of America's first tariff act),[1] the era of high protective tariffs began during the Civil War. Protective duties were lavished on industries as compensation for internal taxes levied on manufactures. In many cases, legislators let the industries determine the level of protection they required (Taussig, 1888, p. 166; Ratner, 1972, p. 31). After the war, Congress eliminated the internal taxes, but they left protective tariffs intact.

By the end of the nineteenth century, the average tariff rate on dutiable items stood at 52 percent and 30 percent on free and dutiable items, respectively.[2] Significant changes in the structure of protective tariffs during the last decades of the nineteenth century were few. For a brief period under the Wilson-Gorman Act (1894–1897), duties on some raw materials were either reduced (iron ore, coal) or eliminated (lumber, raw wool). Also during the last decades of the nineteenth century, duties on agricultural products went up progressively. Protective duties on agricultural products were viewed, in part, as compensation to farmers for the high prices they paid for protected manufactures. In some cases, they were also meant to stem the flow of Canadian agricultural exports to the United States. Significant among the taxed items were wheat, corn, barley, and

1. Although insignificant when compared with protective measures enacted later, duties for cotton industries in Pennsylvania and Massachusetts, which had been protected under state acts prior to 1789, were part of America's first tariff package. Other tariff concessions were made for hemp, nails, iron manufactures, and glass. (See Taussig, 1888, p. 15, Pincus, 1977, p. 9).

2. Because of the general price rise between 1897 and 1909—the period the Dingly Tariff Act was in force—and because of the use of specific as opposed to ad valorem rates, the average tariff rate over the 1897–1909 period was 46 percent on dutiable and 26 percent on free and dutiable goods (see Ratner, 1972, p. 40).

wool and other textile materials, such as hemp and flax (Taussig, 1910, pp. 274–75).

The protective blanket of American tariffs grew to encompass most manufactures. Congress typically imposed tariff rate increases on manufactured items that still entered the United States in large quantities despite existing duties (e.g., fine textiles). Tariff reductions for manufactures, on the other hand, were usually nominal. Tariff rates were reduced (never eliminated) on items that ceased or nearly ceased to be imported into the United States. Thus, these reduced rates still remained prohibitive.[3]

Compensating Tariffs

The existence of compensating duties demonstrates at once the imperatives of a policy process based on logrolling and the complexity of the American tariff system. The process of logrolling works when everyone stands to gain something, and the mutual exchange of support assures that everyone will get what he/she wants. Representatives of western agricultural states exchanged their support for protective tariffs on manufactures for protective tariffs on agricultural products, most notably raw wool. With the exception of the three years the Wilson-Gorman Act was in effect, imports of raw wool were taxed during the last half of the nineteenth century, and the United States was quite exceptional in this respect among countries of "advanced civilization." In fact, the duty on raw wool has been deemed "the most characteristic feature of our protective system" (Taussig, 1910, p. 292). Likewise, representatives in industrial states exchanged their support for protective duties on raw wool for duties on woolens that would compensate manufacturers for the rise in production costs experienced as a result of the duty on the raw material.[4]

Compensating duties were separate from and in addition to protective duties; thus, they greatly complicated the already complex tariff schedules. A compensating duty was generally levied as a specific tax based on an estimate of the amount of raw wool required to make a pound (in some cases, a yard) of cloth and on the current raw wool duty.

---

3. A notable exception to this general pattern was the reduction on dinnerware—part of the Wilson-Gorman Act of 1894. The rate on fine china (a big import item) was reduced from 60 to 35 percent. The rate on cheaper qualities went from 50 to 30 percent. The Dingly Act (1897) restored the duties of 1890. (See Taussig, 1910, p. 304.)

4. Import taxes on inputs for American manufacturing were not limited to raw wool, and their impact on the effective level of protection given to U.S. manufacturers was significant. In his study on nominal and effective tariff rates during the late nineteenth century, G. R. Hawke (1795) concludes: "There was much less increase in the protection given to U.S. manufacturers between 1879 and 1904 than is commonly believed. . . . [I]ncreased tariffs on inputs to many industries offset such increases in tariffs on individual outputs as took place" (p. 98).

The compensating system for wool and woolens was initiated in 1861 but began in earnest in 1867. The wool and woolens tariff of 1867 levied a specific duty on raw wool and a compensating duty on woolens, as well as a protective ad valorem tax. Over the years the compensating system became more elaborate, distinguishing between finished products for purposes of calculating the compensating duty; cheaper goods required less raw wool per pound of cloth than expensive ones, and this was reflected in the compensating duty. Meanwhile, the protective element of the woolens tax escalated from 35 percent in 1867, to 40 percent in 1883, to 50 percent in 1890, and to 55 percent in 1897 (Taussig, 1931, p. 333).

The Democrats under President Grover Cleveland temporarily (1894–1897) dismantled the system when they were able to place raw wool on the free list in 1894. Under the Wilson-Gorman Act, the compensating duty on woolens was eliminated, but the protective duty remained (Taussig, 1910, pp. 293–94).

The ability of the American commercial policy process to generate tariff policies for revenue, indiscriminate protection, and compensation is evident. Yet as early as the 1870s this was not enough. The United States confronted two major problems during the last decades of the nineteenth century. Between 1870 and 1900, American policymakers had to cope with the problem of revenue surpluses, and they also had to find a way to promote trade expansion. These problems recast the policy goals pursued in this issue area.

Resolving Nineteenth-Century Revenue and Trade Problems

Nineteenth-century advocates of tariff reform were handicapped in their efforts to achieve their objective. The impact of these handicaps was evident when officials addressed the problem of revenue surplus and when they tried to promote trade expansion. First, the imperative for tariff reform was not considered critical by all policymakers, and vehicles of reform were typically sidetracked to further other goals. It was not unusual for detractors of tariff reform to manipulate the proposed instruments of policy change to thwart the drive for reform. Second, characteristics of American politics of the late nineteenth century (viz., subservience of Congress and the president to "constituent" political parties) circumscribed the opportunities for reform.[5] Thus, tariff reform was stymied by political parties that used the tariff issue to attract electoral support but

5. This argument is similar to that made by Stephen Skowronek (1982). He considers "the universe of risks, incentives, constraints and opportunities" that informed the nineteenth-century attempts in the United States to create a merit civil service, to regulate the railroads, and to create a national military.

when in office inevitably chose to sacrifice tariff reform in order to satisfy constituent demands for protection.

Revenue and the Tariff Commission

The idea of a nonpartisan body created to study the impact of tariffs on the domestic economy and to make policy recommendations based on its findings predates the Progressive movement. The early attempts to use a commission to resolve tariff-generated revenue difficulties, however, are not illustrious.

Advisory bodies are effective only if their advice is heeded, and in this regard the revenue and tariff commissions of the nineteenth century were not. The record of the Revenue Commission demonstrates the point. Toward the end of the Civil War, Congress created a Special Revenue Commission. David A. Wells was appointed commissioner of the revenue. His task was to recommend changes in the tax and tariff structure in the aftermath of the war. In 1867, Wells recommended a moderately protectionist tariff reform. He suggested duty reductions on raw materials such as scrap iron, coal, lumber, hemp, and flax. He also recommended changes of duty for spices, chemicals, dyes, and dye-goods. Duties on manufactures were to remain basically unchanged (Dobson, 1976, p. 57; Kenkel, 1983, p. 15). Congress failed to pass the bill and abolished the Revenue Commission in 1870. Partially explaining this course of events is the fact that, by 1870, Wells had become a staunch advocate of free trade, and these views disturbed a largely protectionist Congress (Dobson, 1976, p. 83).

In the face of repeated Treasury surpluses in 1880, 1881, and 1882 and growing pressure to do something to relieve them, President Chester A. Arthur recommended and Congress authorized the appointment of a temporary tariff commission to advise on tariff reform. The creation of such a commission in 1882, however, was not a serious attempt to promote tariff reform. In reality, it was a device designed to forestall, not promote, such reform. President Arthur appointed nine protectionists to the commission, including, as president, John L. Hayes, secretary of the Wool Manufacturers Association. Moreover, the commission's report was scheduled for submission in December 1882, *after* Congress had adjourned. It was only the Democratic victory in the November election that prompted President Arthur to call a special session of Congress to give the Republicans one last chance to consider tariff reform before the Democrats took control in March 1883 (Kenkel, 1983, p. 26).

Not surprisingly, reform advocates dismissed the highly partisan body. They criticized Arthur's appointments, and they criticized the commission's methods of investigation, which were "as inconsistent and haphaz-ard as Congressional logrolling" (Kenkel, 1983, p. 25). Ironically, when the commission's report concluded "that a substantial reduction of tar-iff duties was demanded, not by a mere indiscriminate popular clamor, but by the best conservative opinion of the country," avowed protection-ists in Congress also dismissed the commission and its recommendations (quoted in Ratner, 1972, p. 34).

The commission recommended a duty reduction of 20 to 25 percent on items like sugar and molasses. It also proposed substantial reductions in duties on raw materials (Ratner, 1972, p. 34). In view of existing reve-nue surpluses, the commission had obviously concluded that traditional revenue-generating duties on items heavily imported into the United States should be scaled back. No rationale, however, was apparent for the overwhelming majority of the commission's proposed rate adjustments. Certainly, the recommendations bore little trace of principles that sup-posedly guided the commission's work. One such principle—that duties should "equalize the conditions of labor and capital" between domestic and foreign producers (*Report of the Tariff Commission*, 1882, 1:4–5)—was particularly abused. Without the time or the resources to conduct inde-pendent investigations, the commission relied on the "expert" testimony of industry representatives to suggest appropriate duties. Moreover, the constraint of time made it impossible for the commission to absorb all of the information acquired through the hearings process. Relevant material was often ignored (Kenkel, 1983, p. 25).

Indiscriminate methods notwithstanding, the Tariff Commission rec-ommended a moderated tariff package to Congress. It failed to pass. Mem-bers of Congress and their constituents from the business community did not accept the commission's findings. When Republican leaders took up the issue of tariff revision in special session in December 1882, they virtually dismissed the commission's report. Instead, Congress passed the so-called Mongrel Act in 1883. American trade policy remained unre-formed—decidedly protectionist and prone to generate surplus revenue.

The advisory commission represented an interesting variation of the pattern of nineteenth-century institutional relations for tariff policy. In principle, it offered officials in Congress and the White House the possib-lity of more informed decision making. In application, however, the idea floundered. In the context of the interorganizational relations of nineteenth-century American political institutions and filtered through the personal cost-benefit assessments of officials occupying positions of authority in these institutions, the commmission could never become a vehicle of tariff (revenue) reform. For some, the commission served to put off serious consideration of tariff reform; for others, it was viewed as a way to reinforce the nation's policy commitment to protectionism. For champions of real reform, the commission was held in disrepute. President Arthur's appointment of such a partisan body (all protectionists) and its reliance on the "expert" testimony of interested parties did much to discredit the commission concept as a means to improve policy. The idea was not seriously considered again until the twentieth century, when it became part of the Progressive framework for policy and government reform.

Trade Expansion and the Role of Party: The Wilson-Gorman Act of 1894

Between 1860 and 1900, the value of American manufacturing increased by more than 500 percent. By 1900, the United States had surpassed all other nations in the production of iron, steel, and coal. In fact, American steel production, "the most convenient single measure of industrial power," was double that of Great Britain by the end of the century. During the same period in agriculture, the production of major crops— corn, wheat, cotton, and livestock—rose by 130 to 150 percent (U.S. Bureau of the Census, 1960, pp. 289, 297, 301–2, 409; Kirkland, 1961, p. 165; Degler, 1977, p. 28). Despite this prodigious growth, the United States experienced thirteen years of depression between 1873 and 1900. Trade expansion became an increasingly important concern for policymakers of both political parties. They viewed increased access to overseas markets as necessary in the face of the boom-and-bust cycles of the domestic economy. They saw trade expansion as a way to moderate these fluctuations (LaFeber, 1963, pp. 17–24; Terrill, 1973).

The concern of policymakers with overseas trade expansion was tempered and shaped by their concern as party leaders with the dynamics of electoral politics. Late-nineteenth-century American politics was characterized by a two-party "equipoise" (Terrill, 1973, pp. 3–13). In national elections, neither the Republicans nor the Democrats commanded a natural majority. Either party could gain control of the national government, and both parties sought to mobilize the electorate around their respective platforms. Thus, although policymakers and party leaders were concerned about trade expansion, they were preoccupied with electoral politics, and in both the tariff figured prominently.

Taking opposite positions on the issue, the two parties focused a great deal of attention on the tariff. The Democrats wanted "Free Raw Materials" and "A Tariff for Revenue Only"; the Republicans championed high protective tariffs. Party rhetoric on the tariff reached its peak in 1887 and 1888. The "Great Tariff Debate" of the election of 1888 commenced when President Grover Cleveland devoted his 1887 State of the Union address to the tariff issue.[6] The decade 1890 to 1900 saw three major tariff revisions, which corresponded with election swings that put the Republicans (McKinley Act, 1890), the Democrats (Wilson-Gorman Act, 1894), and the Republicans (Dingly Act, 1897) in control of the national government.

Tariff reductionists in the Democratic party wanted tariff reform in order to lower taxes; eliminate, once and for all, the persistent Treasury surplus; and promote trade expansion. The tariff reductionists designed this strategy to shore up a shaky electoral coalition of New England manufacturers (free raw materials, trade expansion) and western and southern agrarians (lower taxes, trade expansion). However, using the tariff issue to secure a winning electoral coalition for the party was different from using party as a means to secure tariff reform. This point is evidenced by the repeated failure of the party in power "to enact a tariff the duties of which confirmed equitably and without glaring exception to the policy which the electorate had intended to establish." The succession of failures gave rise to "the maxim of politics that a tariff revision in the year of an election is fatal to the party which makes it" (Page, 1924, pp. 1–2). Thus, when the Democrats regained control of Congress and the White House in 1892 and sought tariff reform, it was an effort unlikely to succeed.

Leading Democrats, including President Grover Cleveland and Ways and Means Committee chairman William Wilson, were determined to enact legislation in accord with the Democratic platform planks. Chairman Wilson and his committee marked up the bill in closed session and insisted that it be reported to the House floor under a closed rule. The closed rule prevented the addition of any amendments except one to kill the bill. Under these procedures, the House passed the bill on a party-line vote (Terrill, 1973, p. 192).

The Senate did not use similar procedural options. Indeed, its predisposition to logroll was intensified by its small size (relative to the House) and its equal representation of the states. Senators from less populated states could exercise disproportionate leverage in fighting for duties that were of interest to them (e.g., raw materials) because their votes could not be ignored. These Senators tended to join forces, and together they constituted a formidable bloc. Senators from industrial states felt obliged to accept duties on raw materials like coal and hides in exchange for support for duties on manufactures (Taussig, 1910, pp. 373–74).

President Cleveland relied on party unity in the Senate to overcome this tendency to logroll and thereby achieve tariff reform. Unfortunately,

6. The Republicans, campaigning on a platform of high tariffs, swept the 1888 elections. But "most voters probably voted without particular regard for the tariff as an issue, although the political leaders believed they did" (Terrill, 1973, p. 119).

he had no way to secure this unity. The Senate proceeded to amend the Wilson bill beyond recognition, and its version largely prevailed in conference. Disappointed with the result of the legislative process, President Cleveland nevertheless noted the modest reductions in the proposed bill and the raw materials (raw wool and lumber) added to the free list. He decided that the bill was at least an improvement on the McKinley Tariff (1890), and he allowed the bill to become law without his signature (Taussig, 1910, chap. 6; Terrill, 1973, chap. 8).

When the Senate passed its version of the Wilson bill, it contained 634 amendments, including ones that removed iron ore, coal, and sugar from the free list. All pretense of party unity was destroyed. The Senate Democratic leadership, most notably Senator Gorman of Maryland, was unsympathetic to the low tariff philosophy represented in the House bill. Democratic Senators could not be compelled to accept the party platform in policy-making.

Cleveland's inability to achieve party unity and therefore tariff reform was due in large part to the rigidly defined universe of institutional opportunities, incentives, risks, and constraints that severely limited the influence that late-nineteenth-century presidents exercised in government and policy-making. Moreover, Cleveland made a bad situation even worse—his leadership was poor and his timing abysmal. President Cleveland sought reform at a time when there was no tariff reductionist in a Senate leadership position and at a time when his influence and patronage leverage were exhausted. His condemnation of the Senate Democrats in a letter read on the House floor precluded any possible House–Senate compromise on the tariff issue (Terrill, 1973, pp. 192–94).

As was noted earlier, the nineteenth-century trade policy process consisted of Congress's legislating tariff rates and the president's negotiating commercial treaties. The discussion of nineteenth-century trade policymaking so far has, for the most part, presumed an appreciation of a whole host of established patterns of intra- and interorganizational relations that facilitated government operations. These patterns prominently featured political parties. American political parties linked the national government with states and localities, and they organized the legislature internally, but they did not insulate government officials from the pressures of particularistic interests. Party ideology in the United States could not prevent the use of logrolling to expedite the legislative process. On the contrary, as the legislative history of the Wilson-Gorman Act demonstrates, legislative politics embraced the logroll as a means of courting local interests, despite the ideology of the Democratic party.

*Power Sharing with the President: Reciprocity as a Means
to Expand Overseas Trade*

In the McKinley (1890) and Dingly (1897) Tariff acts, the Republicans endeavored to make commercial policy an instrument of foreign policy in order to promote exports. Although the reciprocity efforts of the Harrison and McKinley administrations yielded disappointing economic results, the political significance of what they achieved should not be overlooked or dismissed. In the reciprocity clause of the McKinley Act and Section 3 of the Dingly Act, Congress relinquished its taxing prerogatives to the president. In the context of bilateral negotiations (i.e., a foreign policy context), the president could act to alter tariff rates. Of course, this delegation of authority was carefully and narrowly defined; it applied only to a small number of specified commodities. But a precedent had been established. The president had been given the authority to negotiate trade agreements that became law without Senate approval. Under appropriate circumstances, members of Congress could be persuaded to share their tariff-setting responsibilities with the president.

At the urging of Secretary of State James G. Blaine, a reciprocity provision was included in the 1890 tariff bill. Blaine wanted to wrest concessions from Latin American countries that would promote trade expansion. Toward this goal, he persuaded a reluctant Congress to include, only provisionally, unrefined sugar, molasses, tea, and coffee on the free list. Republican members of Congress had wanted these items imported duty-free on an unconditional basis to eliminate the specter of revenue surplus. They agreed to amend the McKinley bill to include Blaine's proviso only at the last minute. Blaine's high standing with his party, his recognized position as a lifelong and uncompromising advocate of protection, and his reputation as a far-seeing statesman help to explain this success (Stanwood, 1903, 2:279).

The reciprocity provision enabled the president to impose duties on sugar, molasses, tea, coffee, and hides "if any country exporting these items to the U.S. imposed duties or other exactions on the agricultural or other products of the United States, which in view of the free introduction of sugar, molasses, tea, coffee, and hides into the United States, he may deem to be reciprocally unjust or unreasonable" (quoted in Taussig, 1910, p. 279). Under the reciprocity clause, the United States negotiated trade agreements with many Latin American exporters of sugar, molasses, tea, coffee, and hides. Only those agreements concluded with Brazil and with Spain for Cuba had any significant impact on American exports (Terrill, 1973, p. 176).

The reciprocity provisions under the Dingly Act were ostensibly more sweeping than their counterparts under the McKinley Act. The Dingly tariff provided for three types of reciprocal trade arrangements. Under Section 3 of the act, Congress allowed minimal concessions without Congressional approval. For equivalent concessions, the United States would reduce duties on such items as brandies, wines, vermouth, and paintings. The president could also retaliate against discrimination by raising the duties on coffee, tea, vanilla, and tonka beans. The McKinley administration negotiated four agreements under these provisions, none of great economic significance (Terrill, 1973, pp. 200–1).

The third reciprocity provision (Section 4) sanctioned the negotiation of trade treaties to lower some or all duties up to 20 percent. These treaties, however, required the approval of the Senate, had to be negotiated and in force within two years of the date the Dingly tariff became law, and would remain in effect for only five years. This section of the Dingly Act did not grant the president any treaty-making authority he did not already possess, and it may even have inspired Congress to set tariff rates higher in anticipation of negotiated concessions. None of the treaties negotiated under Section 4 of the Dingly Act (known as the Kasson treaties) were ratified by the Senate (Laughlin and Willus, 1903, chap. 10).

Given the constraints within which nineteenth-century policymakers operated, Secretary of State Blaine's achievement was remarkable. He derived an acceptable formula whereby the president shared Congressional rate-setting authority. He also succeeded in convincing important Republican leaders, including William McKinley, that reciprocity was the key to overseas trade expansion. Unfortunately, the intent of his reform was sidetracked in 1897. Under the reciprocity provisions of the Dingly Act, the president was given little additional negotiating authority, but these provisions served to justify the imposition of extraordinarily high tariff rates.

Comparing Nineteenth- and Twentieth-Century Reform Initiatives

It is not mere coincidence that the methods for institutional change employed in the twentieth century resembled those used to pursue tariff reform in the nineteenth. The specific bureaucratic and political mechanisms used to insulate the trade policy process were distinctively American. As specific applications of the possible insulation strategies, the party, commission, and power-sharing alternatives grew out of the American political experience. Because the institutional setting remained fundamentally unchanged, policymakers of both centuries faced the same repertoire of reform vehicles.

Several factors, however, distinguish the significance of the twentieth-century experience from that of the nineteenth in terms of trade policy-making. First, in the later period the reform imperative became more universally recognized. In addition, the complexity of the trade policy dilemma was better understood, and the proposition that tariff reform entailed institutional change was increasingly accepted. Second, the political environment of the early twentieth century had altered in important ways. The late-nineteenth-century patterns of governmental interorganizational relationships were disrupted. Elected officials in the legislative and executive branches of government gained an independence from party that they had not enjoyed in the previous era.[7] This newfound independence gave salience to reform initiatives at all levels of government and in policy areas as diverse as resource management, banking, and the tariff. These factors allowed reform-minded policymakers to pursue policy-making changes in trade as well as in other issue areas.

Although their proposals were reminiscent of earlier reform initiatives, the efforts of twentieth-century policymakers were informed by well-developed reform agendas. These agendas, or cognitive frameworks, were forged as pragmatic responses to perceived limitations of nineteenth-century policy-making. This made twentieth-century reformers more ambitious than their nineteenth-century counterparts. They had learned from the experience of their nineteenth-century counterparts, and given altered political realities, they could hope for greater success.

7. This new independence has been attributed to the realigning election of 1896. No longer did the two major parties compete equally in national elections. The Republicans commanded a natural majority. (See Walter Dean Burnham in Chambers and Burnham, 1967.)

CHAPTER FOUR

Reform through Party:
The Underwood Act of 1913

With the Underwood Act, the Democrats delivered tariff legislation that substantially reflected the tariff reduction policy long proclaimed in the Democratic party platform. The tariff victory was the first in President Woodrow Wilson's efforts to implement his New Freedom program. It also represented a triumph for Wilson's vision of party government in the United States. This vision saw party as the key to cooperative relations between the executive and legislative branches of government and as the bulwark against special interest influence in policy-making.

Wilson's conception of party, however, ran counter to well-established patterns and practices in American politics. During the early years of the Republic, the lack of constitutional provisions for presidential succession had compelled Congress to provide a solution in its nominating caucus. The caucus was a group of legislators organized for the principal purpose of capturing the presidency by legitimating and promoting its candidates.[1] Inherent in this solution was a fusion of powers because the Congress was the president's constituency. Moreover, the succession issue fed into all of the policy issues involving the federal government. But party development changed all this. In the Jacksonian period, parties established control of the presidential selection process. The development of "modern" political parties after 1828 gave the presidency a power base independent of Congress. At the same time, however, party development served to reinforce the constitutional separation of the executive and the legislature. Political parties in the United States "institutionalized *real* separation of powers" (Lowi, 1967, pp. 247–48, emphasis in original; Binkley, 1962).

1. The first nominating caucus met in 1804; the last, in 1824. Each was held under Republican auspices (i.e., "by legislators claiming loyalty to Jeffersonian principles"). The Federalist or other opposition parties held no nominating caucus in the Capitol. (See Young, 1966, p. 114.)

Political parties in America also came to control the organization and administration of Congress and most state legislatures. Parties in Congress functioned as "conduits" and "cumulators" of narrow interests. They relied on logrolling to facilitate the legislative process (Lowi, 1964; 1967, p. 274).

Thus, in 1913, Wilson confronted an enormous challenge. He not only had to close the institutionalized gap between president and Congress, but he also had to fashion the instrument of special interests—the political party—into government's instrument of insulation from those interests. His first opportunity as well as his first test was tariff reform.

Between 1897 and 1909 there had been no general tariff revision. Years of economic prosperity (until 1907) and uninterrupted Republican control of the national government help explain this phenomenon. Moreover, Theodore Roosevelt had exchanged Congressional assurances of action on railroad regulation for his promise not to push tariff reform (Blum, 1977, pp. 75–86).[2] The lack of government activity on the tariff during this period did not mean, however, that the tariff issue was a dormant one. Economic developments guaranteed agitation on the tariff front.

One important development was the growth of large-scale business organizations and trusts in industry, transportation, finance, and to a lesser extent in labor (Faulkner, 1951, p. 153). Several factors compelled captains of industry to pursue large-scale operations. First, technological breakthroughs and innovations (such as advances in power-generating machinery and machine tools) made large-scale production possible. In addition, as overhead costs escalated with the acquisition of new equipment, large-scale production became more than possible; it became necessary. Second, large-scale production required a large market. The development of transportation networks provided American industry access to such a market. Finally, the corporate form of organization "permitted orderly capital subscription procedures under which capital could be fed into the enterprise on a defined installment plan" (Faulkner, 1951, pp. 154–55; Hurst, 1956, p. 17). In this way, the capital requirements for large-scale industry, which were beyond the resources of any single individual or partnership, could be met.

Trusts were a feature of the American economy before 1897. The onset of the rapid movement toward consolidation in industry, however, coincided

2. The Republican leadership in Congress steadfastly opposed tariff reform because the political risks were too great. Speaker Joseph Cannon commented, "We know from long experience that no matter how great an improvement the new tariff may be, it almost always results in the party in power losing the following election" (quoted in Anderson, 1973, p. 96).

with the adoption of the Dingly Tariff Act, the tariff bill that resulted in the highest tariff rates in history to that time. Protectionist tariff policy had contributed to the formation of trusts in a few cases prior to 1897, and it is entirely possible that inordinate protection encouraged the formation of monopolies, but the popular characterization of the protective policy as the "mother of all trusts" was, at best, overdrawn.[3] Harry O. Havenger, president of the American Sugar Refining Company, coined the phrase in testimony before the Industrial Commission in 1901, and, evidence to the contrary, it became a widely held belief and a rationale for tariff reform during the first decade of the twentieth century (U.S. Industrial Commission, 1900–1902).

The rising cost of living also contributed to the growing discontent over the tariff. Living costs rose 7 percent between 1898 and 1901 and 17 percent from 1902 to 1907. They continued their upward swing after the panic of 1907. By 1914, the cost of living was at least 16 percent above the period 1906–1909 (Leschier and Brandeis, 1935, pp. 55–61). Scholars attribute this rise in general price levels to an increase in the money supply (i.e., gold supply) due at first to favorable trade balances, which resulted in an influx of $120 million in gold in 1898, and sustained by mining efforts in South Africa, Australia, and Alaska (Faulkner, 1951, p. 23). The circumstance of rising prices was a welcome reversal in the long downward trend of prices that had prevailed since the Civil War (Faulkner, 1951, p. 6). It helped to restore confidence in the economy and to promote an upward swing in the business cycle at the turn of the century.

Wages, however, lagged behind the cost of living, and in general, wage earners hardly benefited from the increased industrial production of the 1897–1914 period. "Such improvements in welfare as labor was able to attain after 1900 came from more plentiful employment, than from wage rates" (Leschier and Brandeis, 1935, p. 61). Advocates of tariff reform exploited the lag in wage increases relative to the cost of living. They successfully connected high tariffs with the high cost of living, and they were able to repudiate the long-standing Republican claim that high tariffs protected the American wage earner's standard of living.[4]

The growth of trusts and the high cost of living fueled ever-increasing demands for tariff reform. Small-scale manufacturers, in particular, com-

---

3. Available evidence suggests there was a connection between tariffs and the formation of trusts in the sugar, tin plate, and steel rail industries (Taussig, 1915, pp. 171–90, 194).

4. Undoubtedly, the Republican defense of protection deserved repudiation. Richard C. Edwards (1970) writes, "When we turn to a systematic study of the protectionist position we find that the Republicans presented a curious model seemingly profound, but at bottom almost a classic case of economic nonsense" (p. 823).

plained that prices of raw materials and semifinished goods were held artificially high by the trusts. They also claimed that trusts stifled competition. Since antitrust legislation had proved ineffective, tariff reform offered another way to restore competition and restrain prices (Mowry, 1946, p. 45; Wiebe, 1962, pp. 14–15, 55–61; Kenkel, 1983, p. 39).

These small manufacturers also wanted a foreign economic policy that would promote trade expansion. Government assistance to establish markets overseas was not required by large manufacturers. These companies had cost, technological, and managerial advantages that made their products competitive in foreign markets. The same advantages did not accrue to small-scale producers who developed an interest in trade expansion during the depression of the 1890s. They viewed overseas markets as alternative outlets for their products when depressed conditions gripped the domestic economy. Through organizations like the National Association of Manufacturers (NAM) and the American Manufacturers' Export Association (AMEA), small and medium-size firms sought government assistance to expand their markets abroad. To this end, they advocated tariff reform (Becker, 1982, pp. ix, 46–47, 65–66, 69).

The economic downturn of 1907 gave momentum to a growing movement for lower tariffs. It badly tarnished the myth equating protection with prosperity, and it fostered increased agitation for a trade expansion policy. The downturn also gave Democrats, who had long denounced Republican tariff policy as a breeder of trusts and as a haven for special interests, an issue to exploit. The Republican leadership could no longer ignore the issue. The movement for lower tariffs had become national and included prominent members of the Republican party.

The Payne-Aldrich Act: The Republican Party Attempts Tariff Reform

Progressive Republicans from the Midwest (most notably, Senators Robert M. La Follette of Wisconsin, Jonathan P. Dolliver and Albert B. Cummins of Iowa, Albert B. Beveridge of Indiana, Joseph F. Bristow of Kansas, and Moses E. Clapp of Minnesota) were the party's most outspoken advocates of tariff reform. The Dingly tariff had not benefited their farming constituencies. Farmers' income had not kept pace with the increase in their production and living costs, and in contrast to important export windfalls in the late 1890s, farmers experienced a declining world market for their products in the early 1900s. American grain exporters, in particular, experienced stiff competition from Argentina, Australia, Russia, and Canada in the European market (Kenkel, 1983, p. 41).

These midwestern Republicans considered themselves moderate protectionists. They sought tariff reform that would eliminate the special privileges enjoyed by eastern manufacturers. Senator Dolliver, for example, urged the repeal of duties that "sheltered monopolies." This "Iowa Idea" was popularized by Senator Cummins (Mowry, 1946, pp. 44–45; Kenkel, 1983, pp. 35–37). Progressive Republicans wanted to curb the excesses of protectionism as manifest in American tariff policy and thereby vindicate the principle of protection.

When President William H. Taft called Congress into special session on March 15, 1909, to consider the tariff question, Republican progressives believed there existed a good chance to achieve tariff reform. The 1908 Republican party platform had included a plank calling for a general tariff revision: "The Republican Party declares unequivocally for a revision of the tariff" (quoted in Mowry, 1946, p. 46). Although the document did not explicitly promise a revision downward, in light of the candidates' statements, people generally considered the party bound to reduce the rates (Mowry, 1946, p. 46). Progressives in the Republican party hoped that President Taft, who had repeatedly endorsed a downward revision during the campaign, would prove a strong ally.

The last time a party in power had advocated a downward revision of the tariff schedules was in 1892, when President Grover Cleveland began his second administration. The Wilson-Gorman Tariff Act reflected the difficulties President Cleveland encountered in pursuing tariff reform. He had to rely on party as the only buffer between senators and the particularistic interests of their constituencies. Cleveland, moreover, lacked resources to compel party unity.

Taft faced a similar situation. To achieve a downward revision in the tariff rates he needed party unity. However, the structure of government did not then and does not now compel party allegiance to a stated program in policy-making and, in fact, encourages legislators to serve the particularistic interests of their local constituencies. Therefore, efforts to achieve party unity must inevitably focus on altering the cost-benefit calculations of party members in Congress so that it becomes more attractive to vote the party program than to serve local interests.

Several instruments for encouraging party unity accrue to the president. Among these, side payments are the most obvious. Early-twentieth-century presidents, for example, could attract Congressional support for their policy programs through aggressive use of patronage. The president could also make direct appeals to the voters. By having attention called to Congressional politics on issues of demonstrated concern to the voters, legislators may be less inclined to abandon their party's stated positions on these issues.

The instruments at the president's disposal for forging party unity have varied in number and effectiveness over time. Presidents in office when their party is the new majority party in Congress have typically been more successful in compelling party unity in policy-making than have presidents in office at other times (Skowronek, 1984, pp. 87–132). The instruments afforded these presidents, however, lose their effectiveness as new representatives and senators develop links with important constituent groups and become less dependent on presidential patronage for their electoral success. Party unity quickly ceases to be a feature of the American legislative process.

In 1909, tariff reform via party was problematic at best. Vigorous presidential leadership held out the only promise of success. Without it, tariff reform under party auspices was not even a remote possibility. Unlike President Cleveland before him, Taft had resources that he could have used to promote Republican party cohesion on the tariff issue. For various reasons, however, he did not. The result was the Payne-Aldrich Act— a law about as distant from the spirit of the Republican party platform plank as was the Wilson-Gorman Act from that of the Democratic platform in 1892.

President Taft called a special session of Congress to take up the tariff issue, but he was never an effective advocate of policy-making reform. Right from the start, Taft missed an opportunity to influence the policy-making process. His tariff message contained no strident demand for downward revision; it merely stated that Congress had been called for the task of revising the tariff.[5] Even without presidential urging, the Payne bill reported to the House on the third day of the session represented a significant attempt at downward revision. It included important decreases from the Dingly heights on pig iron, machine tools, agricultural implements, lumber, print paper, and sugar, and it fairly reflected the position the president had espoused in his campaign speeches. Midwestern repre-

---

5. In this regard, George Mowry (1946) writes, "Busy with some inconsequential politics in Ohio, Taft in his usual manner had failed to write the trenchant message he had originally planned. It was a poor beginning, indeed, to treat so explosive a matter as tariff reform in this casual manner" (p. 46). Donald E. Anderson also comments on Taft's missed opportunity to demonstrate leadership. He explains it as the result of his "lack of political imagination" and his "policy of harmony." Taft did not want to alienate potentially cooperative Congressional leaders with empty rhetoric (Anderson, 1973, p. 104).

sentatives and progressives expressed satisfaction with the bill (Mowry, 1946, p. 47).

At the president's request and over the objections of House Speaker Joseph Cannon, coal, hides, and iron ore were placed on the free list.[6] Taft, however, rarely intervened in the tariff-making process. At only one other time did the president involve himself in the process. To placate Representative Joseph W. Fordney (Congressional spokesman for the beet sugar growers), Taft submitted a letter to Congress pledging no further reductions in the sugar duty, provided 300,000 tons of sugar from the Philippines was annually admitted duty-free (*Congressional Record*, 44:333). The president's practice of nonintervention did not adversely affect the passage of the Payne bill. The House passed it on a party-line vote on April, 9, 1909.

The moderate Payne bill, however, experienced metamorphosis in the Senate. The bill reported to the Senate floor by Senate Finance Committee chairman Nelson Aldrich contained 847 amendments, over half of substantial importance. It reimposed duties on iron ore, hides, and coal. It increased the duties on numerous articles, including lumber, sugar, iron and steel goods, cottons, hosiery, and other manufactures. It eliminated the Payne bill's provision for an inheritance tax as a means to recoup lost tariff revenue and inserted a provision for maximum and minimum tariff rates.[7]

Many of the changes substituted specific for ad valorem duties; some shifted the dividing line in the progression of specific duties. The actual significance of these changes was often difficult to ascertain. (See Payne's statement in *Congressional Record*, 44:4384.) They tended, however, "to tighten the extreme protective system and were likely to embody jokers— new rates of real importance, advantageous to particular producers and concealed in the endless detail" (Taussig, 1910, p. 376). Statistics compiled at the request of Senator La Follette by the Bureau of Statistics of the Department of Commerce actually indicated that the Aldrich amend-

6. Speaker Cannon maintained a low profile throughout this phase of the legislative process. In return for Taft's support in his effort to retain powers as Speaker, Cannon promised to carry out the pledges of the Chicago platform. He forgot this pledge, however, when the bill went to conference. (See Mowry, 1946, p. 42, and Anderson, 1973, pp. 99–101.)

7. An Insurgent-Democrat coalition threatened to pass a progressive income tax after the inheritance tax provision was eliminated from the Payne bill. Senator Aldrich feared the success of such a coalition, and he asked the president to intervene. Under the circumstances, Taft obtained Aldrich's support for a corporation tax and a constitutional amendment legalizing an income tax. The tax and the amendment passed. The Sixteenth Amendment was ratified February 25, 1913 (see Anderson, 1973, pp. 108–9; for a sense of business reaction to the corporation tax, see Wiebe, 1962, pp. 196–97.)

ments increased the average ad valorem rates from 40.21 percent under the Dingly Act to 41.77 percent (*Congressional Record*, 44:2752–2832).

Despite Aldrich's surreptitious tactics, the bill's true nature was not disguised. Ringing opposition sounded from Senators La Follette, Dolliver, Cummins, Beveridge, and Clapp. Their speeches before the Senate were heavily laced with references to the party platform and party responsibility. They claimed that in opposing the bill they were fighting the president's battle. In the words of two senators:

I cannot refrain from entering a personal dissent from the proposition that it was the purpose of the President in calling this Congress or the purpose of the party in practically ordering the Congress to be called together in its platform of last year, either to leave the Dingly tariff act as it is or to increase its rates.

[Congress] certainly was not called into session to increase the tariff. There was not a voice raised upon that proposition. It certainly was not called into existence to let the tariff stand exactly as it did because an extraordinary session of Congress was not necessary for that purpose. (*Congressional Record*, 44:1460–61)

The president, however, who had promised a downward revision in the campaign remained mute.

Taft was disturbed by the Aldrich bill. He is reported to have remarked to his secretary of the navy, "I fear Aldrich is ready to sacrifice the party [on the tariff issue] and I will not permit it" (quoted in Pringle, 1964, 1:432). Yet Taft voiced no opposition to the Aldrich bill when it was presented to the Senate. When Aldrich threatened to lower the tariff on products of interest to wavering senators, Taft did not use his patronage power to counter Aldrich's tactics. Progressives had to be content with Taft's promise to veto the tariff bill if it was not to his liking (La Follette, 1953, 1:273). The president, however, did not publicly threaten to veto the bill, and expert opinion at the time declared it unlikely that he would exercise his veto power (Anderson, 1973, p. 113).

Taft lobbied for the House version when the bill went to conference. He had been advised by Senator Henry Cabot Lodge that the Conference Committee offered the best opportunity for the president to influence the legislative process (Mowry, 1946, 55–56; La Follette, 1953, 1:273). While this style of executive-legislative interaction suited the president, his efforts were too little, too late.

The only Republican moderate on the committee was Sereno E. Payne, chairman of the House Ways and Means Committee. In their selection of committee members, Speaker Cannon and Senator Aldrich had skipped over several capable moderates. Payne walked out of conference on several occasions when his House colleagues voted unanimously to set aside the House bill and accept the Aldrich rates (Mowry, 1946, p. 62).

During the course of the committee's existence, the president moderated his demand for lower duties, asking only for free raw materials and reductions in the woolen, glove, and hosiery schedules. Speaker Cannon, however, threatened to adjourn the House with the bill still in conference if these reductions were incorporated into the conference report. Meanwhile, western senators pledged to oppose the bill if the duties on raw materials were reduced or rescinded. Ultimately, the threat of a presidential veto did have some impact on the proceedings. Taft obtained free hides and reductions on glass, lumber, coal, and iron ore. In addition, oil was put on the free list, and reductions were made on some steel and iron goods (Taussig, 1910, pp. 400–8).

Taft's victory was a minor one. In the end, Aldrich and the conservatives scored a victory for high protection. The House acquiesced in 522 of the Senate amendments. The Senate yielded on 124. The other 201 amendments were compromised. Except for some new administrative features, which included a tariff board to help the president implement the maximum-minimum rate provision, the bill did not differ from previous Republican tariffs. In fact, many of the Dingly Act's schedules, including the infamous woolen schedule (Schedule X) were left largely unchanged (Taussig, 1910, pp. 400–8).

Taft tried to persuade the progressive Republicans to support the president and the party by voting for the Payne-Aldrich bill; he did not succeed. Following the lead of the progressive senators, twenty House Republicans voted against the bill (*Congressional Record* 44:4755).

American political parties could not oversee tariff reform. The Republican party in 1909, like the Democrats in 1894, could not achieve tariff reform. The Republican party platform pledge to revise the tariff could not assure a downward revision. The party was divided on the tariff issue, and the progressives were in the minority. To achieve significant changes in the tariff schedules, they needed the diligent support of the president. Only the president could possibly persuade wavering senators to support the moderate protection position of the progressives. He needed to counter the Senate leadership's threats by using patronage leverage. This the president refused to do.

Several explanations have been offered for Taft's seeming complacency on the tariff. It has been suggested that his restricted view of the appropriate exercise of presidential authority kept him from using patronage leverage. He did not want to infringe on the legislature's prerogatives (Pringle, 1964, 1:424–25; Skowronek, 1982, pp. 173–74). Another interpretation suggests that Taft's actions on the tariff issue reveal his conservative bias. According to this argument, Taft's unwillingness to use patronage to defeat the Aldrich bill cannot be explained by his conception of the limits of presidential authority. When it came to supporting conservatives against progressives on other issues, Taft was perfectly willing to exercise presidential prerogatives (Mowry, 1946, p. 55 n).

Whether it was his "neo-Madisonian" conception of institutional relationships or a bias toward conservatism that inspired Taft's leadership, any action he took on the tariff was bound to antagonize some part of his party. His decision not to alienate Senate powerhouse Aldrich was understandable but costly. Taft was never able to regain the trust of the progressives in his party. Other events would drive Teddy Roosevelt and the progressives to split from the party in 1912; however, the tariff trouble set the tone for the rest of Taft's term. Moreover, the Republican failure to deliver a moderate tariff gave the Democrats an issue to exploit. The Democratic party won control of the House of Representatives in the midterm elections.

The New Nationalism versus the New Freedom on Tariff Reform

Certain broad social, political, and economic issues defined progressivism and its policy goals during the early decades of the twentieth century. These goals included providing the underprivileged with a larger share of the nation's wealth, making government more responsive to the wishes of the voters, and regulating the economy in the public interest (Wiebe, 1962, p. 211). Progressives disagreed, however, about how to address these issues. The election of 1912 showcased opposing visions of a Progressive America and opposing views about tariff policy and policy-making.

The political philosophy of the New Nationalism espoused by Theodore Roosevelt and his Progressive party was provided by Herbert Croly in his *Promise of American Life* (1909). According to Croly, there had been two divergent views in American thought of the role the federal government should play. The first was that of Alexander Hamilton: government should intervene directly to alter existing economic relationships and to establish new ones. The second, the Jeffersonian view, held that government should practice a policy of laissez-faire toward economic activity. The weak Jeffersonian government had become identified with democracy, equal rights, and opportunity. Croly, however, recommended that the progressives abandon their prejudices against strong government and accept Hamiltonian means to secure Jeffersonian or democratic ends (pp. 28–29, 44–45, 153).

Theodore Roosevelt translated Croly's recommendations into a pragmatic framework for action laced in rhetoric. He wrote:

Our country—this great republic—means nothing unless it means the triumph of popular government and in the long run an economic system under which each man shall be guaranteed the opportunity to show the best that there is in him. . . . The national government belongs to the whole American people and where the whole American people are interested, that interest can be guarded effectively only by the national government. The betterment we seek must be accomplished, I believe, mainly through the national government. (Roosevelt, 1910, pp. 3, 27–28)

The New Nationalism, as represented in the Progressive party platform, advocated social, political, and economic reforms (Link, 1954, p. 16 n). Among its economic reform proposals, the Progressive party called for a federal trade commission to regulate business and industrial activity. It also called for the creation of a permanent tariff commission that would set rates on a scientific basis and guarantee that the benefits of protection accrued to workers as well as to employers.

Progressives like Roosevelt did not want to abandon protectionism. In their opinion, America's rapid industrial growth and the relatively high standard of living enjoyed by American workers proved the value of the policy of protection. They believed, however, that the policy had been exploited by special interests at the expense of the public good. Protection had become something considerably less than principled policy. It was the privilege of entrenched interests (Roosevelt, 1910, pp. 109–10). Moreover, the old, established method of tariff making by its very nature could not restore the public interest in tariff making. With reference to the Payne-Aldrich bill, Roosevelt wrote: "I am not at all sure that it was possible under the old methods to get any other result. I am very much afraid that the trouble was fundamental; in other words, that it is not possible, as Congress is actually constructed to expect the tariff to be well handled by *representatives of localities*" (quoted in Anderson, 1973, pp. 119–20; emphasis in original). The Progressive party endorsed the creation of a permanent, nonpartisan tariff commission that could determine tariff rates without reference to any special interest. The tariff commission would calculate rates of duty according to a cost of production standard.

The idea of a cost-of-production standard had long been popular among protectionists, who had often used it to rationalize proposed tariff rate increases (Taussig, 1910, pp. 364–67). A variation of the idea had been incorporated into the 1904 Republican platform. It called for tariff rates to equalize foreign and domestic costs of production plus a reasonable profit. The Republicans, however, did not endorse a tariff commission in 1904 or 1908. Party stalwarts rejected any proposal that might result in tariff reductions, no matter how moderate. In 1912, the Progressive party refined the cost standard and interpreted it to mean tariff adjustment by commission to equalize labor costs (Roosevelt, 1910, p. 111).

In contrast to the New Nationalism, the New Freedom embodied a neo-Jeffersonian brand of progressivism. Solving the social, political, and economic ills in America required a restoration of freedom—a restoration of laissez-faire. As chief architect of the New Freedom, Woodrow Wilson believed the authority of the federal government should be used only to eliminate special privileges, to liberate individual energies, and to preserve and restore competition in business (Link, 1954, p. 20):

> [W]e are going into the garden to weed it. We are going into the garden to give the little plants air and light in which to grow. . . . We are only in there to see to it that the fertilization of intelligence, of invention, of origination is once more applied to a set of industries now threatening to be stagnant because threatening to be too much concentrated (Wilson, 1916, p. 125).

Fundamental to the New Freedom program was tariff reform.[8] The New Freedom denounced protective tariffs as government subsidies to industry provided at the expense of the taxpayers. According to this view, tariffs fostered trusts and thus restricted competition; they contributed to stagnation and inefficiency in industry, and they had "robbed Americans of their independence, resourcefulness, and self-reliance" (Wilson, 1916, p. 125). Tariffs also greatly impeded the expansion of American commerce abroad: "The tariff was once a bulwark; now it is a dam. For trade is reciprocal; we cannot sell unless we also buy" (Acceptance Address (1912), *Public Papers of Woodrow Wilson*, 1925, 2:471).

The New Freedom Democrats rejected the commission alternative for tariff reform, claiming that such a commission would serve only to legitimate the policy of protectionism. The cost-of-production standard also was dismissed. Since tariffs to equalize foreign and domestic production costs were nearly impossible to calculate (Wilson, 1916, p. 112), any attempt to use this standard in tariff making was merely a rationalization for high tariffs. The New Freedom advocated nothing less than the dismantling of the American protective system, which "cuts us off from our proper position in the commerce of the world, violates the just principles of taxation, and makes the Government a facile instrument in the hands of private interests" (Wilson, First Inaugural (1913), *Public Papers*, 1925, 3:3–4).

The election of 1912 saw the Republican party vote split between the Old Guard and the Bull Moose. Theodore Roosevelt and the Progressive party failed to attract progressive Democrats and failed to establish the

---

8. So strong was Wilson's commitment to tariff reform that in 1912 he was thoroughly prepared to make it the "dominant issue" of the campaign (see Baker, 1946, 3:97.)

new party on a firm and lasting basis. Woodrow Wilson and his party scored a major victory at the polls.

President, Congress, and Party: Wilson's Alternative Framework for Governance

Woodrow Wilson recognized the economic and political necessity of a phased reduction in tariff rates. To avoid economic disruptions and uncertainty, he advocated "a fixed programme upon which every man of business can base his definite forecasts and systematic plans" (Address before the Economic Club (1912), *Public Papers*, 1925, 2:437). Such a course was as much a political necessity as an economic one. Tariff reform was a popular campaign slogan but had proved to be political dynamite for those who seriously pursued it. For legislators, support for tariff reform in principle tended to give way to support for the duties of concern to constituents. This axiom of American tariff making had been demonstrated by the Democrats in 1894 and by the Republicans in 1909. Even groups like the NAM, organized to pursue (among other goals) tariff reform as a means to eliminate economic uncertainty and promote trade expansion, resisted attempts to tamper seriously with the American protective system.[9] Therefore, the task the new Democratic leadership faced in 1913 as it confronted the issue of tariff reform was indeed formidable. Wilson and the Democratic leadership needed to organize the forces of public opinion behind tariff reform, draw together the diverse elements of Congress, and see to it that the influence of lobbies was resisted.

Wilson's plan for a "fixed programme" of tariff rate reductions implied a new scheme for tariff policy-making. The existing process had not generated a thoroughgoing downward revision in over sixty years. It could not be expected, therefore, to produce a series of them. Wilson's scheme, however, extended beyond tariff-making. He envisioned a new mode of operation for government as a whole. Wilson believed that responsible government based on executive leadership and executive-legislative cooperation would yield policy of "constructive choice rather than of compromise and barter" ("The Making of the Nation," *Public Papers*, 1925, 1:335).

Wilson maintained that the constitutional system of checks and balances gave well-organized special interests the opportunity to dominate the policy process. He believed that "leaderless government" was the

9. The NAM advocated the creation of a tariff commission and a program of reciprocity to promote trade expansion. The organization, however, continually reaffirmed its commitment to protection, and this commitment superseded its advocacy of commission and reciprocity (see Becker, 1982, pp. 76–82, 86–87.)

basic defect of the American system ("Leaderless Government," *Public Papers*, 1925, 1:336–67). In his view, only if the executive and the legislature could be drawn closer together and the executive given a chance "to approve himself a statesman" could the "motive power of government" be nationalized (ibid., p. 358). Before 1900, Wilson championed the adoption of a parliamentary system to attain responsible government in the United States. The presidency of Theodore Roosevelt, however, caused Wilson to reevaluate the potential for leadership and responsible government under a presidential system.

In 1908, Wilson wrote: "Leadership and control must be lodged somewhere; the whole art of statesmanship is the art of bringing the several parts of government into effective cooperation for the accomplishment of particular common objects" (Wilson, 1921, p. 54). Wilson believed the president could effect such cooperation because the president is the nexus between party and public opinion. As the only national representative, he could interpret the public will and thus lead the nation: "If he lead the nation, his party can hardly resist him" (Wilson, 1921, p. 69).

The question facing President-elect Wilson was with which "party" in Congress he should cooperate. Wilson had proclaimed himself a progressive and originally intended to work only with those who shared his principles ("Only Progressives," *Public Papers*, 1925, 3:27). The progressives, however, were divided between the two major political parties. The organization bosses and the machine in his own party were as much opposed to him and the issues he stood for as were the Republican bosses. Most of the organization leaders had opposed him at the party's 1912 nominating convention in Baltimore (Baker, 1946, 3:100). Still, Wilson decided not to attempt to build a new coalition of progressives; he decided instead to remain the leader of the Democratic party, but he intended to regenerate it along progressive lines (Link, 1956, pp. 153, 157).

Wilson boldly asserted leadership of his party and of Congress. He claimed that as president he represented the will of the people, and he used public opinion as a spur on Congress. Wilson established his position as national spokesman through the effective use of oratory and public messages. In this way he could galvanize popular support for his party and program against the assaults of private interests and the Republican opposition.[10]

In day-to-day legislative matters, Wilson proved equally effective as leader. Before his inauguration, Wilson conferred in person and corresponded with committee chairmen and Democratic leaders about the gen-

10. Only one time between 1913 and 1917 did Wilson appeal to the people over Congress on a matter of importance. The occasion was the debate over military and naval expansion in 1916. (See Link, 1956, p. 152.)

eral structure of the legislative program. After he assumed office, he gave careful consideration and attention to the details of the proposed legislation. He met frequently with members of Congress, he mediated disputes that threatened to disrupt the Democratic ranks, and he did not hesitate to use patronage to keep the House and Senate caucuses in line (Link, 1956, p. 153). Wilson demonstrated, however, a willingness to compromise on principle if such compromise was necessary to assure his legislative package. He permitted, for example, Postmaster General Burleson to make the numerous local postmaster appointments based on traditional party criteria (i.e., deferring to the suggestions of relevant members of Congress) rather than progressive ones (Baker, 1946, 3:43–47; Link, 1956, p. 159).

Circumstances aided Wilson's attempt to lead a cooperative Congressional majority. During his first term, there was no rival leader in Congress. In 1910 the House of Representatives adopted new rules that deprived the Speaker of control over the routing of bills and committee appointments. These changes, in effect, destroyed one of the most important counters to the president and created a leadership vacuum that the president could fill. In addition, 114 of the 290 Democratic members of the House in 1913 were serving their first terms. They were eager to please the Democrat in the White House because their future careers depended in no small part on patronage and the administration's success. Moreover, the veteran Southerners in both houses realized that the fate of their party depended on their success in achieving the reforms the nation demanded, and they therefore accepted the president's leadership. Finally, a majority of the senators of both parties were progressives, and this cushioned the narrow Democratic majority in the Senate (Link, 1956, p. 148).

Wilson's methods of leadership and the prevailing state of interorganizational relationships yielded remarkable results during his first term. For a time he effectively fused the legislative and executive branches of government. He used party to insulate the policy process and achieved the bulk of his legislative program—tariff reform, banking and currency reform, and business regulation—during the first eighteen months of his administration.

Overcoming Special Interests through Party:
The Underwood Tariff Act

Wilson first demonstrated the potential viability of responsible party government in the United States on the tariff reform issue. The Democrats in Congress passed a bill that revised tariff rates downward—a goal that had eluded policymakers for many years. The Democrats' victory was most impressive in the Senate, which had proved the graveyard for previous reform attempts. The Democrats held ranks against intense lobbying efforts aimed especially at conservative senators of the South and West. The Democrats' campaign for tariff reform, however, began in the House of Representatives. Although not unexpected, victory in the House was not assumed by the president nor by Congressional leaders.

In the American political system, parties compete with local interests for the votes of "representatives of localities." To achieve responsible party government, therefore, the party leadership must either increase the benefits and/or decrease the costs of voting the party line or decrease the benefits and/or increase the costs of defecting. On the tariff reform issue, President Wilson successfully kept the cost-benefit ratio favorable for party government.

Wilson confirmed his determination to shepherd personally tariff reform legislation through Congress even before he called for the special legislative session. He met with Ways and Means Committee chairman Oscar W. Underwood on December 31, 1912, to discuss the legislative timetable for tariff reform. Underwood assured him that hearings would be over and the legislation drafted by mid-March (*New York Times*, January 1 and 2, 1913).

The proposed bill that Wilson and Underwood discussed on March 24, 1913, revealed a genuine desire to reduce rates of duty on manufactured products, but it fell short of thoroughgoing reform. The bill imposed duties on all farm products, retained protection for leather boots and shoes, and imposed a 15 percent duty on raw wool. The committee had incorporated these duties into the bill in response to pressure, largely from farm, livestock, and sugar spokesmen, and in anticipation of doubtless trouble in the upper house if such concessions to southern and western interests were not offered (Link, 1956, pp. 179–80).

Such concessions, however, also invited logrolling. Compromise on some items to gain votes would lead to bargains and more concessions to hold the votes of other legislators. Mindful of this possibility as well as his party's pledge to reduce the cost of living, Wilson insisted, on April 1, 1913, that any proposed tariff legislation provide for free food, sugar, leather, and wool. He promised to veto the bill if it were not rewritten to include these changes. The only compromise the president would admit was one that would reduce the sugar duty from 1.9 cents per pound to 1 cent per pound for three years. After this time sugar would enter duty-free. The president's ultimatum worked. After years of denouncing Republicans for not producing results on the tariff issue, the prospect of a similar fate helped to persuade the Ways and Means Committee to rewrite the bill (*New York Times*, April 2 and 6, 1913).

Congress convened on April 7, and the president addressed a joint session on the tariff a day later. There were rumblings that the president's speech before Congress—the first in 113 years—violated the "separation of the powers,"[11] but it eloquently communicated Wilson's resolve to establish himself as leader of a cooperative majority in Congress and to underscore his idea of an appropriate tariff policy for the United States:

I am very glad indeed to have this opportunity to address the two houses directly and to verify for myself the impression that the President of the United States is a person, not a mere department of the government hailing Congress from some isolated island of jealous power, sending messages, not speaking naturally and with his own voice—that he is a human being trying to cooperate with other human beings in a common service. . . .

We must abolish everything that bears even the semblance of privilege or of any kind of artificial advantage and put our business men and producers under the stimulation of a constant necessity to be efficient, economical, and enterprising, masters of competitive supremacy, better workers and merchants than any in the world. (*Congressional Record* 50:130)

Wilson's address called attention vividly and dramatically to the cause he was championing; it focused public attention on the upcoming struggle with Congress, and it stimulated speedy action in the House of Representatives.[12]

The critical phase in the bill's progress through the House was the debate of the Democratic caucus. The Democratic leadership successfully defeated efforts to restore the wool and sugar duties, and only twelve members signaled that they would not be bound by a caucus rule commanding all Democrats to support the Underwood bill in its entirety.[13] The bill was reported to the House on April 22 on a strict party vote, and following debate, the House approved the bill 281 to 139. Only five Democrats (four from Louisiana) defected from the majority.

In contrast to the Payne-Aldrich Act, the Underwood bill used only ad valorem rates, and it contained no "jokers" that could surreptitiously protect special interests. The bill lowered the average ad valorem rate to 29 percent and greatly expanded the free list (Link, 1956, p. 192).[14] To offset the anticipated decrease in customs revenue, the Underwood bill included a provision for an income tax—the first such tax under the Six-

11. Conservative Democrats voiced the most criticism. See *New York Times*, April 8, 1913.

12. For a sense of public reaction to Wilson's address, see Baker, 1946, 3:110.

13. The twelve were excused because they had given pledges to their constituents (see *New York Times*, April 12, 13, 17, 20, and 22, 1913).

14. The average ad valorem rate under the Payne-Aldrich Act was between 37 and 40 percent.

teenth Amendment. Representative Cordell Hull of Tennessee drafted the provision, and he considered it an important attempt to shift the tax burden from the lower and middle classes to the rich. It imposed a "normal" tax of 1 percent on personal and corporate incomes over $4,000 and an additional "surtax" of 1 percent on incomes between $20,000 and $50,000, 2 percent on incomes between $50,000 and $100,000, and 3 percent on incomes over $100,000 (*Congressional Record*, 50:503–15).

Wilson faced a stiffer challenge in the Senate. The upper house had sabotaged all previous attempts at an honest revision since the Civil War. Moreover, the ranking Democrat on the Finance Committee, Furnifold M. Simmons of North Carolina, had voted for the Payne-Aldrich Act in 1909 and was known to oppose tariff revision that would "unduly threaten" the cotton textile industry. His sentiments were echoed by his North Carolina colleague, Leo S. Overman. Other Democrats in the Senate also voiced reservations about tariff reform. Senator Charles S. Thomas and Senator-elect John F. Shafroth of Colorado declared that they would have to oppose any sizable reduction in the sugar rates (*New York Times*, November 30, 1912).

Despite the obstacles presented by intense lobbying, Wilson's prospects for successfully uniting party members in the Senate were better than those of the last Democratic president because his opportunities and incentives to exert executive leadership were greater than Cleveland's (Skowronek, 1982, p. 174). Unlike Cleveland, who confronted opposition from Finance Committee chairman Gorman, Wilson secured the support of Senator Simmons for tariff reform by withdrawing his objections to Simmons's appointment as chairman of this powerful committee (Baker, 1946, 3:102). Wilson also encouraged and benefited from the heightened levels of publicity surrounding the tariff battle in the Senate. Most notably, he launched a full-scale public attack against special interest lobbies.

Wilson deplored the influence that lobbyists for special interests had exerted in tariff making in the recent past: "Their influence is direct, personal and pervasive. . . . They have as powerful a machinery ready to their hand as the government itself" ("The Tariff Make Believe," *Public Papers*, 1925, 2:138). On May 26, determined that tariff legislation in 1913 not suffer a fate similar to that of previous tariff bills, he issued a public statement:

I think the public ought to know the extraordinary exertions being made by the lobby in Washington to gain recognition for certain alterations of the tariff bill. Washington has seldom seen so numerous, so industrious, or so insidious a lobby. . . . It is of serious interest to the country that the people at large should have no lobby and be voiceless in these matters, while great bodies of astute men seek to create an artificial opinion and to overrule the interest of the public for their private benefit. . . . The Government in all its branches ought to be relieved from this intolerable burden and this constant interruption in the calm progress of debate. (*New York Times*, May 27, 1913)

The Senate Republicans saw this as an opportunity to embarrass the Democrats, and on May 27, they called for an investigation. A resolution was introduced by Senator Cummins of Iowa, calling for a committee "to investigate the charge that a lobby is being maintained in Washington or elsewhere to influence proposed legislation now pending before the Senate" (*Congressional Record* 50:1758). They wanted to force the Democrats to either resist an inquiry or to proceed and risk proving that Wilson's charges were groundless. This was made clear when the Senate minority leader hastily withdrew his objections to the formation of such a committee (*Congressional Record* 50:1758–59). Wilson, however, welcomed the investigation. A surprised Democratic majority, therefore, approved a slightly amended version of the Cummins resolution.[15]

The investigation's most explosive revelations concerned the sugar lobbies. It revealed, for example, that the lobby organized by the beet sugar manufacturers had spent more than a half million dollars over a twenty-year period in the fight against free sugar (Link, 1956, p. 190).

Revelations about the sugar lobbyists notwithstanding, the committee found little evidence of actual wrongdoing. It did find enough lobbying activity, however, to vindicate the president and prove his charges. In fact, the president's action accomplished exactly what he intended. It centered the nation's attention on the tariff struggle, and it made it extremely difficult in light of the committee's findings for any Democrat to reject tariff reform. On July 7, forty-seven of the forty-nine Democratic senators pledged in caucus to vote for unequivocal tariff reform.

The bill that was reported out of the Finance Committee approved the controversial wool and sugar schedules and included numerous additional reductions that were not part of the House version. The debate on the amended Underwood bill was, however, protracted. The Senate Republicans wanted to stall for time; they wanted to delay for as long as possible consideration of the banking and currency legislation then pending in the House (Link, 1956, p. 190).

Although they supported some of the aims of the proposed legislation, the Insurgent Republicans (as Republican party progressives were called) vigorously debated the bill. They felt alienated by the strict party

15. The Democrats insisted on changing the wording of the provision requesting information from the president, and they also insisted on giving control of the inquiry to the Judiciary Committee (see Link, 1956, p. 189.)

stance Wilson had maintained throughout the bill's preparation (La Follette, 1953, 1:459, 472–73). During the course of the debate, therefore, they challenged the "progressive" character of the Democrats' bill. The Insurgents charged that the concept of a revenue tariff was retrogressive. It meant a fiscal policy that threw the heaviest tax burden on the lower and middle classes. They argued that only the graduated income tax was a truly democratic instrument of taxation:

> With regard to a tariff for revenue. . . . I believe it is obsolete, unjust, and intolerable. If tariff duties are not levied to equalize conditions of production . . . they ought not to be levied at all. . . . We have reached a stage in our development when the great majority of humane students of public affairs believe the taxpayers should contribute to the expenses of the government according to their ability to bear the burden rather than according to their necessities. (Remarks of Senator Cummins, *Congressional Record* 50:2557)

Senators Bristow of Kansas and La Follette of Wisconsin introduced amendments to increase the combined income tax on large incomes (*Congressional Record* 50:3805–6, 3819). Both measures were defeated, but the income tax issue unsettled some Democrats. Senators Vardaman of Mississippi, Ashurst of Arizona, Thompson of Kansas, and Reed of Missouri insisted that the Democratic caucus meet in special session to consider the La Follette amendment, which called for a maximum tax of 10 percent on all net incomes above $100,000. They claimed the support of a majority of Democratic senators, and they demanded that the Finance Committee approve the La Follette amendment (*New York Times*, August 29, 1913). Because of the strong support in the caucus for the amendment, Simmons and the other Democrats on the Finance Committee offered a compromise that would raise the maximum combined income tax to 7 percent on incomes over $500,000. The caucus accepted the compromise when it became known that the president supported it (*New York Times*, September 2, 1913).

The Senate debate continued through September 9. The Democrats held their ranks and defeated all Republican sponsored amendments. The final vote on the bill was 44 to 37, with only two Democrats (the senators from Louisiana) defecting from the majority (*Congressional Record* 50:4617).[16] The Conference Committee approved 427 of the 674 Senate amendments, compromised on 97, rejected 151, and disagreed on 1 (Link, 1956, pp. 194–95). Both houses voted to accept the conference report, and on October 3, 1913, President Wilson signed the Underwood bill into law.

The new law attempted to lower the cost of living for consumers and

---

16. Senator La Follette voted with the majority.

to abolish excessive profits to giant industries. Moderate protection to "legitimate" industries, however, remained a feature of American tariff policy.[17] Besides the provision for an income tax, the features of the 1913 tariff act included a great expansion of the free list. Raw wool, iron ore, pig and scrap iron, steel rails, lumber, coal, farm products (e.g., wheat, flour, corn, corn meal, cattle, eggs, milk, flax, hemp, and tea), and some manufactures (e.g., leather boots, shoes, wood pulp, print paper, and gunpowder) were to be admitted duty-free. Moderate reductions were achieved in the rates on many manufactured products, including woolens, cottons, linens, earthenware, glassware, bar iron, steel bars, and tinplate. Some schedules remained virtually unchanged or were raised (e.g., tobacco, liquor, silks, and other luxury items). The act also provided for free sugar after May 1916. In 1915, however, Congress voted to retain the sugar duty (Taussig, 1931, pp. 409–46; Ratner, 1972, pp. 44–46; *New York Times*, September 30, 1913).

Tariff-making Reform through Party: Institutional Change or Variation on the Existing Pattern of Institutional Relations?

In debate on the Underwood bill, Senate Republicans repeatedly called attention to the manner in which the tariff legislation was being handled by the Democratic party:

[A]fter months of secret work the Democratic Senate has presented the pending bill. It was brought forth in the darkness of the secret caucus chamber. . . . I can not understand how Senators . . . can submit to the dictates of their party leader against their publicly and privately declared convictions. Has party fealty and caucus rule reached that stage when they can control the consciousness and votes of United States Senators?

I do not know that it will do any good for me to call attention to this matter, as our friends on the other side seem to be disposed to maintain the bill as it now stands no matter what suggestions may be made. . . . It seems to me that our friends on the other side are blindly disposed to keep what they may call their consistency apparent on the record.

I do not believe in legislating by means of a caucus. We are elected to come to the Capitol and legislate according to our own views of what will be for the benefit of the people of this country and no one has the right to surrender his views either to a secret caucus or to any individual, however prominent.[18]

---

17. The Underwood Act sought a "competitive tariff," one in which rates would be fixed at a point where foreign competition might still be effective (see Underwood's remarks, *Congressional Record* 50:328–32).

18. Excerpts of remarks made by Senators Townsend (R., Mich.), Bradley (R., Ky.), and Gironna (R., N.D.). (*Congressional Record* 50:2808, 2847, 2863.)

It was clear to members of Congress and to astute observers that the pattern of institutional relations that had defined the policy process for tariff making had been altered or at least obfuscated by Wilson and the Democrats. In 1913, policy was not made by "representatives of localities" but by party members committed to a policy platform. Party overcame the structural predisposition of Congress to logroll. Party imperatives significantly diminished the usually potent influence of narrow, special interests in tariff making.

The Underwood Act was a tremendous legislative success. It remains the only *legislated* downward revision of the twentieth century—the only legislated tariff revision since the Civil War in which the predisposition to logroll was mitigated. The act lowered the average rate of duty on all imports to 8.8 percent and on dutiable imports alone to 26.8 percent. Tariff rates were not to achieve the low levels of the 1913 act again until 1957 (Dobson, 1976, pp. 18, 24).

The legislative successes scored by the president and Congress through party in 1913 (and in 1914), however, did not result in or from institutional change. In fact, Wilson sacrificed whatever opportunity he had in 1913 for institutional change to guarantee the success of his legislative program. By choosing not to build a new progressive party and by deciding to work within the existing Democratic party organization, Wilson gave up his only chance to establish permanent party government.

Instead, Wilson chose an excellent short-term strategy. He made intelligent use of circumstances that favored reform through legislative action. First, despite the fact that the Democrats were a disparate group, including in their ranks conservative Southerners as well as progressives, there was in 1913 and 1914 a policy program they could agree upon. "For several years the major alternatives in tariff, banking, and trust legislation had been before the public" (Wiebe, 1962, p. 127), and with regard to the tariff in particular, the Democratic position had been known for years. Second, because the Democratic party coalition did not command a natural majority in the electorate, the Democrats welcomed a strategy designed to broaden the base of their coalition. If their control of the national government was to endure after the repair of the Republican schism, the Democrats needed to achieve legislative success. Third, newly elected Democrats in Congress were inclined to support the president's legislative package. They had to establish themselves in their districts, and to this end, they relied on presidential patronage, and they accepted the president's leadership.

These factors promoted party unity, and Wilson took full advantage of them. Such factors, however, are not permanent characteristics of American politics. They have typically emerged after a party achieves electoral success following an earlier disaster (1856–1860, 1913–1914, 1933–1935).

The party in a "redevelopment" phase is more innovative, and leaders "are temporarily more susceptible to real mass opinion; the separation of powers is temporarily ineffective" (Lowi, 1967, p. 274 n). For the 1913–1914 period, the fundamental agreement on policy dissipated after the New Freedom legislation had been passed. The tariff issue demonstrates the point dramatically.

In no way could the Underwood Act be considered free trade legislation, but its moderation of tariff rates, expansion of the free list, substitution of ad valorem for specific duties, and provision for an income tax to reduce the government's dependence on customs receipts clearly represented a liberalization in policy and a new departure for the United States. Its projected impact—a reduction in living costs, an elimination of exorbitant corporate profit, and an increase in U.S. involvement in the world economy without injury to domestic industry—was supposed to keep tariffs off the political agenda for a while. Instead, the outbreak of war in Europe, by disrupting normal world trade, rendered the Underwood Act inoperative and kept tariffs and tariff making in the political spotlight.

The tariff surfaced as a major issue in the 1914 Congressional elections. Democratic losses in 1914 and Republican predictions that at the end of the war the United States would be a dumping ground for products of revitalized European industries rekindled the tariff debate within the Democratic party.[19] Some Democrats came to advocate the creation of a tariff commission. They viewed a commission either as a means to deal with international economic uncertainty or as a means to outflank the Republicans at the polls. To other Democrats, however, such a proposition remained antithetical to long-standing party principles on the tariff. When Wilson came to endorse the creation of a tariff commission (for reasons that will be explored in the next chapter), he was opposed in Congress by members of his own party.

Although the 1913–1914 experience was not perpetuated and did not result in party being established as a permanent instrument of insulation in policy-making,[20] the importance of Wilson's achievement for American

19. Democratic losses in 1914 can be attributed to an economic downturn in 1914 and to the disintegration of the Progressive party and the return of its members to the GOP (see Link, 1956, p. 468; Becker, 1982, p. 87).
20. Walter Dean Burnham (Chambers and Burnham, 1967) comments on the "insulative function" of the fourth party system (1894–1932, excepting the "special case" of 1912) in "Party Systems and the Political Process." He uses the concept of insulation much more broadly than it is used here: "The chief function of the fourth party system . . . was the substantially complete insulation of elites from any attack by the

politics should not be underestimated. "Wilson's leadership," one scholar writes, "combined force, clarity, and the art of the possible" (Wiebe, 1962, p. 127). He was flexible when necessary and unyielding when it served his purposes. He held together a legislative coalition through major economic reforms. He remains the archetype of the "Legislative President" (Wayne, 1978, pp. 15–16), and as such he helped to lay the foundation of the modern American presidency.

It is evident in hindsight that the tenor of legislative-executive relations was being transformed. Congress would come to expect, even depend on, the president as the source of legislative initiative. This development began with Theodore Roosevelt, fully emerged under Woodrow Wilson, and was solidified under Franklin D. Roosevelt. It was a product of important modifications in the American party system after 1896 that freed the president from dependence on the party and created new opportunities and incentives for executive leadership (Skowronek, 1982, pp. 165–76).

The lack of fundamental institutional change establishing party government in the United States, however, prevented the president from exercising legislative leadership in any sort of permanent way. Institutional change toward party government implies that party programs consistently take precedence over special interest concerns, but given the U.S. Constitution, such programs can never be structurally mandated. In the United States, the government does not fall when party members in Congress defect from the party line; the party imperative is an electoral, not a policy one. Only to the extent that legislators can calculate that their election chances are better served will they choose party unity over local interests in policy-making. Policy-making through disciplined policy parties, therefore, has never been more than a transitory phenomenon.[21] As parties deteriorate, the periods of effective president–Congress cooperation and coordination become shorter and shorter. Thus, the president now has important legislative responsibilities but little leverage (save his claim to represent public opinion) over the legislature (Skowronek, 1982, pp. 288–89).

---

victims of the industrializing process, and a corresponding reinforcement of political coalitions favoring an exclusively private exploitation of the political economy" (p. 301).

21. The last major attempt to forge a policy party in the United States was made by FDR:

[I]n the party purge of 1938, Roosevelt suggested that a new party might lend coherence to relationships among the President, Congress, and the bureaucracy. He attempted to use New Deal patronage appointments to prod recalcitrant Democrats into line behind his programs, but the Democratic Congress would have none of it. The Hatch Acts formally removed federal civil service from electoral politics, and stunted the further development of this revival of party government. (See Skowronek, 1982, p. 288.)

Conclusion: The Party Alternative and Its Implications for Trade Policy

Intrinsic to the idea of party government is a strategy for insulating the policy process from the pressures of particularistic interests. Intrinsic to the party alternative as applied in 1913, however, was also a strategy for foreign economic policy—unilateral liberalization. The party alternative provided no instruments to guarantee reciprocal action by trading partners. Woodrow Wilson and other advocates of this alternative simply assumed that American actions to liberalize its commercial policy would be matched abroad. Yet history had demonstrated that this was unlikely. The unilateral action taken by Great Britain in the 1840s to lower its barriers to trade (e.g., the repeal of the Corn Laws), for example, was not reciprocated. The nineteenth century's "Golden Age of Free Trade" began only after Britain negotiated with France to conclude the Cobden-Chevalier Treaty (1860) (Stein, 1984). In all probability, therefore, the party alternative, by itself, could not have sustained a policy of trade liberalization.

The Commission Alternative and the Scientific Tariff: The Tariff Commission, 1916–1929

Under the conditions that characterized the world economy during the post–World War I period, American foreign economic policy attained a global importance. These policies were inextricably linked to the successful resolution of major international economic problems—repayment of loans, reconstruction, stabilization of exchange rates, and reparations. Specifically, the imperatives of the international situation demanded that the United States adopt a trade policy that encouraged more imports. Scholars of the period analyzed the situation in the following way:

[T]he United States up to 1914 a debtor nation has become the world's creditor. Such a condition implies the receipt of payments from the debtor, either in gold, in securities, or in goods. Payment of our enormous balances in gold is out of the question. Payment in securities implies a continuance of the war condition of our trade—an outward flow of capital and goods, an excess of exports over imports. . . . [E]ventually, trade balances augmented by the new borrowings must be paid in goods. Our imports must increase, our excess of exports disappear. (Bullock, Williams, and Tucker, 1919, p. 234)

Encouraging imports required a policy process that could achieve some form of trade policy liberalization. In 1919 this was something American policymakers had yet to accomplish. In 1913 extraordinary circumstances enabled Democrats in Congress to use party as a policy instrument, and they produced the moderate Underwood bill. The Democrats, however, were unable to hold ranks on subsequent matters relating to tariff policy liberalization. In 1915, for example, they oversaw the reinstatement of the duty on sugar.

Wilson's attempt to establish party government failed because the constellation of domestic political factors that permitted early legislative successes dissipated before the end of his first term in office. Yet even had

Wilson successfully orchestrated a change in the nature of executive-legislative relations via party government, it is unlikely that the resultant policy process would have provided a sufficient answer to America's trade policy dilemma. The focus of the debate on the Underwood bill was squarely on domestic political and economic issues. Foreign policy concerns were, at best, tangential to the debate. The complexities and implications of the dual character of trade as both domestic and foreign policy were, if not unappreciated, certainly underappreciated by Wilson and his cohort. They simply assumed that American actions to lower protective barriers would be matched abroad and thus afford American exporters new opportunities in overseas markets.

Certain Republican leaders had proved more cognizant of the dual character of trade policy. Witness the successful efforts of Secretary of State James G. Blaine to see enacted reciprocity and trade treaty provisions in the 1897 Dingly Act. However, at the turn of the century, the principle of reciprocity had to vie with the idea of scientific tariff making for the allegiance of reform-minded Republicans. Debate about the two alternative paths for tariff-making reform figured prominently during the presidency of William Howard Taft. The debate reemerged with the outbreak of World War I. For the first time, with the war, the potential impact of world economic woes on the national economy grabbed the attention of leaders and relevant constituents of both political parties.

The Tariff Commission became the focal point of policy-making changes of the post–World War I period. Although it was originally created in 1916 to be an advisory body to Congress and the president as officials in both institutions confronted new economic contingencies, competing views abounded on the appropriate role of the commission. Democrats like Wilson reluctantly accepted the need for an advisory body. Republican progressives envisioned a rate-setting commission that would "take the tariff out of politics" and determine rates scientifically. Members of the National Foreign Trade Council (NFTC, representing large manufacturers and prominent bankers) and the American Manufacturers' Export Association (AMEA—representing "high tech" manufacturers) considered the Tariff Commission a means for producing policies conducive to import and export expansion. Standpat protectionists fought for a policy process flexible enough to respond to the vagaries of an uncertain international economic environment, but at the same time, they wanted to keep the protective system fully intact.

The dynamics of policy-making reform yielded a trade policy process for the 1920s that was decidedly more detached from the pressures of particularistic interests than the previous one had been. The Fordney-McCumber Act of 1922 included provisions for tariff rate adjustment outside the traditional legislative process. The Tariff Commission was authorized to investigate and compare costs of production between domestic and international producers. Based on the results of these investigations, the Tariff Commission was to recommend to the president tariff rate-adjustments of up to 50 percent. The new rate adjustment system was supposed to eliminate the indiscriminate quality of legislated duties and instead produce more scientific tariffs. It was also supposed to add flexibility to the tariff schedules so that the United States could respond promptly to changing economic conditions at home and abroad. In addition, the new policy process would allow foreign producers fair and equal access to the American market.

This new policy process was, in many respects, an innovative alternative to tariff making by Congress. It was, however, doomed to failure because, in practice, the new policy process was neither flexible nor scientific. The inflexibility of the process guaranteed the preservation of American protectionism at a time when the world's economic well-being required an American policy of import expansion. Moreover, it made Congressional reintervention in the policy process inevitable. When enough members considered existing tariff schedules inappropriate, Congress would again undertake a general revision.

Inflexibility became the salient characteristic of the so-called flexible tariff system of the 1920s. This inflexibility had two dimensions. The first stemmed from the procedural difficulties associated with the administration of the new tariff rate adjustment system. These difficulties included (1) determining methods for case selection, (2) establishing and interpreting criteria for cost-of-production comparisons, and (3) finding and gaining access to the requisite information about production costs. Each of these worked against infusing flexibility into the tariff-making system. In fact, they guaranteed that the implementation of the flexible tariff provisions of the Fordney-McCumber Act (1922) would leave unaltered most of the tariff rates specified in the act.

The second dimension of inflexibility was a feature of the approach to foreign economic policy inherent in the institutional design of the flexible tariff system. This approach precluded policymakers from pursuing reciprocity agreements as an alternative or additional means to reduce tariff levels. Tariff reductions through reciprocity arrangements with trading partners had come to be viewed as antithetical to the principle of scientific tariffs. As established in the 1922 act, the flexible tariff system stipulated that individual tariff changes could be made only after the Tariff Commission conducted a comparative cost-of-production investigation and determined the appropriate rate for the item in question. Thus, when scientific rate adjustment proved unworkable, the institutional design for trade policymaking rendered it impossible for policy-makers to seek tariff reduction through some other avenue, such as reciprocity arrangements.

The failure of the scientific tariff-making experiment in the 1920s demonstrates the limitations of a policy-making design when it is used in service to a cognitive framework that aims to justify anachronistic principles. This chapter examines the factors that shaped the tariff-making methods and policies featured in this experiment. Prominent among these factors were the competing ideas about and approaches to American foreign economic policy. This chapter considers these contending cognitive frameworks. It examines the pre–World War I debate about the appropriate role for government (and particularly the role for reciprocity arrangements) in promoting the sale of products overseas as well as the coincident and often conflicting efforts to establish a tariff commission. This analysis is accomplished through reexamination of the Payne-Aldrich Act (1909) and through examination of the 1911 attempt to establish reciprocity with Canada. The chapter also analyzes the impact of wartime economic uncertainty on the commission movement and the political dynamics surrounding passage of the Fordney-McCumber Act (1922). Finally, the chapter explores the ramifications for American politics and international relations of a policy process that achieved insulation but remained ineffective.

This chapter showcases the complexities and uncertainties of policy-making reform. Change advocates with competing cognitive frameworks contend in a political environment where individual officeholders make decisions about altering existing patterns of policy-making based on personal calculations of costs and benefits. Whether or not institutional change results from a successful episode of policy-making reform so that an alternative pattern of institutional relations is established depends largely on the policy produced.

It is from the policy product that the lessons of policy-making reform are derived. Officials can learn to accept and even to embrace a new policy process if they deem the policy product a success. However, if they judge the policy a disaster, these same officials can easily conclude that the effort to reform policy-making is misguided, and they recommit to the long-standing patterns that have historically characterized policy-making in the issue area. The case of the tariff-making reform movement of the early decades of the twentieth century is an exemplar of the consequences of perceived policy failure on policy-making reform.

The Tariff-Making Reform Movement, circa 1910: Reciprocity and Scientific Tariffs, Complementary or Competing Frameworks for Tariff-Making Reform?

Tariff-making reform[1] became an issue during the first decade of the twentieth century. The drive for such reform grew out of the depression of the 1890s, the explosion of trusts that followed in its wake, and the moderate protectionist dissatisfaction with the policy in place—the Dingly Tariff of 1897. Support outside government for tariff-making reform came principally from a vocal group of small- and medium-scale manufacturers and within government from Republican progressives.

The manufacturers supporting tariff-making reform were protectionists. They believed in privileged access for American producers to the national market, but they were unhappy with a protective system that enabled trusts to charge their American customers higher prices than their international ones. NAM activist and tariff reform advocate Herbert E. Miles, for example, was one of the businessmen who saw a causal connection between high tariffs, trusts, and increasing prices. A small-scale but prosperous producer of carriages and agricultural implements, Miles estimated that the difference between the price he paid for steel and the price overseas customers paid for the same good was roughly equal to the amount of duty on steel imports (Stone, 1952, p. 4; Kenkel, 1983, p. 48). He concluded that tariff-making reform was necessary to reduce tariffs and thereby restore competition and eliminate excessive profit in industries like steel.

These smaller manufacturers also wanted government assistance in marketing their own products overseas. During the depression of the 1890s comparatively small firms looked to overseas markets as the answer to an "overproduction" problem. In their view, the American industrial economy produced too many goods to sustain price levels that produced the desired profit. Their inability to control their industries' output and prices forced them to seek other arrangements (viz., overseas markets). They wanted the government to act on its "open door" proclamations. They wanted a policy that would promote fair and equal (if not preferential) treatment of American goods in international markets (Becker, 1982, pp. 46–47). The Dingly Tariff Act failed on this account; the treaties nego-

---

1. I distinguish between tariff reform and tariff-making reform. Tariff reform refers to a fundamental revision of the tariff schedules. Tariff-making reform refers to the alteration of the policy process whereby tariff rates are determined in order to achieve tariff reform.

tiated under the reciprocity provisions of this act were left unratified by the Senate.

Progressive Republicans from the Midwest, the "Insurgents" of their party, made up another group of protectionists who were dissatisfied with American commercial policy. They supported the creation of a commission to achieve tariff-making reform. They envisioned a commission that would rationally determine tariff rates and thereby secure equitable treatment for the agrarian and industrial interests of their region (Freidel, 1970, pp. 86–89; Kenkel, 1983, pp. 51–52).

Concerns for judicious and equitable tariff making and government-aided access to foreign markets, however, were shared neither by "tariff for revenue only" Democrats nor by the Republican leadership of Congress. The Democrats felt that the creation of a permanent tariff commission would serve only to legitimate the policy of protectionism. They also believed that the only aid Americans required to gain access to overseas markets was a substantial downward revision in tariff rates. Meanwhile, the Old Guard Republicans considered the tariff-making reform movement an affront to their leadership and competence. They jealously guarded their tariff-making prerogatives (Kenkel, 1983, p. 52).

Tariff-making reform and government-assisted trade expansion were also not the concerns of the owners and operators of the large firms that dominated American manufactured exports nor of numerous small firms that had no interest in marketing their products abroad. The hundred largest companies in America accounted for 81 percent of manufactured exports in 1913 (Becker, 1982, p. 13). These firms (e.g., U.S. Steel, Westinghouse, Singer) had technological, managerial, and cost advantages that enabled them to develop foreign markets without government assistance. They were even able to maintain these markets under growing nationalist sentiment abroad.[2]

In contrast to the large firms that were basically indifferent to tariff-making reform efforts, many producers with a home market orientation questioned the desirability of such reform to promote trade expansion. They feared any tampering with the American protective system. They viewed overseas markets as too costly in terms of what would have to be given up by reducing tariffs and opening the domestic market to imported products (Becker, 1982, p. 42).

At the turn of the century, therefore, advocates of tariff-making reform expressed a minority opinion. Effective leadership and organization,

---

2. In the face of tariffs and patents designed to combat the "American invasion," U.S. companies marketed more intensely, often relying on foreign employees and developing branch manufacturing abroad (see Becker, 1982, pp. 50–51).

however, allowed them remarkable visibility. During the Congressional hiatus on tariff-making (1898–1909), they attracted increasing support for their general goals of lower duties, scientific tariff making, and trade expansion. Their organizations also provided forums for a growing number of critics of tariff making in the United States.[3]

The tariff-making reform movement, however, suffered from internal disagreements over specific goals and priorities. Supporters of tariff-making reform had difficulty reconciling their differences on issues like the anticipated role and responsibilities of the Tariff Commission: Should it be established as a bureau within the newly created Commerce Department or should it be established as an independent commission? Should it be an advisory or a rate-setting body? In addition, they differed on the subject of reciprocity: Should the United States continue to pursue reciprocity arrangements with trading partners even after the disappointment over the Kasson treaties? How should the principles of reciprocity and scientific tariff making be reconciled and coordinated? These disagreements enabled opponents of tariff-making reform to practice a strategy of divide and conquer, and thus they contributed to the failure to establish a permanent tariff commission as part of the Payne-Aldrich Act of 1909.

The Payne-Aldrich Act, in one fashion or another and with very little success, addressed the three general goals of tariff reform: revision of tariff schedules, trade expansion, and scientific tariff making. As was discussed in the previous chapter, the 1909 tariff revision did not result in the desired downward adjustment of rates. The same legislative pitfalls that had sabotaged every other attempt to reform tariffs in the post–Civil War period also beset the 1909 effort. Concerns about trade expansion were addressed in the Payne-Aldrich Act by the creation of a dual-rate tariff schedule. The stated tariffs were declared the minimum tariff of the United States. To these rates, 25 percent was to be added on imports from countries that "unduly discriminate" against the United States (Taussig, 1931, p. 403).[4] As for scientific tariff making, the Progressive Republicans and their supporters in the commission movement failed to secure a permanent tariff commission in 1909. They could only gain approval for the appointment by the president of an unspecified number of advisors. These

3. Organizations that supported tariff-making reform included the National Association of Manufacturers (NAM), the American Reciprocal Trade League, and the National Tariff Commission Association (NTCA, created in 1909 expressly to garner business support and to lobby Congress for the establishment of a tariff commission). (See Kenkel, 1983, pp. 48–55.)

4. The additional tariff was not a 25 percent increase in the existing rates but rather 25 percent of the value of the imported goods (see Taussig, 1888, p. 403).

advisors were to help the president administer the dual-rate provisions of the Payne-Aldrich Act. All direct references to scientific tariff making or to cost of production equalization were eliminated by the Conference Committee (Kenkel, 1983, pp. 63–64).

President Taft used his minimal authority to appoint advisors under the Payne-Aldrich Act to create the Tariff Board. Taft envisioned the board as more than an aid for administering the antidiscrimination provisions of the 1909 act. He wanted the board to dabble in scientific tariff making. It would investigate whether the tariffs in place made equal domestic and foreign costs of production. Taft hoped to use the Tariff Board to mend the intraparty rift that had emerged during the tariff battle of 1909 and to diffuse public criticism of the Republican-sponsored tariff legislation. He saw the board as a way to placate the Insurgents' demand for tariff-making reform and at the same time demonstrate to the conservatives that the activities of a tariff board or commission would not compromise the party's commitment to protectionism. His strategy failed because at the same time he pursued reciprocity with Canada. In the context of negotiations with Canada, he willingly ignored the rate-setting principles he otherwise advocated (cost-of-production equalization). The blatant inconsistency in Taft's trade policy further alienated him from the Insurgents of his party. It also gave the Democrats an issue to exploit until the general election.

The Tariff Board became embroiled in a partisan conflict over Canadian reciprocity. The conflict sank the Tariff Board, discredited reciprocity among tariff-making reform advocates, and helped to wreck the Republican party. Thus, although short-lived (1909–1913), the board, its activities, and its role in the political dynamics of the Taft administration shaped the course of American foreign economic policy during the 1920s.

Its first task was to assist the president in administering the maximum and minimum rate provisions of the 1909 act. Section 2 of the act stipulated that an additional 25 percent penalty duty would go into effect on April 1, 1910, unless the president declared that a country did not discriminate in any way against American products. Working in tandem with the Bureau of Trade Relations of the State Department, the board found only one American product that received unfair treatment in European markets—cottonseed oil.[5] Attempts to secure equitable treatment for this product were unsuccessful (Kenkel, 1983, pp. 65–66).

5. American seed oil exports to Europe remain a contentious issue between the United States and its European trading partners. Witness the recent imbroglio over discrimination against American seed oil imports and the threatened retaliation by the United States in the form of increased duties on white wine imports from Europe.

Other American exports entered under the best possible terms in all but three of the most important commercial countries. Canada, France, and Germany had multiple tariff schedules. Since the United States did not have reciprocity agreements with them, American exports were not entitled to the lower rates. To avoid additional duties, however, France continued to apply its minimum rates on most dutiable American goods. Germany also agreed that American products would enjoy the same rates that were extended to European countries with which it had signed conventions. Negotiations with Canada went beyond the question of penalty duties; the two countries began talks on a reciprocity agreement (Kenkel, 1983, pp. 65–66).

The Tariff Board recommended against the application of penalty duties, and Taft concurred with this judgment. On March 28, 1910, Taft declared the minimum rates to be in effect. He proceeded to ask Congress for additional funds for the Tariff Board. He wanted the board to investigate the foreign and domestic costs of production on dutiable articles. He believed that the results of such an investigation could serve as the basis for a "new and proper revision of the tariff." He cautioned Congress not to expect immediate results, *and* he advised against any attempt to adjust rates until the board had determined the appropriate duties (Richardson, ed., 1897–1914, 16:7408, 7427).

Over the objections of the Democrats and ultraprotectionist groups like the American Protective Tariff League, the Republicans provided $250,000 for the Tariff Board. Most Republicans made the decision to fund the Tariff Board reluctantly. Although they had not created a permanent tariff commission and had merely appropriated funds for the president's advisors, they disliked the idea of surrendering the initiative in tariff legislation. They hoped, however, that the Tariff Board would placate the Insurgents in their party, who had opposed the Payne-Aldrich Act. The Republicans also hoped that by funding an investigation of tariff rates they could eliminate the issue from the 1910 campaign (*American Economist*, September 17, 1909, p. 136; May 13, 1910, p. 217; May 27, 1910, p. 245; July 10, 1910, p. 268).

Their political maneuverings were for naught. The Republican party did take a beating at the polls in the Congressional elections of November 1910, and the Payne-Aldrich Tariff Act was indeed cited as one reason for the party's poor showing.[6] The House went Democratic by a 68-vote majority for the first time in sixteen years. The Republicans retained control of the Senate, but they lost eight important seats.

6. The party also paid the price for the calamity of the Balinger-Pinchot row, the president's close relationship with the conservative Congressional leadership, and a year of bad press (see Anderson, 1973, p. 135).

The reversal of their collective political fortunes put pressure on the Republicans to act. Behind-the-scenes pressure from the president, intense lobbying by the National Tariff Commission Association (NTCA),[7] and growing interest among Republicans in Congress put tariff-making reform on the legislative agenda of the lame duck session.

Taft persuaded Congressman Nicholas Longworth, Theodore Roosevelt's son-in-law, to introduce the administration's bill establishing a permanent tariff commission with extensive powers of investigation (Anderson, 1973, p. 145). Taft felt that he had to disassociate himself as much as possible from the proposal. He did not want White House sponsorship to incur Insurgent opposition. He also persuaded Henry Cabot Lodge of Massachusetts, a convert to the commission idea, to refrain from simultaneously introducing a similar measure in the Senate so that the Longworth bill would not be jeopardized (Anderson, 1973, pp. 145–46; Kenkel, 1983, p. 73). Conservatives and Insurgent Republicans joined in support of the reform proposal, but in the end, shrewd parliamentarians who were either opposed to the bill or were interested in other issues defeated the commission proposal.

After receiving the House version, the Senate Finance Committee delayed consideration of the bill and then only reluctantly permitted Senator Lodge to report it with several amendments. Senate Democrats who opposed the idea of a tariff commission on the grounds that it would institutionalize protectionism filibustered for three days, so the amended bill reached the House in the closing hours of the session. Speaker Cannon suspended a roll call on the bill and heeded Ways and Means Committee chairman Payne's request to withdraw the measure to permit the passage of some last-minute appropriation bills (*Congressional Record*, 46:3331–33, 3787, 3887–88).

Despite Congressional rejection of a permanent commission, it approved additional funds for Taft's "advisors" and, in effect, sanctioned their investigation of the Payne-Aldrich tariff rates. Taft used the opportunity to appoint two additional members to his board—both Democrats. He wanted the bipartisan group to demonstrate the effectiveness of the proposed (and rejected) tariff-making reform (Kenkel, 1983, p. 75).

While he was trying to demonstrate through the Tariff Board the via-

---

7. Initially, the NTCA enjoyed the financial and organizational support of the NAM. The organizations, however, soon clashed on certain issues. One point of dispute was whether the proposed tariff commission should be granted the authority to examine industrialists under oath and to study the books of firms. The NAM broke with the NTCA in 1909 when it rescinded its support for a tariff commission in order to underscore the organization's unequivocal support for protectionism. (See Becker, 1982, p. 81; Stone, 1952, p. 66; National Association of Manufacturers, *Proceedings*, 1909, pp. 66, 150–54, 1766–77.)

bility of scientific tariff making, however, Taft was also ardently pursuing a reciprocity agreement with Canada. The president viewed the successful negotiation of such an agreement as "good statesmanship" and as "a great step toward a commercial union with Canada." So convinced was Taft of the benefits to be gained from reciprocity with Canada that he was willing to compromise his commitment to scientific tariff making in the context of the agreement.

The reciprocity agreement drastically lowered trade barriers between Canada and the United States, and it was part of Taft's long-range policy of trade expansion. The agreement had been secured by Secretary of State Philander Chase Knox in secret negotiations. The president and the Canadian prime minister, Wilfred Laurier, pledged to recommend to their respective legislatures the tariff rates that they had agreed on. Importantly, the agreement had the same legal standing as any ordinary tariff bill; it did not require the two-thirds Senate majority of a conventional treaty (Anderson, 1973, p. 136).

On January 26, 1911, President Taft presented the agreement to Congress. Basically, the agreement called for freer trade on agricultural products of the West and Midwest in return for sizable reductions on manufactured exports from the East. Because the agreement was negotiated without reference to cost-of-production figures, reciprocity with Canada conflicted with Taft's commitment to duty levels that equalized domestic and foreign costs of production. The only cost investigation for the industries affected by the reciprocity bill was one for pulp and paper. Unfortunately, this report was published too late to affect the negotiations. Taft had no reports that justified the rate changes negotiated on the more than three hundred items in the agreement.

The agreement appeared to confirm the Insurgents' suspicion that farmers did not receive the same benefits from protection as did manufacturers. With the exclusion of farm products from protection by the terms of the agreement, opposition to the policy and party spread across the agricultural sectors of the country. Insurgents and standpatters alike demanded that the president withdraw the negotiated agreement until the Tariff Board was able to investigate the probable impact of the proposed changes (Kenkel, 1983, pp. 76–77).

When Taft realized that the reciprocity agreement might be sidetracked in the closing minutes of the session, he threatened to call a special session of Congress to consider the reciprocity issue. Few Republicans believed that the president would commit political suicide by calling a Democratic House into session nine months before it was necessary. Few realized, however, the depth of Taft's commitment to reciprocity: "My judgment before I sent in the message (and even now it hasn't changed) was that this will blow me up politically, but I think that ultimately there will come a realization that it will help our country and the question of parties is not quite so important and still less the question of personal political fortunes" (quoted in Anderson, 1973, p. 137). With assurances from the Democratic House leadership that the Democrats would pass the reciprocity bill, Taft called for the special session the day after the 61st Congress adjourned. The reciprocity bill passed in special session, but internal politics in Canada prevented the agreement from ever going into effect.[8]

In the months following the reciprocity battle, the Democrats worked with the Insurgent Republicans to pass several tariff-revision bills. The Democrat–Insurgent coalition passed bills to lower the duties on wool and woolens, on cotton manufactures, and on sundry manufactured items— the so-called farmers' free list. These the president vetoed somewhat ironically on the grounds that the Tariff Board had yet to report its cost findings (Pringle, 1964, p. 60; Richardson, ed., 1897–1914, 17:7625–27, 7636).

The Tariff Board was a casualty of the political struggles of the Taft administration. It died when appropriation bills for fiscal 1913 omitted its funds. Interestingly, however, in the struggles that embroiled the Tariff Board, the utility of the cost-of-production standard for scientific tariff rate adjustment was never seriously questioned. This standard became an important feature of the flexible tariff provision of the 1922 Tariff Act even though the board's pioneering reports comparing foreign and domestic costs of production revealed the serious drawbacks of using such comparisons for rate setting purposes (Kenkel, 1983, p. 70).

Reciprocity was also a casualty of Taft's political struggles. Unlike the president, most of the members of Taft's party did not accept the idea of privileged access to American markets for whatever reason. Only the palest reflection of former reciprocity provisions appeared in the Underwood Act of 1913, and provisions for negotiation of special reciprocity agreements were eliminated entirely from the Fordney-McCumber Act of 1922. Because Taft did not link concessions offered in the context of a reciprocity agreement to results of the Tariff Board's efforts to determine cost-equalizing duties, reciprocity agreements became viewed as antithetical to the preservation of protection in America and to the principle of scientific tariff making. More important, since the activities of the Tariff Board were overshadowed by the battle over Canadian reciprocity, it was the idea of reciprocity, not scientific tariff making, that was discredited as a means to lower American tariffs and to expand overseas trade

8. The Liberal government of Sir Wilfred Laurier, forced to dissolve Parliament over the reciprocity issue, was defeated at the polls on September 21, 1911. The victorious Conservative party had raised the specter of American annexation as a major campaign issue. (See Anderson, 1973, pp. 144–45; Stewart, 1982.)

(USTC, 1919; McClure, 1924, pp. 96–105). For reform advocates, scientific tariff making remained a viable approach to tariff-making reform.

War and Economic Uncertainty: The Establishment of the Tariff Commission

Following the collapse of the Tariff Board and the Democratic victory in November 1912, the movement for a tariff commission experienced a setback. The several amendments to create a tariff commission introduced during the debates on the Underwood bill were defeated. Most Democrats, including President Wilson, believed that a tariff commission was nothing more than a way to institutionalize the policy of protectionism— "a scheme to reduce protectionism to a science" (Houston, 1926, 1:196, *Congressional Record* 50:765, 770–71, 4353, 4393, 4397–98).

Although they were opposed to duties to equalize costs of production, the Democrats did appropriate funds for a limited study of foreign and domestic production costs by the Bureaus of Foreign and Domestic Commerce in the Department of Commerce. The funding of these studies may have helped to diffuse temporarily support for a tariff commission (Kenkel, 1983, p. 95; Becker, 1982, p. 86).

War in Europe restored the campaign to establish a permanent tariff commission. The business community feared the uncertainty that characterized the international economic environment. Business leaders expressed concern that once the war ended, European manufacturers would attempt to dump goods on the American market in order to undercut American industry and regain lost trade.

Business groups interested in international trade voiced concern that a postwar division of the world into regional markets would encourage discrimination against American exports. The Paris Economic Conference aggravated these concerns. Held in June 1916 and attended by the Allied Powers, it rejected the concept of commercial competition in an open economy. Despite Allied disclaimers of any intention to discriminate purposely against the interests of neutral nations, conference resolutions calling for politically organized regional markets worried business leaders and politicians. The National Foreign Trade Council was particularly vocal in its opposition to the conference resolutions (Kaufman, 1974, pp. 165, 168).

More than ever before, there was a need for careful policy-making. The United States needed to be able to respond to policies inimical to American interests and at the same time encourage trade expansion. Numerous business publications called for the establishment of a permanent tariff commission. The commission proposal was overwhelmingly endorsed in a referendum conducted by the U.S. Chamber of Commerce. Indeed, by late 1915, among business organizations only the ultraprotectionist American Protective Tariff League opposed the creation of a tariff commission (Kaufman, 1974 151–52; Becker, 1982, p. 82).

President Wilson came to endorse the idea of a tariff commission. He explained that the war would lead to a need to study new conditions. Wilson argued that a commission would provide valuable information on the actual operation and impact of the tariff laws:

A year ago, I was not in favour of a tariff board. . . . Then the only purpose of a tariff board was to keep alive an unprofitable controversy. . . . But the circumstances of the present time are these: There is going on in the world an economic revolution. No man understands that revolution. . . . No part of the business of legislation with regard to international trade can be undertaken until we understand it. (Speech before the Railway Business Association, June 27, 1916, quoted in Houston, 1926, 1:197–98)

There was also an element of political expediency in Wilson's conversion. He wanted to attract votes from those who had cast their ballots for the Progressive party in 1912. He also wanted to eliminate the tariff issue from the campaign of 1916—something he had failed to do during the midterm election of 1914 (Becker, 1982, p. 87; Kenkel, 1983, pp. 113–14).[9] A provision for the establishment of a permanent tariff commission was made part of an emergency revenue bill, which President Wilson signed into law on September 8, 1916.

The commission would have six members, appointed by the president and confirmed by the Senate. No more than three of the commissioners could be of the same political party. The commission would investigate and report annually to Congress and the president. These reports were to assess the administrative and fiscal effects of the tariff on the prevailing commercial conditions between American and foreign producers, including their comparative production costs and any evidence of unfair trade practices. Unlike the Tariff Board, the commission would be able to subpoena witnesses and compel testimony.

Republican Progressives in the Senate failed to make the Tariff Commission a rate-setting body. They also failed to have its cost-of-production function emphasized. These Progressives were successful, however, in amending the bill to provide for presidential appointment of the commission's chairman and vice chairman. The amendment was designed

---

9. The creation of the Tariff Commission did not remove the tariff question from partisan debate. Republican presidential candidate Charles Evans Hughes emphasized the need for a return to protectionist policies at the war's end, and he asked the voters to return to power the party of protectionism.

to promote good relations between the commission and the executive (*Congressional Record*, 53:12018–23, 13794–98, 13845, 13848–51).

The establishment of the Tariff Commission demonstrated the growing preoccupation of policymakers with the conditions of international trade. Some hoped that economic cooperation would provide the basis for a lasting peace, but a pervasive fear of dumping, export subsidies, and foreign trade cartels compelled even the visionaries to acknowledge the need for protection under circumstances of unfair competition. The Tariff Commission would assure informed policy-making by Congress in an uncertain postwar period.

Under the leadership of Chairman F. W. Taussig, the charter members of the commission scrupulously avoided any infringement on Congress's prerogative to set rates.[10] Taussig and the other commissioners believed that they could remedy the deficiencies in existing legislation and improve the tariff-making process without suggesting duties for particular imported items. The commission would address broad questions of commercial policy (USTC, *First Annual Report*, 1917, pp. 10–12, 15–19).

The Tariff Commission under Taussig's chairmanship had a significant impact on the foreign economic policy of the United States. During the years immediately following its creation, the commission produced a complete revision of the customs administrative laws. The revision was enacted as part of the Tariff Act of 1922 (the Fordney-McCumber Act). The Tariff Commission's policy recommendations for countering unfair trading practices and discrimination were also incorporated into trade legislation during the early 1920s. The antidumping statute incorporated the Tariff Commission's recommendations and strengthened the existing antidumping law,[11] which had not provided adequate provision against dumping, nor reasonable procedures for its detection. Antidumping legislation was enacted as Title II of the act passed on May 27, 1921. The Anti-dumping Act of 1921 authorized the secretary of the treasury to impose a special dumping duty when he found that imports entered the United States at less than fair market value and when these imports were liable to injure a domestic industry.[12]

In its report on reciprocity and commercial treaties (submitted to Con-

10. The original members of the Tariff Commission were Frank W. Taussig, chairman (1917–1919); Daniel C. Roper, succeeded shortly by Thomas W. Page; David J. Lewis; William Kent; William S. Culbertson; and Edward P. Costigan (see USTC, *First Annual Report*, 1917, pp. 3–4).

11. Antidumping provisions were part of the revenue bill signed into law on September 8, 1916. This was the same legislation that created the Tariff Commission. See USTC, *Third Annual Report*, 1919, pp. 10–12, and Kaufman, 1974, pp. 169–70).

12. Find the text of the Anti-Dumping Act of 1921 in USTC, *Dictionary of Tariff Information*, 1923, pp. 279–82.

gress in February 1919), the commission recommended that the United States adopt a policy of nondiscrimination: "[It] should be the policy of our Government to offer equality of tariff treatment to all who grant like treatment to the United States and its products and to penalize with a higher tariff those countries which refuse us equality of treatment" (USTC, *Third Annual Report*, 1919, p. 13). Under the leadership of the Senate Republicans, the U.S. Congress adopted this policy:

In short, Senators, we would base the commercial policy of the United States upon the twin ideas of granting equal treatment to all nations in the market of the United States and of exacting equal treatment for the commerce of the United States in foreign markets. We do not believe that the United States should pursue a general policy of special bargains and special reciprocity treaties. (Comments by Senator Smoot, *Congressional Record* 62:5881)

Section 317 of the Fordney-McCumber Act empowered the president to defend American exports against discrimination by enabling him to levy "defensive" or penalty duties on products of countries that discriminated against American products.[13]

Although the Tariff Commission influenced American commercial policy as evidenced in the changes of the customs administrative laws, the Anti-Dumping Act, and Section 317 of the 1922 Tariff Act, it could not alter the fundamental character of the trade policy process. It had no role in the tariff rate-setting process. Therefore, it did not alter the pattern of institutional relations that had defined the trade policy process for so many years. The rate setting procedures that characterized the revisions of 1883, 1890, 1894, 1897, and 1909 again operated unencumbered when the Republicans in Congress undertook a general revision in 1921–1922. The Fordney-McCumber Act raised average ad valorem rates on dutiable imports to 38.2 percent (up from 26.8 percent).[14] In contrast to previous revisions, however, the act's flexible tariff provision was supposed to eliminate the excesses and inconsistencies produced by the logroll.

The Scientific Tariff-Making Experiment: Section 315 of the Fordney-McCumber Act

Recapturing control of government in 1920, the Republicans strove to assure a return to "normalcy." For commercial policy this meant a return to the policy of protection. However, for many Republicans and Republican supporters, the unbridled protectionism produced by the existing tariff-making process was an unacceptable policy outcome.

13. The text of Section 317 is reprinted in McClure, 1924, pp. 23–26.
14. Taking into account all imports, the 1922 act raised average ad valorem rates to 13.9 percent.

Large segments of the business community wanted "judicious" levels of protection but feared indiscriminate rate setting by Congress. Radical shifts in tariff levels were always unsettling to the business community. Now prominent business organizations were also convinced that excessive protection would discourage exports and curtail foreign trade expansion. The Chamber of Commerce, the NAM, the AMEA, and the NFTC advocated tariff-making reform to provide for flexible rate setting (Becker 1982, p. 13; Kenkel, 1983, pp. 152–53). The Chamber of Commerce endorsed a plan that would have had tariff rates determined by a board. The Tariff Commission would supply board members with reliable information upon which the specific determinations could be made (Chamber of Commerce, *Referendum*, no. 37, 1921).

Astute Republicans saw the general revision as a political booby trap that would compel members of Congress to extend protectionism to all who demanded it and yet lead to Republican party losses at the polls. This is what had happened to the Republican party in 1910. Given the existing policy process, the public cry for tariff reform could not be assuaged. Thus, while voters failed to organize on behalf of tariff reform, they cast their ballots against members of the party that failed to deliver it. Republicans sought a way to turn this potential liability into an asset. They endorsed the flexible tariff idea. Protective tariffs could be assigned in the usual indiscriminate manner, but a flexible tariff provision would, in principle, eliminate the inconsistencies of Congressionally determined tariff rates.

Tariff Commissioner William S. Culbertson presented the plan for a flexible tariff system to President Warren G. Harding in a series of memoranda, and he persuaded the president of its merits. Culbertson advocated reasonable protection that equalized the conditions of competition between American producers and their overseas counterparts. The experience of the Tariff Board did not deter him. He believed that the commission could compare the difference between foreign and domestic production costs and that this would determine a proper equalizing duty. He proposed to let the president adjust rates in accordance with that formula. Culbertson maintained that flexibility would ensure against trade-stifling protectionism, provide for adjustment to changing trade conditions, and obviate the need for subsequent Congressional revisions (Culbertson, Memoranda for Harding, October 13 and 18, 1921; April 24 and September 5, 1922; Papers of William S. Culbertson, Library of Congress).

Culbertson also understood the political desirability of an elastic tariff, with its promise of revision by experts. Harding and Secretary of Commerce Herbert Hoover accepted Culbertson's arguments. They agreed that an elastic tariff would at least create the illusion of moderation necessary to prevent a voter backlash in 1922 (Page, 1924, pp. 1–2; Sinclair, 1966, p. 57, 231). In his first State of the Union message, Harding publicly endorsed the flexible tariff plan:

Every contemplation, it little matters in which direction one turns, magnifies the difficulty of tariff legislation, but the necessity of the revision is magnified with it. Doubtless we are justified in seeking a more flexible policy than we have provided heretofore. I hope a way will be found to make for flexibility and elasticity so that rates may be adjusted to meet unusual and changing conditions which can not be accurately anticipated. . . . I know of no manner in which to effect this flexibility other than the extension of the powers of the Tariff Commission, so that it can adapt itself to a scientific and wholly just administration of the law. I am not unmindful of the constitutional difficulties. These can be met by giving authority to the Chief Executive, who could proclaim additional duties to meet conditions which the Congress may designate. (Harding, "First Annual Message," in Israel, 3:279–82)

The president's endorsement came after the House of Representatives had passed its version of the tariff bill. Thus, the House bill did not include a flexible tariff provision. The House bill was noteworthy, however, because it included a controversial provision for American valuation of imports. Although foreign valuation—"actual cost at the place of exportation" (USTC, *Dictionary*, 1923, p. 282)—had long provided the dutiable base for imports entering the United States,[15] a plan for American valuation gained growing acceptance, especially among staunch protectionists, during the early 1920s. Proponents of the plan argued that foreign valuation at a time of depreciating foreign exchange rates risked undervaluation of imports. Opponents countered by noting that price levels abroad had risen by approximately the same amount that exchange rates had fallen, and therefore the continued use of foreign valuation would not decrease the amount of duty revenue (USTC, 1921; Gersting, 1932, pp. 19–20). Nevertheless, Section 402 of the Fordney bill provided for a complete change to the American valuation base (*Congressional Record* 61:4198).

Senate amendments to substitute a flexible tariff system for American valuation were among the Finance Committee's 2,082 amendments of the Fordney bill. Most of these amendments (in typical Senate fashion) offered tariff increases to numerous special interests (Hicks, 1960b, p. 56). The four amendments sponsored by Senator Smoot of Utah, however, proposed a fundamental alteration of the tariff-making process—the process epitomized by the other 2,000-plus amendments.

15. Two exceptions are notable. America's first tariff act (1789) provided for American valuation. This practice lasted six years. American valuation also was practiced for two months under provisions of the Tariff Act of 1833. (See Gersting, 1932, p. 17.)

Section 315 (the final form of the flexible provisions sponsored by Smoot) had no antecedent in American tariff legislation. For the first time in history, the president was given the power to raise or lower tariff rates by up to 50 percent in order to equalize foreign and domestic production costs. The changes made under the section were to be permanent; they were designed to eliminate general tariff revisions by Congress. These changes took the process of tariff rate adjustment out of the Congressional arena, and they gave to experts a significant role in the rate-setting process. The provisions of Section 315 would serve to insulate the trade policy process from interest group pressures. They represented a significant departure from the pattern of institutional relations that had previously dominated commercial policy-making.

A predominantly Republican majority passed Section 315 because it appealed to both the moderates and the staunch protectionists in the party. Some Republicans who had supported American valuation were persuaded that Section 315 provided a more rigorous method for protecting the home market from the vagaries of the international market than did American valuation.[16] For staunch protectionists, President Harding eased acceptance of the flexible tariff by his appointment of two uncompromising protectionists to the Tariff Commission (Kenkel, 1983, p. 159).

Those who feared that American valuation would result in the imposition of prohibitive tariffs considered the provision for a flexible tariff a moderating measure. Senator Smoot, for example, expected the president to reduce "the majority of the rates" and thus provide "reasonable access" to the American market for foreign exporters (*Congressional Record* 62:35, 5876–77, 5881).

Still other moderates supported the flexible provisions because they offered judicious protection while correcting the excesses of the logroll. Senators Arthur Capper of Kansas and Robert L. Owen of Oklahoma were among those who expressed this opinion (*Congressional Record* 62:9151).

Clearly a major factor weighing in favor of the provision was the expectation of repeated tariff revisions in response to changing conditions in the international economy and the recognition of the political costs associated with general revisions. The Republican party did not want to be victimized by the trade policy process as it had been after the passage of the Payne-Aldrich Tariff Act (*Congressional Record* 652:9071, 11154, 11211).

Commissioner Culbertson was influential in solidifying support for Section 315 throughout the Senate's and the Conference Committee's consideration of the bill. He persuaded President Harding to come out against an amendment to make the grant of extraordinary power a temporary

16. See remarks of Senator McCumber, *Congressional Record* 62:5763–64.

provision to be reviewed by Congress. He briefed Senator Smoot and fed him with arguments. He also fought to preserve for the Tariff Commission a major role in the rate setting experiment (Culbertson, Memorandum for Smoot, April 20, 1922; Memoranda for Harding, May 4 and August 10, 1922, Papers of William S. Culbertson, Library of Congress).

In the Senate and Conference Committees the role of the Tariff Commission was challenged on two grounds. The first was the constitutionality of delegating tax adjustment authority to an independent commission. Congress had delegated railroad rate-setting authority in the Hephurn Act to the Interstate Commerce Commission, but delegating authority to tax was considered a more questionable proposition (Gersting, 1932, p. 67). To get around the issue, Culbertson suggested and Harding agreed that Congress should delegate tariff adjustment authority to the president—the president to make these adjustments based on the cost of production information provided him by the Tariff Commission. In the Senate debate, Section 3 of the McKinley Tariff Act (1890) was cited as constitutional precedent. This provision had allowed the president minimal rate adjustment authority; under specified circumstances, he could remove items like coffee, tea, and hides from the duty-free list (U.S. Senate, 67th Cong. 2nd Sess., 1922, S. Rep. 595, p. 4; *Congressional Record* 62:5874–81, 11189). The issue was not definitively settled until April 9, 1928, when the U.S. Supreme Court ruled (J. W. Hampton and Co. v. the U.S., 276, U.S. 394 [1927]) in favor of the constitutionality of Section 315.

The ability of the Tariff Commission to maintain impartiality in its investigations was also questioned. Senator McCumber, chairman of the Finance Committee, worried that to designate the commission as principal advisor to the president would involve it in factional disputes. Culbertson, however, believed that the commission would be immune to pressures. He convinced President Harding that the Tariff Commission should be the source of information on all tariff matters. The bill passed by Congress granted considerable powers of investigation to the Tariff Commission (*Congressional Record* 62:11229).

Although Harding, Culbertson, and the majority of Congress approved Section 315 in its final form, support for the tariff-making reform measure was not universal. The majority of Congressional Democrats opposed the reform on a variety of grounds. They objected to the enactment into law of the Republican party's principle of protection—cost-of-production equalization. Some also questioned the claim that Section 315 instituted scientific tariff making. Senator Simmons, senior Democrat on the Finance Committee, noted, for example, that the president was not bound by the Tariff Commission's findings and that he was free to respond to whatever interests he deemed worthy (*Congressional Record* 62:5885, 5999, 6493–502, 7108–9, 11155, 11205–6, 11234, 11596).

These criticisms turned out to be prophetic. The cost-of-production standard—its interpretation and its implementation—and the Chief Executive—his unwillingness to execute faithfully his legislative mandate—resulted in a flexible tariff system that was neither flexible nor scientific.

Scientific Tariff Making in Practice

Section 315 required the Tariff Commission to conduct a cost-of-production investigation before any tariff adjustment could be made. The commission was given practically a free reign in deciding how the final cost-of-production figures should be derived. The section specifically mentioned several cost elements that were to be included, but substantial commission discretion was granted in that part of the statute that allowed the commission to consider "any other advantages or disadvantages in competition." [17] Under that grant of authority, it was possible for the commission to find in almost any case a cost difference that would warrant the maximum increase in duty permissible under the section. How the Tariff Commission chose to interpret the cost-of-production guidelines, therefore, became critical in the operation of the flexible system.

Another important matter was deciding what to investigate. The criteria the commission used to select its cases would determine the scope of the flexible tariff experiment. Should the commission respond to industry petitions? Should the commission systematically investigate items in the tariff schedules? Should the commission restrict its investigations to those requested by the president?

The Tariff Commission was divided on these important questions. The three remaining Wilson appointees (William S. Culbertson, Edward P. Costigan, and David L. Lewis) were Progressives. They wanted to encourage fair competition between domestic and foreign products in the American market. This meant rate levels that equalized costs. They had no intention of employing the cost standard to erect an impenetrable tariff wall around the American market. They also believed that the flexible tariff was a great reform—a substitution for legislation dictated by special interests. They wanted to revise thoroughly the tariff schedules and intended to conduct cost investigations of the major industries (Kenkel, 1983, p. 162).

In contrast, the Harding appointees, especially Thomas O. Marvin and

17. The text of Section 315 is reprinted in Gersting, 1932, pp. 87–89.

William F. Burgess, were against relaxing American protectionism.[18] They thought that proper protectionism guaranteed the preeminent position of every American producer in the home market. They were against the idea of fair competition, and thus they opposed the principle of duties based on differences in production costs if it permitted the entry of some competing foreign goods. Whenever possible they used commission discretion to inflate domestic cost figures and recommend tariff rate increases. They also opposed a system-wide application of the cost standard. They preferred to be directed by industry petitions and presidential directives (Gersting, 1932, p. 112; Larkin, 1936, p. 24; Kenkel, 1983, p. 163).

President Harding was reluctant to intervene. To side with either the progressives or the staunch protectionists risked stirring up controversy within the Republican party. He had already aroused the suspicions of the progressives by appointing Marvin chairman of the commission. Before his death in August 1923, however, he did help the commission reach a compromise on the decision criteria for choosing cases. On April 21, 1923, after a conference with the Tariff Commission, President Harding issued a statement: "Petitions and applications for the increase or reduction in rates are to be considered in accordance with the Executive Order of October 7th to determine whether formal investigation is warranted. If the nature of the subject so requires, the Commission will exercise power to limit inquiry or broaden it to include related subjects" (quoted in Gersting, 1932, p. 71). The commission agreed to begin twenty-nine cost investigations, some on insignificant items but some on important industries, including cotton hosiery, pulp logs, and sugar (Kenkel, 1983, p. 166).

Cost-of-production investigations presented many difficulties for the staff of the commission. Small-scale producers seldom kept accurate records, and information obtained from one producer was seldom comparable to information collected from other producers. Moreover, manufacturers usually produced more than the single item in which the commission was interested, and this demanded the apportionment of overhead and other general charges.

In the absence of records, agricultural costs proved most difficult to determine. It was often necessary to estimate a money value where no money was paid out for family labor, for articles produced on the farm, and for maintenance of farm animals. The whole process required months

18. Thomas O. Marvin was the secretary of the Home Market Club of Boston. William F. Burgess was a member of the board of directors and former president of the International Pottery Company of Trenton, New Jersey. He was chief lobbyist for the U.S. Potters' Association, and he had represented potters' interests at tariff hearings since 1894. (See Schattschneider, 1935, pp. 186–87; White, 1938, p. 29.)

of field and office work (USTC, *Thirteenth Annual Report*, 1929, pp. 17–28; Gersting, 1932, pp. 78–138).

The commission's staff also encountered perplexing difficulties collecting cost-of-production data overseas. Foreign manufacturers resisted the suggestion that American experts could, in a brief visit, determine the production costs of each item they produced. They were reluctant to reveal data on costs, prices, and profits (Kenkel, 1983, pp. 169–70).

Concern about the lack of progress on the foreign investigations led the commission to send Commissioners Costigan and Glassie abroad to report on the situation. They found that the commission surveys irritated European manufacturers and governments, that there was widespread skepticism that they would lead to a relaxation of restrictive duties, and that the commission's agents were suspected of industrial espionage (USTC, *Tenth Annual Report*, 1926; USTC, "Proceedings," October 28, 1924, June 23, 1925, September 27, 1927).

When it was impossible to collect sufficient data, the commission inferred costs from invoice prices on the assumption that they most likely equaled, if they did not exceed, costs of production. The commission also came to use a simple weighted average to estimate the domestic and foreign costs of a particular item (USTC, *Thirteenth Annual Report*, 1929, pp. 17–18; Gersting, 1932, pp. 86–119).

The commission often made two recommendations to the president based on different interpretations of the data. In the report on wheat requested by the president, the commission offered two interpretations of the data and made two rate-adjustment recommendations. The protectionists elected to average costs based on the single year 1923. Because the year 1923 was a particularly bad one for wheat growers in the United States, the protectionists on the commission concluded that the flexible tariff system could not provide the required level of protection. They settled for recommending the maximum possible increase in the existing tariff rates. The progressives used a three-year average (1921–1923). They also recommended a tariff rate increase, but they found the flexible provisions fully adequate to meet the farmers' protection requirements (USTC, 1924, pp. 6, 26–29, 37–39).

The sugar investigation also was divisive. The progressives and protectionists clashed on the issue of conflict of interest and commission procedures. The progressive commissioners, understanding the importance and visibility of the sugar case, were determined to make the investigation the proving ground of the tariff-making reform. Culbertson, Costigan, and Lewis decided for the sake of procedural integrity that Commissioner Glassie should not participate in the sugar investigation. They saw a potential conflict of interest in Glassie's participation because his wife had inherited some shares in a sugar company (USTC, "Proceedings," December 19, 1923). Of course, the move to exclude Glassie was opposed by the other commissioners. They argued that since the Tariff Commission served only as an advisory body and not as a quasi-judicial one, the conflict of interest concerns of the progressives were groundless. President Coolidge accepted the protectionists' argument and supported Glassie's participation (Glassie, 1925, pp. 329–435; 442–66).

The progressives would not be dissuaded. To Culbertson, Costigan, and Lewis, Glassie's participation in the sugar investigation was tantamount to a return to tariff making by representatives of special interests. They challenged Glassie to excuse himself at the opening of the public hearing on January 15, 1924. Glassie stood firm until Congress intervened. The Independent Appropriations Act included a provision that withheld the salary of any commissioner who participated in an investigation when there existed a conflict of interest (USTC, "Proceedings," January 15 and 16, 1924; *Congressional Record* 64:5527; USTC, *Eighth Annual Report*, 1924, p. 41). Under penalty of law, Glassie withdrew from the sugar investigation.

Constituting a temporary majority on the Tariff Commission, the progressives recommended that the duty on raw sugar be reduced. The dissenting opinion submitted by Marvin and Burgess maintained that the prevailing sugar duty did not equalize the higher cost of sugar produced from beets, but they did not specify an increase because they claimed the commission lacked the information to make such a recommendation. In reaching that conclusion, Marvin and Burgess disregarded seemingly relevant information. They clearly wanted to discredit the commission's report. This became even more apparent when they complained to Coolidge about the procedures followed in the investigation (USTC, 1926, pp. 69–70, 106–7, 135; USTC, "Proceedings," May 26, July 9, 19, August, 7, 1924).

The commission's reports on wheat and sugar were not unique. Most of the reports under Section 315 demonstrated a considerable difference of opinion within the Tariff Commission. Gradually, that dissension grew less and less as the progressives were replaced on the commission with men whose views on the tariff and Section 315 paralleled those of the president and the staunch protectionists already serving on the commission (Gersting, 1932, pp. 171–73).

The achievement of a more cohesive commission did little to improve operation of Section 315. Time consumed on frivolous applications and the difficulties of obtaining cost information continued to impede progress. Between 1923 and 1930 the Tariff Commission sent only forty-seven reports to the president (Kenkel, 1983, p. 168).

Effective administration of Section 315 was further confounded by a president who was not committed to tariff-making reform. President Coolidge praised the protectionism of the Fordney-McCumber Act and maintained that Section 315 should be used only when there were "inequalities of sufficient importance." He believed that constant adjustment of duties would disturb business and jeopardize prosperity (Slemp, 1926, p. 141; Larkin, 1936, p. 28; White, 1938, pp. 344, 371, 385). He therefore refused to enforce the flexible provisions of the law vigorously; he avoided and delayed decisions.

Coolidge did not act on the commission's report on sugar for months. He waited out the 1924 election, not wanting to alienate either consumers or producers with his determination. It was not until July 1925 that he announced his intention to leave the sugar duty unchanged. His procrastination had created havoc in the sugar trade as buyers and sellers waited for the new duty to be announced. More important, his decision to reject the commission's recommendation and leave in place the rate that was the product of lobbying and logrolling undermined the credibility of the tariff-making reform experiment. The obvious motives underlying the president's actions in the sugar case demonstrated how susceptible scientific rate adjustment was to political manipulation.

On two other occasions in the five-and-a-half years he adjusted tariff rates under Section 315, Coolidge announced his rejection of the Tariff Commission's recommendations for tariff rate changes, leaving the existing rates in place. In thirty-three other instances, he opted to change the existing rates after Tariff Commission investigations. He increased rates on twenty-eight items and lowered them on five. For fifteen other articles, however, Coolidge made no announcement at all; he simply did not act one way or the other on the commission's recommendations (Gersting, 1932, p. 171; Kenkel, 1983, p. 168).

Coolidge also demonstrated his lack of commitment to tariff-making reform with his annual reappointment of Thomas O. Marvin as chairman of the Tariff Commission. Chairman Marvin worked to make the flexible tariff an "instrumentality for raising rates." He expedited cases when he anticipated a maximum increase in the duty and prolonged investigations if he suspected a rate decrease (Kenkel, 1983, pp. 189–90).

The problems associated with the administration of the flexible tariff program did not go unnoticed in Congress.[19] In March 1928, the Senate organized a committee to investigate the activities of the Tariff Commis-

---

19. Commissioner Costigan drew attention to the problems of the Tariff Commission in a speech before the American Economic Association in December 1925. He asked the Senate to withhold confirmation of two Coolidge appointments to the commission, and he asked Congress to investigate commission activities. (See *Congressional Record* 67:1389–90.)

sion. It recommended in May 1928 the repeal of the flexible tariff provision (*Congressional Record* 69:10547).

The concept of flexible tariff rates was resurrected by President Herbert Hoover. He insisted that Congress's revision of 1929 include a provision for rate adjustment. Since the flexible tariff system was supposed to have obviated the need for tariff revision by Congress, the very fact that Congress deemed revision necessary was an admission that the flexible, scientific, tariff system had failed.

The Smoot-Hawley Tariff Act of 1930 is significant because it *did not* represent a departure from long-standing American commercial policy and policy-making methods. The return to Congressional tariff making acknowledged the failure of the tariff-making reforms introduced in 1922. The reforms that were supposed to produce scientific tariffs, promote foreign trade, and eliminate the need for general tariff revisions by Congress accomplished none of these goals.

Institutional Change and the Trade Policy Process of the 1920s

Tariff-making reform had emerged as an issue around the turn of the century. It was supported by influential business organizations and progressive Republicans. The movement was able to come to fruition in the early 1920s because international economic uncertainty, a product of the war, impressed upon members of Congress the necessity for flexible tariffs. In addition, the Republicans were sensitive to public criticism of traditional tariff-making methods. They feared a voter backlash if the effects of the Congressional logroll were not mitigated somehow. Despite these favorable circumstances, the tariff-making reform package that passed Congress in 1922 did not wholly reflect the designs or the desires of longtime reform advocates.

The trade policy process that emerged from the Tariff Act of 1922 achieved insulation. The locus of policy-making was shifted from Congress; narrow, particularistic interests were distanced from the task of tariff rate setting. Under the provisions of Section 315, such interests could petition the Tariff Commission for an investigation. But under the new process there was no guarantee that a petition would result in an investigation. In fact, most petitions did not. Out of more than six hundred formal requests, the Tariff Commission instituted only eighty-three investigations (Kenkel, 1983, p. 168). Moreover, there was no guarantee that an investigation would lead to the desired outcome. Interest groups were further divorced from the rate-setting process by Congressional action that stipulated the withholding of salary for any commissioner who participated in an investigation when there was a question of conflict of interest.

Insulation of the trade policy process, however, did not result in a scientific tariff, a flexible tariff, or an effective commercial policy for the United States—the stated goals of tariff-making reform. The dynamics of the policy-making reform process produced factors that precluded the fulfillment of these goals. First, the new trade process was not fully detached from the political arena. The new process would not "take the tariff out of politics." Appropriate rates would be determined by an independent commission of experts, but the decision to act on the determination would be the president's. The constitutionality issue figured prominently in this regard. Also, backers of the proposal figured that staunch protectionists would more likely accept the tariff-making reform if it integrally involved an avowed protectionist (i.e., President Harding).

Second, the goals of tariff-making reform were not unanimously endorsed by the officials authorized to carry out the legislature's mandate. President Harding's appointment of avid protectionists to the Tariff Commission was a scheme contrived to attract the standpatters in Congress to the reform proposals, but the appointees' lack of commitment to tariff-making reform could only sabotage the flexible tariff system. Animosity to tariff reform on the part of the commissioners and President Harding's successor led to delays and infighting among the officials authorized to implement the new trade policy process. The lack of commitment also fed suspicions at home and abroad that the flexible system was nothing more than an elaborate ruse to forestall real and much needed tariff reform.

Most important, however, the flexible tariff system was doomed because Congress attached rate adjustment under the new process to an ambiguous cost-of-production equalization formula. Interestingly and somewhat ironically, the stipulation that rate adjustments be made according to this standard was not the result of political machinations in Congress. Rather, it was on this one point—the adoption of the cost-of-production standard—that Section 315 of the Fordney-McCumber Act satisfied progressive reformers. The formula of cost-of-production equalization had been an integral feature of their reform plans for a long time. This aspect of their cognitive framework remained fixed despite the revelatory experience of President Taft's Tariff Board.

The Tariff Board had demonstrated that the calculation of production costs for each of the thousands of dutiable items was a monumental and tedious process. The experience of the Tariff Board proved that the cost standard was an unsuitable basis for a thorough revision of the tariff schedules. The range and variety of costs among producers also precluded the determination of a single figure that would represent the difference between foreign and domestic costs. Experts could and did calculate and justify an average difference between foreign and domestic costs, but any decision to fix a duty equal to that average was inherently political and not scientific. A duty equal to the average difference in costs would not protect the least efficient and would protect the profits of the most efficient.

Even though the standard in actual application was variously interpreted, it rarely resulted in a downward rate adjustment. Thus, the cost-of-production standard did nothing to encourage imports at a time when this was vitally important to the world economy. The prospects for a stable international economy were considerably dimmed by an American commercial policy that eschewed tariff rate reduction except under the provisions of the not-so-flexible tariff program.

Yet in spite of the disaster of American commercial policy, the trade policy process that emerged in the 1920s embodied significant innovation in policy-making. A role for the president and the Tariff Commission in tariff rate setting had been firmly established. Even as Congress reasserted its tariff-making prerogatives (1929–1930) and a repetitive sequence began again, President Hoover successfully battled to preserve presidential rate adjustment. The experience of 1922 to 1930, however, demonstrated that this policy-making innovation had to be divorced from the principle of cost-of-production equalization and the pretense of scientific tariffs. Presidential rate adjustment needed to be used in service to a commercial policy based on reciprocity.

CHAPTER SIX

Power Sharing with the President: The Trade Agreements Act of 1934

In 1934 the United States charted a new course in its international economic relations. It adopted a commercial policy based on reciprocal trade agreements and the unconditional most-favored-nation (MFN) principle. Such a policy presumes "a strong industrial nation which wants to secure markets for a broad sweep of its manufactures . . . [the strong nation] can afford to risk injury to some industries in order to obtain these larger markets" (Gardner, 1964, p. 40). It also presumes a policy process that is removed from the pressures of particularistic interests.

Through the scientific tariff-making experiment of the 1920s, the trade policy process had achieved insulation. The experiment failed, however, because it accomplished none of the goals for which it had been created. It did not secure a judicious revision or even review of the tariff schedules. In fact, the Tariff Commission investigated less than a hundred items among the thousands of dutiable products in the tariff schedules. The experiment, therefore, failed to provide a workable alternative to tariff rate setting by Congress. It did not lead to increased access for imports to the American market. Besides being an incredibly ponderous means to revise tariff rates, the rate-adjustment experiment was tied to an inherently protectionist principle (cost-of-production equalization). If anything, it helped to further restrict access to the American market. The rate-adjustment experiment certainly did not work to promote American exports abroad. Rather, it engendered suspicion and distrust on the part of foreign businesses and governments. And in terms of trade expansion, a bad situation was made worse by policymaker rejection in the 1920s of reciprocity treaties or agreements as a component of the American program of trade expansion.

The Trade Agreements Act changed all this. Although it was an amendment to the ultraprotectionist Smoot-Hawley Tariff Act (1930), the trade agreements program was itself not inherently protectionist. In addition, it restored as an integral part of American foreign economic policy the pursuit of reciprocity arrangements with trading partners.

What was equally important, the Trade Agreements Act proved a firm foundation for a new trade policy process, one in which tariff rate adjustment would be accomplished through bilateral agreements that would not require Congressional approval. This was the case despite the fact that the legislation delegated negotiating authority to the president for a three-year period only. In important ways, moreover, the necessity to secure from Congress periodic renewal of the trade agreements program facilitated the development of the new policy process.

The necessity to secure renewal cued the executive branch about the possible repercussions of antagonizing too many domestic interests. American officials sought to maximize the economic benefits of the agreements while minimizing the potential for domestic economic disruption. Their success in accomplishing this goal was due in part to the Smoot-Hawley tariff schedules, which provided an excessively high negotiating base.[1] It was also due to the careful preparation that preceded each negotiation. An elaborate bureaucratic infrastructure of executive committees, agencies within the State and Commerce Departments, and the Tariff Commission supplied useful data on trade between the United States and potential negotiating partners. This information assured that concessions offered in negotiations when generalized under MFN agreements would not result in unacceptable import levels.

Periodically renewing the trade agreements program also facilitated social learning. Renewals gave Congress the opportunity to assess the advantages and disadvantages accompanying this new pattern of institutional relations in trade policy and to explore new legislative options in the policy-making process. These options permitted Congress to respond to the pressures of interest groups without legislating tariffs. Congress could alter the terms of the president's negotiating authority; it could stipulate procedures to ensure that the concessions offered did not result in injury to domestic industries (e.g., peril point); and it could legislate procedures whereby domestic interests could seek relief from import competition (e.g., escape clause). Although these procedures sometimes originated in the executive branch, when adopted by Congress, they provided new ways for legislators to approach trade policy and assured the perpetuation and institutionalization of an insulated trade policy process.

The trade policy process that emerged after 1934 had strengths and weaknesses that not only shaped American foreign economic policy but also in-

---

1. Under the Tariff Act of 1930, the level of duty on all imports was 19 percent (up from 13.9 percent under the Fordney-McCumber Act of 1922). The level of duty on dutiable imports was 55.2 percent (up from 38.2 percent in 1922).

fluenced the course of international economic relations in the post–World War II period. The failure to establish an International Trade Organization (ITO) and the structure of the General Agreement on Tariffs and Trade (GATT) can only be explained in the context of the parameters of the American trade policy process. An understanding of the Trade Agreements Act—the policy it embodied and the process it engendered—is, therefore, pivotal to an understanding of the postwar world economy.

This chapter examines the Trade Agreements Act. It considers why and how reciprocity became established as the directing principle and motive force of American trade policy. It also analyzes the social learning that resulted in the emergence of new policy process for trade. Finally, it discusses the implications of this emerging policy process for the establishment of a liberal economic order in the post–World War II era.

The United States in the World Economy: The Search for Policy

Trade expansion became a goal of American foreign economic policy in the late 1800s. Reciprocity implemented by special treaties was the Republican strategy to expand trade. In 1890 the Republican Congress authorized the president to remove selected items from the duty-free list if concessions were not forthcoming in trade negotiations with the countries of Latin America. U.S. officials hoped to achieve favorable treatment through negotiation for American manufacture exports.

Reciprocity provisions were not included in the Democratic tariff bill of 1894. Democratic leaders argued that trade expansion would be the natural outcome of lowered tariffs because other countries would follow the American lead and lower their own tariff barriers. A policy promoting trade agreements or treaties in which concessions are reciprocally offered and special bilateral trade arrangements created was anathema to Democrats, who in principle advocated universal free trade.

When they returned to power in 1897, the Republicans again incorporated reciprocity provisions into their tariff legislation. The Dingly Act permitted tariff adjustment by the president for a few specified items (Section 3). It also authorized (Section 4) a three-year period for negotiating trade treaties (the high tariff schedules of the Republican bill were jacked up to still higher levels in anticipation of these negotiations). None of the trade treaties concluded under Section 4 of the Dingly Act, however, went into effect. None of them received Senate ratification (Laughlin and Willus, 1903, chap. 10).

The reciprocity issue was revived in 1910, when President Taft made reciprocity with Canada a major goal of his administration. The reciprocity agreement was part of Taft's long-range policy of trade expansion. The agreement with Canada had been secured by Secretary of State Philander Chase Knox in secret negotiations. The president and the Canadian prime minister, Wilfred Laurier, pledged to recommend to their respective legislatures the tariff rates that they had negotiated. The agreement had the same legal standing as any ordinary tariff bill. It did not require the two-thirds Senate majority of a conventional treaty (Anderson, 1973, p. 136).

On January 26, 1911, President Taft presented Congress with the agreement. It drastically lowered trade barriers between Canada and the United States. The agreement called for freer trade on agricultural goods of the West and Midwest in return for sizable reductions of Canadian duties on manufactured exports from the U.S. East.

The terms of the agreement generated great political controversy. Since they accorded Canada tariff concessions on numerous agricultural products, these terms seemed to confirm the suspicions of self-proclaimed Insurgent Republicans like Robert M. La Follette that farmers did not enjoy the same benefits from protection as did manufacturers. In addition, the agreement had been negotiated without reference to cost-of-production figures. Reciprocity with Canada, therefore, conflicted with Taft's commitment to a level of protection for American producers that equalized domestic and foreign costs of production. This point did not go unnoticed by Insurgent Republicans, who demanded that the president withdraw the proposal until cost investigations could determine the probable impact of the proposed tariff rate change (Kenkel, 1983, pp. 76–77).

Despite such objections, Taft continued to push reciprocity with Canada. Most members of his party, however, did not accept the idea of privileged Canadian access to American markets. Traditionally, Republicans had regarded reciprocity as a vehicle to gain access to foreign markets. In their view, reciprocity agreements that resulted in import competition for American industry or agriculture were undesirable—an unintended consequence of the trade expansion policy. Special reciprocity agreements became viewed as antithetical to the preservation of protection in the United States and to the principle of scientific tariff making through the cost-of-production formula.[2]

The financial and commercial changes in the international economy brought about by World War I transformed the circumstances in which Americans sold in the world. During the war years and postwar period, the United States had tremendously increased its level of production and

2. Only the palest reflection of former reciprocity provisions is found in the Underwood Act of 1913. Provisions for negotiation of special reciprocity agreements were eliminated entirely from the Fordney-McCumber Act of 1922. (See USTC, 1919; McClure, 1924, pp. 96–105.)

foreign trade. Its industrial output doubled in less than seven years, between 1914 and 1921, and its foreign trade in manufactures increased from $165.5 million (1900–1914) to $1,272 million (1915–1925) (Becker, 1982, p. 158).

In the initial postwar period, American goods were in demand; they were important to European reconstruction. However, the lack of foreign exchange made it difficult for Europeans to buy American products. The situation was complicated by debt obligations that put more foreign currency in American hands. The imperatives of the situation demanded that the United States adopt a commercial policy that encouraged more imports.

In 1922 the United States chose to adopt a commercial policy based on the principles of fair competition and nondiscrimination. It proposed to open the American market to the extent that no producer was threatened by import competition. The notion of "fair competition" was implemented through the flexible, scientific tariff system. The United States also offered equal access to the American market for everyone. The practice of according privileged status in the American market through reciprocity agreements and treaties was eschewed. The policy of "nondiscrimination" was implemented along with penalizing provisions (Section 317) to assure equality of treatment for American exports (Davis, 1942, p. 211). As part of its policy of nondiscrimination, in 1923 the United States adopted the diplomatic counterpart to Section 317. The United States began to negotiate agreements with its trading partners seeking mutual unconditional MFN treatment.[3]

Policymakers' concern with discrimination was consistent with the changes that had occurred in the composition of American imports and exports. Between 1919 and 1931, crude materials for the manufacture of such products as automobiles became important. Moreover, recovery in Europe would eventually threaten the increasingly high levels of American manufacturing exports. American goods were often competitive with and not complementary to European goods and would thus be vulnerable to discrimination in markets with exclusive tariff systems: "Countries which predominantly export manufactured articles are much more vulnerable to retaliation than countries which import manufactured articles and export raw materials" (Gregory, 1921, p. 480).

This concern about the potential impact of discrimination against American products in overseas markets led policymakers to question the

3. Such agreements were concluded with Brazil, Germany, Nicaragua, Guatemala, Dominican Republic, El Salvador, Czechoslovakia, Poland, Estonia, Finland, Hungary, Greece, Spain, Lithuania, Latvia, Rumania, Haiti, Honduras, Norway, Austria, and Turkey (see USTC, 1933, pp. 15–16; Davis, 1942, pp. 104–5).

advisability of maintaining the long-standing commitment to a conditional MFN clause. Under the conditional variant, a third party was not automatically accorded the concessions offered to others. Instead, the third party was offered the opportunity to qualify for these concessions. In 1923, therefore, the United States became willing to automatically extend concessions to third parties with which it had MFN agreements. However, because the United States had rejected in the Fordney-McCumber Act (1922), the policy of negotiating special reciprocity arrangements with its trading partners, all nations, even those entitled to MFN treatment, were subject to the same high tariff levels. Nevertheless, American officials did hope to benefit from the concessions extended in negotiations between other countries and secure new markets for burgeoning American exports (Tasca, 1938, pp. 117–20; Davis, 1942, p. 106).

American leaders particularly wanted to circumvent the British system of imperial preferences. They wanted U.S. producers to share equal access to the markets, raw materials, and investment opportunities in Britain's colonial empire. American leaders also battled against the French two-column tariff, which, "aside from imperial preference," was defined as the most difficult obstacle to obtaining the widest possible markets for American goods (Partini, 1969, p. 244).

Given the nonnegotiability of American tariffs, the efforts to establish MFN relations with foreign countries failed. Germany was the only major nation with which the United States was able to conclude an unconditional MFN treaty before April 1933 (USTC, 1933, pp. 15–16). The two major discriminatory systems, the British system of imperial preferences and the French two-column tariff schedule, remained unchanged. A policy offering an extremely high, autonomous tariff implemented by penalty duties (U.S. policy under the 1922 Tariff Act) could not be successful. It appeared coercive and, more important, it offered nothing to Britain or France, in particular, in exchange for sizable concessions: access to their home and colonial markets.

The policy of fair competition as administered through the flexible tariff program also failed. The elastic interpretation of fair competition greatly restricted, not expanded, foreign access to the American market; and along with the contingent duty clauses of the 1922 Act, it engendered hostility in the international community (Taussig, 1933, pp. 307–405). Under the operation of Section 315, duties were changed on only thirty-eight items; there were thirty-three rate increases and five decreases. In some cases the flexible tariff aimed to increase duties on items for which no comparable articles were produced in the United States (Kenkel, 1983, p. 173).

With access to American markets restricted, the United States was able to export in the interwar period only by granting loans. During the period 1924–1930 the average annual merchandise export balance for the United States was $764,000,000. The average net payments on all service transactions, including interest and dividend items were $260,000,000, thus leaving an average annual balance of approximately a half billion dollars. The average estimated amount of funds made available to foreigners during this period as a result of long-term capital transactions was $497,000,000 (Culbertson, 1937, p. 190).

When the loans dried up, beginning in 1928, as American investors turned toward the lucrative stock market (Ashworth, 1952, p. 190), Europeans no longer had the foreign exchange to purchase American products. The collapse of foreign credit (1929–1932) precipitated the collapse of world trade. Shrinking foreign trade hit the United States particularly hard because the high wartime levels of production and the resulting export expansion that continued through the 1920s had grown well beyond domestic needs.

The first year of the New Deal did not bring a new American foreign economic policy. The National Recovery Act (NRA) and the Agricultural Adjustment Act (AAA) were Franklin D. Roosevelt's "first-tier" options for recovery. Promoting trade expansion and international cooperation were not top priorities in 1933. The domestic planners did not want recovery jeopardized by "internationalist" policies. This "go it alone" orientation was apparent in the protectionist provisions of the NRA and AAA as well as in Roosevelt's repudiation of the currency stabilization program proposed at the July 1933 London Economic Conference (Gardner, 1964, pp. 22–30; Kenkel, 1983, p. 241). Only when New Deal domestic planning failed to bring immediate results did the administration turn toward a more internationalist approach to recovery. In 1934 the administration adopted a policy of trade expansion advocated by Secretary of State Cordell Hull.

A longtime proponent of liberalism in international economic relations, Hull favored "any action or agreement that would lower tariff barriers, whether the agreement was multilateral, signed by many or all nations, whether it was regional, embracing only a few, or whether it was bilateral, embracing only two" (Hull, 1948, 1:356). In 1916, Hull had endorsed a program by which all nations would agree to lower their tariff barriers to the same extent. He held to this formula throughout the 1920s and up to the London Economic Conference, where he proposed a worldwide tariff truce. He was pragmatic enough to recognize, however, that it would be "folly to go to Congress and ask that the Smoot-Hawley Act be repealed or its duties reduced by Congress" (p. 358). The inevitable result would have been still higher tariff rates. Hull decided to try to secure the enactment of a bilateral trade agreement program that embraced the principles of nondiscrimination and equality of treatment.

When Congress adopted the Trade Agreements Act, it endorsed an approach that would not only enable the United States to lower its tariffs but would also promote the establishment of a liberal economic order. By delegating to the president authority to negotiate tariff concessions bilaterally, the Trade Agreements Act offered an alternative to policy-making through party or through commission. Moreover, in marked contrast to those of either party or commission, the policy strategy inherent in the "power sharing" alternative was that of trade liberalization. The commission alternative embodied a policy strategy that would inevitably preserve protectionism, and even if it could be achieved, the traditional trade policy approach of the Democratic party (exemplified in the Underwood Act of 1913) would not have yielded multilateral trade liberalization.[4] Such liberalization is the product of tariff bargains, not of unilateral reductions: "[F]ree trade is not a game at which one can play—more than a single country must lower its tariffs before a free trade regime can be said to exist" (Stein, 1984, p. 364). The Trade Agreements Act offered the possibility for generalizing the concessions negotiated in specific bilateral agreements because third-party countries accorded unconditional MFN status would enjoy the benefits of these concessions.

On this point the case of Great Britain in the nineteenth century is illustrative. In the late 1840s Britain reduced its tariffs unilaterally.[5] The "golden age of free trade," however, did not begin until the British had concluded the Cobden-Chevalier Treaty (1860) with France. The United States faced a similar imperative. To redirect the course of international economic relations toward liberalization, the United States needed to conclude trade agreements with the major trading nations of the world; then, to extend liberalization, these nations would have to conclude agreements with each other.

---

4. This observation assumes that national economies have significant investment in "transaction specific assets for trade" and that conditions for trade between states resemble a "Prisoners' Dilemma" situation (see Yarbrough and Yarbrough, 1987.)

5. Beth V. and Robert M. Yarbrough (1987) explain Britain's commitment to unilateral trade liberalization by noting Britain's small investment in transaction-specific assets for trade. Britain needed to export manufactures and import raw materials in an environment in which there were multiple buyers and few, if any, alternative suppliers of the manufactures Britain exported and multiple suppliers of the raw materials it needed. Under these conditions, Britain was not compelled to guard against or to practice "opportunistic protectionism." Investment in transaction-specific assets for trade, however, increased rapidly during the twentieth century. Unilateral liberalization ceased to be a viable policy option for any state in this changed world economy.

The Democrats Chart an Uncertain Course: 1932–1933

When the Democratic party took control of the House of Representatives as a result of the Congressional elections of 1930, they lacked any semblance of unity on the critical foreign economic policy issues confronting the United States. By the early 1930s, Democrats in increasing numbers were advocating explicitly protectionist commercial policies. Some influential Democrats did remain committed to the liberal trade principles espoused by Woodrow Wilson, but even these liberal diehards understood the futility of attempting to lower the Smoot-Hawley tariff rates through traditional means in the middle of a depression.

The party was equally ambivalent about delegating rate-adjustment authority to the president. Democrats uniformly rejected the provisions for a flexible tariff system of the Fordney-McCumber and Smoot-Hawley Acts. However, their motivations varied. Some Democrats objected to presidential encroachment into Congressional prerogatives. Others simply rejected a system that had been poorly administered and had clearly failed.

The Collier bill, passed by Congress before the 1932 election, demonstrates the Democrats' ambivalence toward the commercial policies enacted by the Republican party during the 1920s. Vetoed by President Hoover, the bill would have rescinded the president's authority to adjust tariff rates as stipulated in the flexible provisions of the Smoot-Hawley Act (*Congressional Record* 75:1524–26, 9115, 9149). It would have had the Tariff Commission make its rate-adjustment recommendations directly to Congress. The commission would have continued to use the inherently prohibitive cost-of-production standard in its investigations, but the Collier bill would have removed artificial restraints on the commission's application of this standard. Under provisions of the bill, the commission could make adjustment recommendations of more than 50 percent (*Congressional Record* 75:1275, 1516, 1524–26).

The lack of party unity on the tariff issue posed a dilemma for those who drafted the 1932 Democratic party platform. The party pundits wanted to adopt a plank that would satisfy uncompromising liberals like Cordell Hull without explicitly endorsing a policy of unfettered liberalism—"[a policy] hardly anyone wanted to see . . . implemented" (Tugwell, 1957, p. 231). Advocating reciprocal trade agreements proved a useful compromise. Cordell Hull (1948) was pleased that he and his associates had won the fight "to keep the Democratic Party from falling into the error of high tariffs" (1:332) while less doctrinaire Democrats were not burdened by a platform promise they would not (and could not) keep.

Franklin D. Roosevelt endorsed the platform plank that called for reciprocal trade arrangements, but he deferred action on the matter until 1934.

This reluctance to act on trade matters must be understood in the context of the policy shifts that characterized the early New Deal.[6] During March and early April of 1933, the administration seemed interested in pursuing international cooperation as part of a recovery program. Secretary of State Cordell Hull and Secretary of Commerce Daniel Roper called for tariff reductions. FDR appeared anxious to participate in preparations for the upcoming World Economic Conference in London, and in late March American officials began negotiations with the British and the French on a wide range of issues (Moore, 1974, pp. 729–30).

The president, however, turned away from the course of internationalism. National recovery became tied to a posture of self-containment. The twin experiments in domestic planning—the NRA and AAA—required insulation from, not cooperation with, the world economy. The NRA fixed industrial prices and wages, which undermined the competitive position of American manufacturers. Public works were supposed to substitute for lost foreign markets. The AAA sought to increase commodity prices by restricted production. Foreign dumping of agricultural products would sabotage this effort (Moore, 1974, p. 739). On the monetary front, Roosevelt adopted a policy of forced devaluation. Deliberate devaluation, along with protective tariffs, locked out foreign goods and made other nations bear the costs of American recovery (Gardner, 1964, p. 27–28; Moore, 1974, p. 743).

A couple of factors help to explain the New Deal's early rejection of international cooperation. First, FDR himself was not firmly committed to internationalism, and neither were key members of his Brain Trust. Raymond Moley, for example, had occasion to remark, "It was not that tariff reduction was *per se* incompatible with the economics of the New Deal that was taking shape, but that there was a crucial question of timing and method" (Moley, 1939, p. 48; see also Hull, 1948, 1:363). Thus, while Roosevelt expressed interest during the first weeks of his administration in exploring the strategy of recovery through international cooperation, he was not so committed to internationalism that he could not abruptly alter course when European statesmen thwarted American proposals.[7]

6. Roosevelt did not delay action on trade agreements legislation because of any Congressional reluctance to delegate additional tariff-rate-adjustment authority to the president. This was made evident in the legislation that established the NRA and AAA. Both pieces of legislation included provisions authorizing the president to restrict imports when they adversely affected domestic industry or agriculture. (See Feis, 1966, p. 262.)

7. In this regard Moore (1974) writes:
Certainly European statesmen thwarted Roosevelt's first impulse toward a cooperative program for worldwide recovery. In response he attempted to extend the New Deal abroad, or depending upon the viewpoint, to facilitate domestic recovery by

Second, the efforts of the administration's internationalists in the State Department (e.g., Secretary Hull, Assistant Secretary Francis Sayre, and Herbert Feis) were hampered because a myriad of government agencies and departments shared responsibility for commercial policy. The State, Commerce, and Treasury departments, the Tariff Commission, the NRA, and the AAA each had a measure of independent authority in the field of commercial policy. This created chaos and conflict within the government about the nature and direction of commercial policy (Hull, 1948, 1: 353; Feis, 1966, p. 263).

The internationalists in the State Department knew that they had to come up with some plan of united control over commercial policy before they could successfully make their case for trade liberalization. Four times between August and October 1933, Secretary Hull brought up the matter without result at cabinet meetings. Only in November did the president become convinced of the urgency of the situation. He approved the establishment of an executive committee on commercial policy. A State Department official would serve as its chairman.[8] The committee would coordinate the administration's commercial policy, and it would serve as vehicle for honing new thinking about trade policy-making.

The initial task of the Executive Committee on Commercial Policy was to draft a trade agreements bill. The committee unanimously endorsed legislation that would authorize the president to enter into reciprocal trade agreements. The committee members agreed that trade treaties that had to be submitted for Senate approval were fated never to be ratified if they contained substantial tariff reductions (Sayre, 1939, p. 56; Hull, 1948, 1:354).

In advocating the delegation of negotiating authority to the president, the executive committee considered the pressing need for such negotiations. The tariff truce agreed upon at the London Economic Conference proved ineffectual. After the conference, nations had increased their tariffs and restrictions. At the same time, moreover, they had negotiated trade agreements whereby the two countries sought to balance exactly their exports and imports. Key members of the executive committee argued that such barter agreements "could not expand commerce but only

---

parallel foreign action. When the French demanded a mortgage on American monetary policy to continue moribund internationalism Roosevelt cut loose from the world economy. (pp. 743–44)

8. Herbert Feis reports that FDR became convinced of the necessity for an executive committee only when pushed on the matter by Acting Secretary of State William Phillips while Hull was participating in the International Conference of American States at Montevideo. Feis suggests that Hull had been ineffectual at stressing the need for united control of commercial policy at cabinet meetings. (See Feis, 1966, p. 262.)

choke it" (Hull, 1948, 1:354). These members believed trade liberalization through bilateral agreements and the application of the unconditional MFN principle represented "the way forward."[9]

FDR, however, was not so unequivocal in his support for a trade liberalization program. In fact, his actions during the first fall and winter of his administration underscore his apparent ambivalence about the matter. A month after he established the executive committee to unify control of commercial policy, he created another interdepartmental body to rival the executive committee. He appointed George Peck chairman of the new committee, whose task was to find markets for agricultural products through either reciprocal trade agreements or barter arrangements (Hull, 1948, 1:354; Gardner, 1964, p. 42; Kenkel, 1983, p. 244).[10]

George N. Peck had served as the first director of the AAA. He saw Hull's trade agreements program as one more sacrifice that the American farmer would be called upon to make for the industrialist. According to Peck, eastern industrialists had historically exploited the farming West. It provided their source of raw materials and their market for overpriced goods. He maintained that the industrialists wanted to continue the exploitation by sacrificing the farmer to the trade agreements program of the secretary of state (Peck and Crowther, 1936, p. 40).

Thus, in early 1934 the nationalist/internationalist debate over the direction of U.S. foreign economic policy had not yet been resolved. However, the battle lines within the administration on the two frameworks for action had been clearly drawn. What remained unclear was the president's position on the issue. No doubt by promoting both approaches, FDR demonstrated his desire to keep options open—perhaps he wanted to impress upon the ardent internationalists that domestic recovery would not be compromised by their vision of peace through trade liberalization;[11] perhaps he simply did not recognize the fundamental incompatibility of the Hull and Peck approaches. But regardless of the policy the administration would eventually choose to employ in its foreign economic relations, the prior matter of method had to be resolved. The president had to secure negotiating authority from Congress before either approach could be implemented.

---

9. This is the theme of Francis B. Sayre's (1939) book.
10. See also Peck to FDR, December 30, 1933, Papers of Cordell Hull, Library of Congress.
11. FDR cautioned Hull in this regard before the secretary of state left for Montevideo in November 1933 (see Hull, 1948, 1:353).

The Democrats Act on Trade Agreements Legislation

There was general agreement within the Executive Committee on Commercial Policy that the traditional system of tariff rate adjustment by Congress could not produce significant rate reductions. Cordell Hull, for instance, criticized the "old system" for tariff rate adjustment and its major deficiency—interest group penetration of the policy process: "[Rate adjustment by Congress] had been the old system; and with the exception of the Underwood Act in 1913, it always resulted in higher tariffs because the special interests enriched by high tariffs went to their respective Congressmen and insisted on higher rates." On this point Hull continued:

Throughout my experience I found many able Republicans in the House and Senate who individually were moderate rather than extremists in their tariff views. . . . But in practice, the chief tariff beneficiaries who had helped finance political campaigns would come to Washington and demand that the rates be increased rather than decreased with the result that Republican leaders of moderate view were obliged to yield to ever rising rates as successive tariff revisions took place. (Hull, 1948, 1:358)

Furthermore, the committee agreed that even if the United States could unilaterally lower its tariff barriers, without reciprocal actions by other countries, the United States could not expand foreign trade. Unilateral action would only open the domestic market to increased import competition (Sayre, 1939, p. 41; Beckett, 1941, p. 5).

The executive committee considered the option of trade treaties. This option had the necessary reciprocal dimension, but it offered no real opportunity for trade expansion. During its entire history, the United States, in spite of numerous attempts, actually completed only three reciprocity treaties. And these three were special cases of countries with which the United States shared geographic or political ties.[12] Practical considerations weighed against any method of tariff adjustment that required the approval or ratification of treaties or agreements by a majority of one or both Houses of Congress.

The committee concluded that only through executive agreements could the United States solve the dilemma of tariff rate adjustment. This option would provide a method for rate adjustment that was insulated from the pressures of particularistic interests, and it would enable the United States to lower tariff barriers in exchange for reciprocal concessions. Proponents of this method of tariff bargaining noted the successful

---

12. The three reciprocity treaties carried through to completion were those with Canada and Newfoundland, effective 1855–1856; Hawaii, effective 1876–1900; and Cuba, effective after 1913. (See Sayre, 1939, p. 50 n; Hull, 1948, 1:354–55.)

record of agreements negotiated under prior authorization of Congress. Under the McKinley Act of 1890, thirteen executive trade agreements were negotiated, and twelve became effective. Under Section 3 of the Dingly Act of 1897, fifteen executive agreements were successfully concluded with eight countries.[13]

The committee was also satisfied that this proposed change in rate adjustment procedures was constitutional. The power to modify the statutory rates of duty by up to 50 percent had been introduced into American tariff practice with the so-called flexible tariff provision (Section 315) of the Fordney-McCumber Act of 1922. In 1928 the Supreme Court upheld this provision. In *Hampton and Co. v. the U.S.* (276, U.S., 394 [1927]), the Court ruled that Congress could delegate to the president the power of tariff adjustment within prescribed limits and in execution of a stated policy. Moreover, the right of the president to enter into binding executive agreements without the necessity of subsequent Congressional approval had also been clearly established. Throughout its history, the United States had entered into executive agreements covering such subjects as commercial and consular relations, MFN rights, trademark and copyright protection, postal and maritime arrangements and the settlement of claims. In several decisions the Supreme Court expressly recognized the validity of such agreements. Within the field of tariff duties, the Court twice upheld the constitutionality of executive agreements.[14]

The committee drafted two versions of the trade agreements legislation in early 1934. The first draft was lengthy. It attempted to define in great detail the policy to be pursued and the principles that should govern the new trade policy process. The committee rejected this initial draft. In reworking the proposal, a suggestion made by George Peck guided the committee's efforts: "Make the bill only two or three pages long and it will stand a better chance" (quoted in Hull, 1948, 1:356). The second draft bill was "much shorter in form, more general in nature, and practical in its approach" (Sayre, 1939, p. 56). It was built around two basic provisions: one sanctioned the negotiation of executive agreements with other states for the purpose of expanding American foreign trade; the other authorized the president to proclaim and enforce tariff rate reductions in the context of such agreements, not to exceed 50 percent of the existing rate (Sayre, 1939, p. 56).

The members of the executive committee rejected the idea of incorporating trade agreement provisions into a general revision of the tariff

13. For the most part, these agreements had little economic significance (see chap. 2, this volume).
14. For a discussion of the constitutionality of trade agreements, see Sayre, 1939, pp. 65–82.

schedules. They understood that a change in the method of tariff rate setting had to precede any change in policy. To avoid an otherwise inevitable general revision, therefore, the committee decided to package the legislation that they hoped would fundamentally alter the process for commercial policy-making in the United States as an amendment to the Smoot-Hawley Act of 1930.

On February 28, 1934, the president presided at a White House conference to consider the draft bill. The conference was attended by Congressional leaders and administration officials. At the meeting the president approved the executive committee's bill and agreed to send it to Congress. Equally important, the trade agreements legislation received the general approval of the Congressional leaders present (Sayre, 1939, p. 56; Hull, 1948, 1:357).

On March 2, 1934, the trade agreements bill was introduced in the House of Representatives, accompanied by a message from President Roosevelt strongly urging its passage. The strategy that administration officials adopted to promote the trade agreements bill was manifest in their testimony before the Ways and Means and Finance committees. They aimed to demonstrate to members of Congress that trade agreements legislation offered the only real opportunity for the United States to restore its foreign trade. They also wanted to convince the members of the legislature that the proposed changes in tariff making merely redirected already existing authority for presidential rate adjustment.

Hearings began in the House Ways and Means Committee on March 8. The first to testify was Secretary Hull: "If it is once agreed that a normal amount of trade among nations is a vital and necessary factor in the restoration of full and stable prosperity, the conclusion seems clear that the proposed policy of bilateral trade agreements offers virtually the only feasible and practicable step in this direction." [15] He used several arguments to support this contention.

Hull noted that all but two European states vested authority in the executive for trade negotiations. The pending legislation would, therefore, delegate to the president an authority on par "with that exercised by the executive departments of so many of the governments for purposes of negotiating and carrying into effect trade agreements" (U.S. House, Hull testimony, p. 5). Moreover, these trade agreements would permit the gradual moderation of the excessive and more extreme barriers to trade. The negotiated reductions would yield economic relations that were mutually beneficial because tariff concessions would not be offered

---

15. Testimony of Secretary of State Cordell Hull (U.S. House, Committee on Ways and Means, 1934, March 8, p. 2).

"blindly or hastily": "[I]t can be stated with emphasis that each trade agreement undertaken would be considered with care and caution and only after the fullest consideration of all pertinent information" (p. 4).

Hull also stressed the imperative for action under conditions of economic emergency. The overriding consideration for Congress and the president as they addressed foreign economic policy issues was the restoration of international trade. When the crisis abated, Congress would have the opportunity to evaluate the methods adopted to deal with the emergency:

There will be ample time and opportunity after the crisis shall have been met and passed and the unprecedented emergency coped with, for a thorough review, re-examination, and discussion of any and all methods, policies, plans, and programs that may have been placed in operation during the panic period in desperate endeavors to curb, control, and cure such condition. (U.S. House, Hull testimony, p. 6)

Administration officials who testified after Secretary Hull likewise emphasized the necessity, feasibility, and practicality of the trade agreements program. Secretary of Agriculture Henry A. Wallace thought the trade agreements program would work to improve foreign purchasing power and that foreign purchase of American agricultural products would "lighten the job of the Agricultural Adjustment Administration" (U.S. House, Committee on Ways and Means, 1934, Wallace testimony, p. 45). He also thought Congress was incapable of acting in the national interest to restore foreign trade: "It seems to me, it is impossible with Congress as a whole, with so many diverse interests involved, with the emergency as it is—it seems to me it is totally impossible for Congress to handle this matter from the standpoint of the national interest" (p. 47).

Daniel C. Roper, commerce secretary, supported the trade agreements bill because it would permit American business to sell abroad with fewer restrictions and without adversely affecting those interests that depended on protection from foreign competition. The bill offered the only solution to the dilemma of a divided business community: "The bill permits an intelligent and objective study of the basic situation in every industry and the negotiation of agreements which it is hoped will open up to us foreign markets now closed to us" (U.S. House, Committee on Ways and Means, 1934, Roper testimony, p. 62).

In his testimony, Roper emphasized the importance of flexibility and speed in the tariff-making process. He pointed out that flexibility had long been a feature of the American tariff system. Under Sections 315 and 336 of the 1922 and 1930 Tariff Acts, the Tariff Commission investigated costs of production and made rate-adjustment recommendations. After such investigations, the president could declare new tariff rates. The process was slow and cumbersome. The United States needed to keep pace with the rapid developments in the world economy. Thus, for all practical purposes, a tariff-making process that featured flexibility without speed was useless. The trade agreements bill promised a process capable of providing both the necessary promptness as well as flexibility (Roper testimony, p. 65).

The trade agreements program also offered a feasible alternative to the existing rate-adjustment process. This point was made by Robert L. O'Brien, chairman of the Tariff Commission. He maintained that since tariff making by the president had already been established, Congress should not hesitate to replace a method of presidential tariff making that had manifestly failed with one that would work: "I do not see why a form of Presidential tariff making which promises some purpose and some results should be regarded with danger and dismay and reluctance, by comparison with a method of tariff adjustment that works in exactly the same scope of power without any results, without any purpose" (U.S. House, Committee on Ways and Means, 1934, O'Brien testimony, March 9, p. 3).

For his part, Assistant Secretary of State Francis B. Sayre painstakingly went over the constitutional precedents. These demonstrated the practical feasibility of the trade agreements alternative to tariff rate adjustment. Sayre argued that the power of the president to regulate commerce had been established in the earliest years of the Republic and that the Supreme Court had repeatedly upheld Congressional delegation of authority in this matter:

At the very outset, in the early days when the makers of the Constitution were still alive and active in the scene, we have an indication [1794] of how far these Constitution makers though it was proper for Congress to give power to the President. With regard to American commerce and trade . . . they allowed the President, not to regulate rates, but to stop altogether the departure of commerce from American ports, through the laying of this embargo.

Moreover, Sayre continued:

The matter went before the courts. It was carried up to the Supreme Court of the United States and in the case of the brig *Aurora* . . . it was held that this was not an unconstitutional delegation of power, that the powers granted were of the kind that Congress could within the limits of the Constitution delegate to the President. (U.S. House, Committee on Ways and Means, 1934, Sayre testimony, March 10, pp. 8–9)

The majority report of the Ways and Means Committee favored the bill, and the House of Representatives passed it on March 29 by a vote of 274 to 111. Some amendments, however, had been added to the House bill. The most important of these set up a definite time limit (three years) for the duration of the proposed act.[16] Apparently, the majority in Congress wanted to guarantee for themselves the opportunity to review the new commercial policy process. The persuasiveness of the administration's arguments notwithstanding, the members of Congress understood that the Trade Agreements Act represented a significant development for commercial policy-making in the United States, and they wanted to closely monitor its administration.[17]

The Senate Finance Committee also amended the bill. An important section was added to assure public announcement of the intention to negotiate a trade agreement. Interested parties could present their views to the president or to his designated agencies. In this way, fears that bureaucratic administration of the trade agreements program would lead to abuse were assuaged (Sayre, 1939, p. 58; Beckett, 1941, p. 11). The bill, together with this and a few other clarifying amendments,[18] was favorably reported by the Finance Committee on May 2, 1934.

During the Senate debate, a succession of amendments was offered by the opposition. These were designed to win the votes of sectional groups and of lukewarm supporters. But they were also framed in such a way as to obstruct the effective operation of the act. One amendment exempted all agricultural tariffs from the provisions of the act; another provided for Congressional approval of each agreement. These and all other crippling amendments were defeated. On June 4, the Senate passed the bill by a vote of 57 to 33 (Sayre, 1939, p. 39). The Trade Agreements Act became law on June 12, 1934, with President Roosevelt's signature.

In its final form the Amendment to the Tariff Act of 1930 authorized the president (1) to enter into executive agreements for the reciprocal reduction of excessive trade barriers, and (2) to make such tariff adjustments within prescribed limits as required to carry out such agreements. These

16. The bill as originally introduced into the House (H.R. 5420) stipulated no time when the act should terminate (see Beckett, 1941, p. 41 n).

17. House members may have been persuaded by some of the arguments presented in the "Minority Report of the Ways and Means Committee." The report contained 24 objections to the bill. Important among these were claims of the unconstitutional delegation of taxing power, the nonexistence of a precedent for the bill, and the "sacrificing" of certain domestic industries to the trade agreements program. The minority report also stated that foreign countries would probably have the advantage in bargaining because their rates were already "padded" for negotiating purposes. (See *Congressional Record* 78:5532.)

18. The most significant of these changed the section stating that the provisions of the act should terminate three years from the enactment to the statement that the president's authority to enter foreign trade agreements should terminate within three years (see Sayre, 1939, p. 58).

limits specified that "no proclamation should be made increasing or de-
creasing by more than 50 percent any existing rate of duty." They also prohibited transferring any article from the dutiable to the free list. Congress
provided this negotiating authority for an initial three year period only.[19]

The Organization and Operation of the Trade Agreements Program

By the time Congress considered renewing the Trade Agreements Act
in 1937, an organizational infrastructure was in place and administrative
and negotiating procedures established. These resulted in the successful
operation of the program. However, success was never a foregone conclusion. Those in the Roosevelt administration charged with the organization
and operation of the trade agreements program confronted a whole host
of difficulties. First, Secretary Hull and his cadre had to deal with the
antagonism of certain administration officials—like George Peck—who
opposed the program's adoption of the unconditional MFN principle. Second, they had to devise an organization and procedures that worked to
achieve the stated goal of the Trade Agreements Act—the restoration of
American foreign trade—without, at the same time, promoting injurious
import competition for domestic industries. Third, they had to demonstrate to members of Congress that the authority delegated to the executive was used judiciously and conservatively; in addition, they had to
convince them that tariff rate adjustment in the context of trade negotiations offered a viable alternative to either legislated tariff adjustment or the
so-called scientific method of the 1920s. Finally, they had to accomplish
all of the above without fundamentally compromising their commitment
to international trade liberalization.

Since Congress had not specified the exact means by which trade agreements would work to expand overseas markets, the debate between Secretary Hull and George Peck was yet to be totally resolved. Peck opposed
the incorporation of the MFN principle into American foreign economic
policy. Support of the policy by such influential groups as the AMEA
and the NFTC notwithstanding, Peck remained convinced that a flood of
unwanted imports would follow the adoption of reciprocal trade agreements. He continued to lobby for barter arrangements with foreign governments. In fact, during November and December 1934, Peck earnestly
pursued the negotiation of a barter agreement with Germany (Hull, 1948,
1:370–71; Gardner, 1964, pp. 42, 99, 102–3).

Alarmed, Hull and his associates countered Peck's maneuvers with

---

19. The text of the Trade Agreements Act is reprinted in Sayre, 1939, p. 205.

a series of memoranda to the president. These memos emphasized the fundamental incompatibility of barter arrangements and the trade agreements program. They also rearticulated the purpose and rationale of the MFN policy. In one memo, for example, Hull defended his commitment to the unconditional form of the MFN principle by stressing the U.S. role in the world economy: "It is manifest that the United States never faced a more outstanding responsibility to furnish the world both a program that is sound and leadership that is alert and aggressive than at this crucial stage while there is yet a chance to save and finally restore a normal economic situation" (quoted in Gardner, 1964, p. 43). In another, Assistant Secretary of State Francis Sayre refuted Peck's contention that adherence to the MFN principle would lead to a flood of unwanted imports. He cited in particular the organization and procedures being established under the trade agreements program that would preclude the possibility of unwanted imports (Hull, 1948, 1:372–74; Gardner, 1964, p. 43).

Their strategy worked. Roosevelt withdrew his approval of the German deal. This squelched any intention Peck had to negotiate similar deals with other countries. In early 1935, Peck's office within the Roosevelt administration was abolished (Hull, 1948, 1:374). Nevertheless, Peck's criticism of the trade agreements policy put administration officials on notice that the program's success depended on whether or not it worked to expand foreign trade without threatening domestic economic recovery. If this goal was not achieved, the program would not survive beyond its original three-year mandate. How the program was organized and how well it operated were, therefore, of critical importance to Secretary Hull and his supporters.

The Creation of a Trade Agreements Organization

With the enactment of the Trade Agreements Program, administration officials chose not to create an independent organization to deal with foreign trade problems and to negotiate trade agreements. To take full advantage of the experience, knowledge, and tried capacity of the trade experts at work in different departments, they decided to build up gradually an interdepartmental organization along the lines of the Executive Committee on Commercial Policy. Various interdepartmental committees were set up for handling specific problems (Hull memorandum, June 29, 1934, Papers of Cordell Hull, Library of Congress; Sayre, 1939, pp. 90–95).

The Trade Agreements Committee supervised the whole program. It was established by the executive committee on June 22, 1934. Its membership included high officials from the Departments of State, Commerce, Agriculture, and Treasury, as well as officials from the Tariff Commission and the Agricultural Adjustment Administration. As the need developed, the Trade Agreements Committee appointed additional subcommittees. These were composed of economists and technical experts from the various departments. "Country committees" prepared detailed studies of American trade with states with which trade agreements were contemplated. "Commodity committees" investigated specific products of particular importance. Other committees were appointed to deal with special technical problems such as exchange controls, quotas, and discriminations (Beckett, 1941, pp. 18–20).

In the State Department, responsible for conducting the actual negotiations, a special section to deal with trade agreements was established in June 1934 as an adjunct to the office of the assistant secretary of state in charge of the program. In 1935, however, with the increasing volume of work, a separate Trade Agreements Division was organized in the State Department. Its chief served also as the chair of the Trade Agreements Committee (Sayre, 1939, pp. 88–89).

In accordance with Section 4 of the Trade Agreements Act, the Committee for Reciprocity Information was created by executive order to provide a practical way for interested parties to present their views about a trade agreement in advance of negotiations. It was composed of representatives from all the departments concerned with foreign trade, and it was to "function under the direction and supervision of . . . the Executive Committee on Commercial Policy." It provided the central point of contact between the public and the interdepartmental trade agreements organization. Most of its members also served on the Trade Agreements Committee, and its chair was the vice chair of the Tariff Commission (Sayre, 1939, p. 87; Beckett, 1941, p. 18).

Before commitments were made in any trade agreements, the Committee for Reciprocity Information solicited the written views of all interested persons and presided at open hearings for oral presentations. After an agreement was concluded, the committee collected information or views concerning its actual operation. The committee systematically analyzed and digested the material presented and distributed it to the governmental agencies involved in the program (Sayre, 1939, p. 87).

Unlike the members of Congress who traditionally conducted hearings on trade issues, the members of the Committee for Reciprocity Information were permanent government officials who were not beholden to particular constituencies. For members of the information committee, there was no necessity for knee-jerk responses to constituent demands for tariff favors. The committee's objective was to acquire information pertinent to specific proposals under consideration and bring this information to the attention of the relevant administration officials. Thus, the Committee for Reciprocity Information worked to insulate the process whereby trade agreements were studied, negotiated, and implemented.

Procedures and Guiding Principles of the Trade Agreements Program

The process of negotiating a trade agreement began with exploratory discussions between representatives of the United States and another country. If these discussions showed potential, the Department of State issued a formal notice of intention to negotiate, together with a list of products considered for concessions. Accompanying the formal notice was an announcement from the Committee for Reciprocity Information indicating in what form written views were to be presented to the committee and when hearings were to be held. The committee turned over the information it collected to the appropriate committees of the trade agreements organization.

The country committee, charged with analyzing the data made available by the Committee for Reciprocity Information and the various specialized committees, launched a commodity-by-commodity study of the items imported from the country in question. Each item was examined as to (1) past tariff treatment, (2) the proportion of imports to domestic production, (3) the status and condition of domestic production, and (4) the possible effects of greater competition on domestic production. The country committee also made detailed analyses of export commodities.

The Trade Agreements Committee next reviewed the report of the country committee and recommended two lists—one of concessions to be requested, the other of concessions to be offered. The recommendations were submitted to the secretary of state and the president for modification or approval. Once the lists were approved, negotiations began (Sayre, 1939, pp. 90–95; Beckett, 1941, pp. 19–20).

In and of themselves, however, these procedures could not resolve the thorny dilemma of reconciling the unconditional MFN principle with the commitment to make no concessions that, when generalized, would threaten domestic industries. They also did not offer a solution for trade agreements officials who were concerned that the MFN principle could compromise American bargaining power in future negotiations with third-party countries. (If by virtue of MFN status a country benefited unduly from an agreement concluded between the United States and another state, it might be reluctant to enter into trade negotiations with the United States because it would judge such negotiations unnecessary and undesirable. It would stand to gain little, and it would be asked to pay for what it had already obtained for nothing.)

American officials resolved these dilemmas by adopting the principle of "chief supplier" as a guide in agreement negotiations. According to this principle, the country that was the chief source of supply for certain commodities was given a reduction in duty on those commodities, provided data revealed that such concessions would not prove injurious to domestic industries. In this way, the major benefit of a modification in the Tariff Act of 1930 was granted to the country with which an agreement was negotiated. Even though other countries received the duty reduction through MFN treatment, the reduction was often of little benefit to them because they did not export large quantities of the concession product to the United States (Beckett, 1941, p. 23).

The use of the chief-supplier rule required overcoming some special difficulties. One such difficulty arose in negotiations with small states, where it was impossible to isolate any commodities for which the small state was the principal supplier.[20] Another problem appeared when two or more countries supplied approximately the same quantity of a given commodity or when two countries were the chief suppliers of the product in alternate years. If a substantial reduction in duty was granted to one country, bargaining power with the other was lost. To avoid such a situation, simultaneous negotiations were sometimes tried. More often, however, a split concession was granted; that is, a small reduction was made in the agreement with the first country, and an additional reduction was offered in the agreement with the second country. This procedure preserved bargaining power with the second country.[21]

Another drawback to extending concessions on the basis of the chief-supplier principle was that concessions in any one agreement were limited to commodities furnished predominantly by the one country, whether or not such commodities were significant in the total trade of the two countries. This led to the inclusion of insignificant concessions and the omission of concessions on some important commodities. In addition, because chief-supplier status was determined by studying past commercial statistics, its application could not easily accommodate the appearance of new products.

Some of these problems were circumvented by reclassification and by the use of customs quotas. Through reclassification, new subdivisions were made in the tariff paragraphs. A concession was then extended to that subdivision in which the negotiating country was the chief supplier. American officials also used quotas in a way that enabled them to extend duty concessions that they would otherwise never have offered.

Reclassifications appeared in each of the trade agreements concluded

---

20. The negotiation of the agreement with Finland is a case in point.
21. This device was used, for example, in negotiations with the Netherlands and the United Kingdom. These two countries were in alternate years the chief suppliers of rutabaga seed. (See Beckett, 1941, p. 23 n.)

before 1940.[22] Careful reclassification provided a way to grant valuable concessions based on the chief-supplier principle while at the same time conserving bargaining power for future negotiations. It also gave flexibility to the process of negotiating trade agreements because it permitted frequent changes in tariff structure. This procedure of reclassification, however, had to be employed conservatively. Too specific a subdivision would, in effect, have denied MFN treatment. Unrestrained reclassification would have made a mockery of this policy, for the generalization of concessions would have offered no possible gain to other countries.

Customs quotas were used to limit the quantity of a commodity that entered the country at a reduced duty during a given period (usually a year) without limiting the quantity of the commodity that entered at the regular rate. All imports in excess of the stipulated quantity were subject to the preagreement rates. This procedure gave assurance to domestic producers that import competition would be restricted. It was most typically used in connection with agricultural products (Beckett, 1941, p. 31).

The Initial Results of the Trade Agreements Program

By the end of the initial three-year negotiating period in 1937, the American government had signed agreements with sixteen countries, including Canada and France. These agreements covered one-third of American foreign trade. Nevertheless, without an agreement with Great Britain, further liberalization was unlikely. Because administration officials had refused to consider accords with Germany and Japan and they had failed to reach agreements with Spain and Italy, they needed to demonstrate that the Trade Agreements Program could lead to successful negotiation with other large countries.[23] Concluding an agreement with Great Britain was considered especially important. Great Britain had been the leading market for American exports absorbing 17.5 percent of total American sales abroad between 1926 and 1930. With the Ottawa Agreements that strengthened and extended the preference system, imperial imports cut appreciably into these sales. Goods from the United States,

22. Reclassifications were made on the basis of value or quality or by specific selection of one product from a general group of products. Approximately one-third of the paragraphs modified by concessions were subject to reclassification. More reclassifications were made in Schedule III, metals and their manufactures, than in any other schedule. The second largest number were made in Schedule VII, agricultural products and provisions. In the agreement with the United Kingdom, ninety-one reclassifications were made—a number that far exceeded the number in any other agreement. (See Beckett, 1941, pp. 27–29.)

23. Although American officials had negotiated an agreement with Germany to extend mutual unconditional MFN status in the 1920s, a decade later the Roosevelt administration refused to negotiate a trade agreement with Germany (see Stein, 1984, p. 277).

which had accounted for 16.1 percent of British imports in 1929, accounted for only 11 percent in 1936 (Kottmann, 1968, p. 117).

American leaders were eager to conclude a trade agreement with the United Kingdom for political as well as economic reasons. The United Kingdom had traditionally been a major market for American agricultural products. An Anglo-American trade agreement would go a long way toward reversing the dissatisfaction with the Trade Agreements Program that had arisen among farm organizations. Farmers voiced concern that increased import competition for farm products would result from the fact that the majority of agreements signed during Roosevelt's first term were with agricultural countries. They resented being sacrificed in order to stimulate industrial exports (Bidwell, 1938, pp. 4–17; Russett, 1963, pp. 49–62, 81–95).

Administration officials, particularly Cordell Hull, were also convinced that Anglo-American cooperation in the economic sphere provided the answer to the international upheaval that followed from Hitler's and Mussolini's rise to power and the Spanish civil war. In this view, the program of trade revival "would either coerce Germany and Italy into cooperating with the democracies or present the example of Anglo-American solidarity to the world as an antidote for contemporary nationalism" (Kottmann, 1968, p. 120).

Repeated American overtures notwithstanding, British officials remained cool to American proposals, and between 1934 and 1937 trade agreement negotiations made little headway. Anglo-American accommodation was stymied by repeated international crises that excited fears of war and commanded the energies of British statesmen. Seeking some kind of rapprochement with Hitler, these statesmen expressed more interest in concluding an economic pact with Germany than with the United States.[24] The prospect for a trade agreement was further compromised by British unwillingness to antagonize the dominions (most notably Canada), which enjoyed tariff preferences in the British market and demanded compensation for concessions offered to the United States (Kottmann, 1968, p. 147).

The impasse forestalling an Anglo-American trade agreement was circumvented when the United States agreed to negotiate simultaneously agreements with Great Britain and Canada. Although all concessions offered were strictly reciprocal, the United States had to accept the reality that if it wanted a trade agreement with Britain and export markets for its

---

24. Anthony Eden favored an Anglo-American economic accord. Other cabinet members believed that in any future conflict, Britain could count on American support and, therefore, they were not convinced that an economic agreement was necessary (see Kottman, 1968, p. 131).

agricultural products, it would have to renegotiate the terms of its trade relationship with Canada. The United States had to make it worthwhile for Canada to relinquish the preferences it enjoyed in the British market. In 1938, American negotiators successfully concluded the two agreements.[25]

The United States and Great Britain signed an agreement in which the British acceded to most of the American substantive demands. However, this agreement and the one between the United States and Canada only slightly weakened imperial preferences. The United States gave in on this issue in order to secure its more immediate objectives. U.S. officials needed an agreement with Great Britain to assure the success of their Trade Agreements Program.

Advocates of the program were anxious to demonstrate that it could attract the participation of the world's major trading nations and that it could benefit both American industry and agriculture. With the Anglo-American trade agreement, they achieved these objectives. Between 1933 and 1937, American officials doggedly pursued their uninterested and preoccupied counterparts in Britain about the possibility of an agreement. Despite their high degree of commitment to an Anglo-American pact, however, these officials never lost sight of the domestic political factors that could sabotage the success of the Trade Agreements Program and the foreign economic policy it supported.

They established an administrative infrastructure and developed procedures that enabled negotiators to implement economically advantageous strategies that minimized domestic dislocations while promoting American exports. These strategies were not abandoned, even in the pursuit of a trade agreement with the United Kingdom. Thus, while the Trade Agreements Program did not serve to lessen worldwide tensions, it did lay the domestic political and international foundations for the creation of a liberal economic order in the years after the war.

The organization and procedures of the Trade Agreements Program worked. Congress renewed the Act in 1937 and thereafter. The committee reports that recommended renewal in 1937 concluded "that the policies adopted in the original act were soundly conceived, that . . . its results demonstrate clearly that favorable progress has been made toward the objective of increased foreign trade" (U.S. Senate, 1937, p. 1), and that "the provisions of the Act have been administered with care and concern and with scrupulous regard to the best interest of the nation and to the

25. The terms of the agreements are discussed in Soward et al., 1941, pp. 212–24; Kreider, 1943.

intent of the Congress in authorizing the Executive to negotiate foreign trade agreements" (U.S. House, 1937, p. 17).

A successful trade agreements program meant effective insulation of the commercial policy process; it created new legislative possibilities for Congress in trade policy-making. The Trade Agreements Program demonstrated that unencumbered by the details of tariff rate adjustment, Congress could achieve its stated policy goals in the area of international trade.

Congress Redefines Its Role in Trade Policy-Making, 1937–1962: Institutional Change as Social Learning

The reports of the House Ways and Means Committee and the Senate Finance Committee on the joint resolution to extend the Trade Agreements Act indicate that members of Congress were beginning to redefine their role in the trade policy process. In this regard, the report of the Senate Finance Committee is most specific:

Under our form of government general tariff policies can be and should be formulated by the legislative branch. . . . To attempt more may often thwart important policies and principles; to attempt to require in every instance Senatorial disposition of the manifold and constantly changing details involved in the carrying out of such policies and principles would frequently be to render the legislative branch incapable of effective exercise of its functions. (U.S. Senate, 1937, pp. 3–4)

The periodic renewals of the Trade Agreements Program provided Congress opportunities to explore new legislative options in trade, which in turn contributed to the institutionalization of the policy process.

Interestingly, the Trade Agreements Act had been introduced and supported in 1934 as an emergency measure. The primary reason for treating the legislation as such was to reduce resistance to it. But the supporters of reciprocal tariff reduction never viewed this as a short-term policy. Neither did they view as temporary or short-term the method for its implementation. Secretary Hull, in particular, felt that given the nature of the tariff issue, nothing but delegated authority to the executive would work to achieve the policy of reciprocal tariff reduction (Hull, 1948, 1:358). However, the Trade Agreements Act was treated as an emergency measure "until thinking had become accustomed to the new policy and the method of carrying it out" (Hawkins and Norwood, 1962, p. 85).

In 1949, the "emergency" tariff-making process established in the Trade Agreements Act was finally accepted as a routine process (a repetitive sequence)—in renewing the act, the language referring to "the present emergency" was removed. The "emergency" label also was omitted from all subsequent renewals of the act (Hawkins and Norwood, 1962, p. 85).

The institutionalization of the new trade policy process also was manifest in the conduct of the protectionist opponents of reciprocal tariff reductions. By the late 1940s, even in their opposition the protectionists operated within the limits of the new process. They did not attempt to resurrect the old system of rate setting by Congress, and in their efforts to limit the tariff-making power of the president, they contributed to Congress's repertoire of legislative options in trade policy-making.

The Trade Agreements Program had always elicited Congressional concern about the impact of negotiated concessions on domestic industries. Administration officials had devised methods to avoid "serious injury" to American producers. These methods included the creation of procedures designed to assure the careful weighing of facts and probabilities with regard to proposed tariff concessions and the use of qualified concessions.[26] However, during the postwar period, the opponents of trade agreements pushed to make what had been a matter of administrative policy a Congressional requirement. Escape clause and peril point provisions became the most important legislative tools for limiting the authority of the president to negotiate tariff reductions under the Trade Agreements Act.

The Escape Clause

A general escape clause that permitted the modification or withdrawal of negotiated concessions in order to remedy serious injury to a domestic industry from increased imports was first included in the 1942 trade agreement with Mexico. In 1945, to expedite approval of legislation to renew and strengthen the Trade Agreements Act, the administration assented to including an escape clause of this kind in future trade agreements. Yet no special procedures for administering the escape clause were delineated by the interdepartmental trade agreements organization. Consequently, complaints of injury brought by domestic industry were handled, along with all other trade agreements matters, by the Trade Agreements Committee (Leddy and Norwood, 1962, p. 125).

This situation, along with the fact that no tariff had been raised as a result of an escape clause action, led protectionist groups and members of Congress to urge specification of the procedures for determining injury. They felt that such specifications would make relief under the escape clause more readily available. One of their most important proposals was to have jurisdiction over the escape clause transferred from the Trade

26. After 1942, these methods included the incorporation of a general escape clause in each trade agreement (see Leddy and Norwood, 1962, p. 125).

Agreements Committee to the Tariff Commission. An increase of protectionist pressure in 1946—the result of Republican success in the Congressional elections—which coincided with preparations for multilateral trade negotiations at Geneva, compelled President Truman to issue an executive order to establish escape clause procedures along the lines specified by the protectionists. The order designated the Tariff Commission as the agency for conducting escape clause investigations. The commission was to recommend action to the president "for his consideration in the light of the public interest" (Executive Order 9832, February 25, 1947).

From 1947 to 1951, the escape clause was administered in accordance with the executive order. During this period, twenty-one petitions for tariff rate increases were filed with the Tariff Commission. One petition was withdrawn, and sixteen others were dismissed after preliminary hearings. Action was recommended to the president in three cases. President Truman increased the tariff in two of the three cases (Leddy and Norwood, 1962, p. 128).

In 1951, during Congressional consideration of legislation to renew trade agreements authority, protectionist dissatisfaction with American commercial policy focused on the escape clause procedures. Protectionists criticized the administration of the escape clause under the executive order of 1947. They pointed out that, although numerous tariff rate reductions had been negotiated in the period since the order was announced, there had been only two cases of tariff rate increases. The protectionists demanded precise rules and guidelines to replace the ambiguous language of the executive order (Leddy and Norwood, 1962, p. 129).

The Truman administration had submitted a bill for renewal of presidential negotiating authority without provision for the escape clause (or peril point). However, the restrictive escape clause provision passed by the House of Representatives forced the administration to change its strategy.[27] To avoid a direct confrontation with Congress and to mitigate the likelihood that the amendments might pass the Senate in the same form as they had passed in the House, the administration decided to concentrate its efforts on securing the revision of the most objectionable features of the escape clause amendments.[28]

---

27. The bill provided for a Tariff Commission determination of serious injury, not only to a "domestic industry" but also to a "segment of such industry." It provided further that "in arriving at a determination in the foregoing procedure, the Tariff Commission shall deem a downward trend of production, employment, and wages in the domestic industry concerned, or a decline in sales and a higher or growing inventory attributable in part to import competition to be evidence of serious injury or a threat thereof." (See U.S. Senate Committee on Finance, 1951, pt. 1, p. 3.)

28. See testimony of Secretary of State Dean Acheson in U.S. Senate Committee on Finance, 1951, pt. 1, p. 8.

Most of the changes desired by the Truman administration became part of the final legislation. The law provided that no tariff rate reduction would remain in effect if "any product upon which a concession has been granted . . . is as a result . . . being imported into the United States in such increased quantities, either actual or relative, as to cause or threaten serious injury to the domestic industry producing like or directly competitive products" (quoted in Leddy and Norwood, 1962, pp. 133–34). Under the escape clause provisions of the 1951 act, the Tariff Commission was required to investigate a petition and report to the president within a year. If the president did not act upon the recommendation of the commission, he was required to report his reasons for not accepting the Tariff Commission's recommendations to the House Ways and Means Committee and the Senate Finance Committee (Leddy and Norwood, 1962, p. 134).

These provisions also specified certain factors that the Tariff Commission had to take into consideration in making its determination of serious injury.[29] In addition, Congress stipulated that the Tariff Commission had to conduct formal investigations on all petitions for escape clause protection from domestic industries. No longer could the commission dismiss petitions after a preliminary investigation.

The Trade Agreements Extension Act of 1955 amended the escape clause. Under the new escape clause provisions, the Tariff Commission could not avoid a finding of injury in cases where the chief cause was not increased imports as long as imports were contributing "substantially" to injury.[30] The new provisions also changed the definition of domestic industry. The Tariff Commission was required to confine its investigation to that portion of the operations of domestic producers that made a similar or directly competitive article. The commission was to disregard market and other factors for other products made by the same company. Another change specified that commission reports be made public immediately. Under the previous statute, these reports were made public sixty days after being sent to the president. The purpose of the change was to enable domestic producers to make their views known to the president while he had an escape action before him (Leddy and Norwood, 1962, p. 141).

The 1958 act also altered escape clause procedures in two important ways. First, it provided for the imposition of higher duties. Duty in-

29. The law provided that the Tariff Commission "without excluding other factors, shall take into consideration a downward trend of production, employment, prices, profits, or wages in the domestic industry concerned, or a decline in sales, higher or growing inventory, or a decline in the proportion of the domestic market supplied by domestic producers" (quoted in Leddy and Norwood, 1962, p. 134).

30. This was an important change because the major part of the economic difficulties of many import-competing industries derived from domestic causes, especially from increasing productivity in more dynamic industries (see Humphrey, 1955, pp. 564–65).

creases up to 50 percent above the rates in effect as of July 1, 1934, were permitted. Before this change, duty increases had been limited to 50 percent above the rates existing on January 1, 1945. Second, the 1958 act allowed Congress to override decisions of the president whenever he refused a recommendation from the Tariff Commission. The president could be overridden within sixty days by a concurrent resolution receiving a two-thirds vote in each house (Leddy and Norwood, 1962, p. 142).

The Peril Point

The peril point was first introduced in the 1948 extension of the Trade Act. It was removed from the 1949 legislation but restored in that of 1951.[31] This provision required the Tariff Commission to determine, in advance of negotiations, precise tariff rates that could be agreed to without threat of injury. The peril point required the president to furnish to the Tariff Commission a list of all products on which the United States was considering granting concessions. The commission had to hold hearings and report to the president the limit to which concessions could be made without threatening serious injury to domestic industries (Leddy and Norwood, 1962, p. 129). These peril point procedures were reminiscent of the old cost-of-production formula, and they clearly reflected the perennial notion of the protectionists that there must be some objective criterion for determining appropriate tariff rate modifications.

The peril point provisions enacted in 1951 also stipulated procedures to be followed if a concession below the peril point was nevertheless granted. The president was required to report his action and the reasons for it to the House Ways and Means Committee and the Senate Finance Committee. The Tariff Commission then was required to send the two committees the portion of its report that the president had ignored. The idea was to put the president in a defensive position if he disregarded peril point determinations (Leddy and Norwood, 1962, p. 130).

Critics claimed there was no precise peril point that could be established in advance of a tariff reduction. They argued that the extent of a rate reduction must be determined by weighing several factors, including the degree of protection enjoyed by the industry as well as the benefits to be gained from the concessions received and other general foreign policy considerations.

This balanced approach for determining appropriate tariff rate reductions was supported by the interdepartmental trade agreements organization that had been established during the 1930s. Therefore, it is not

---

31. It is interesting to note that in both years members of the Democratic party held majorities in Congress and occupied the White House.

surprising that the critics of the peril point also objected to the new role of the Tariff Commission in the peril point procedures. By making the Tariff Commission the guardian of protected interests and by giving it a prominent role in the rate-adjustment procedure, the peril point provision upset the interagency balance inherent in the trade agreements organization. The minority report of the House Ways and Means Committee (1948) pointed out that "other governmental agencies with responsibilities with regard to the effects of the tariff on domestic industry and national security are subordinated to the Tariff Commission" (U.S. House, Committee on Ways and Means, 1948, p. 10).

Peril point advocates in 1948 and again in 1951 maintained that the provision simply guaranteed what the administration had already promised—that no concession would be granted if serious injury would be the result. They argued that peril point procedures would develop more confidence in trade agreements because the peril point was applied before the agreement was concluded. Finally, proponents of the peril point provision argued that it would be a double check on the escape clause (Leddy and Norwood, 1962, p. 131).

Prior to 1934, the American commercial policy process could not accommodate a policy of trade liberalization. All of this changed when Congress delegated to the president authority for tariff rate adjustment. Congress, however, never made commercial policy the exclusive domain of the executive branch, and as the escape clause and peril point illustrate, in important ways the legislature continued to shape its course.

Reminiscent of the cost-of-production formula, the peril point procedures required the Tariff Commission to determine, in effect, the minimum tariff necessary to prevent injurious import competition. The escape clause specified standards and procedures to be implemented by the Tariff Commission whereby American producers could qualify for relief from increased imports. These standards for protection replaced protection itself (i.e., tariffs) as the political issue of concern to members of Congress. Decisions about individual tariff rate increases would be made by experts and be based on specified standards without reference to any particular interest.

The peril point and the escape clause demonstrate the ability of Congress to redefine its role in the commercial policy-making process. They show that Congress developed ways to respond to protectionist pressures without legislating tariffs. They also show how Congress grafted vestiges of the failed scientific tariff experiment (the commission alternative) onto a policy process characterized by rate setting by the president. This served to further insulate the trade policy process.

The successful effort of Congress to redefine its role in the trade policy process aptly showcases the dynamics of the process of institutional change. Individual members of Congress had come to realize that their interests were better served by a policy process in which Congress articulated the broad contours of policy and specified the criteria and procedures for implementing it. In their efforts to identify criteria and procedures that would both perpetuate trade liberalization and address the concerns of domestic industry, organizations and practices established during the interwar period figured prominently. Specifically, the Tariff Commission and its procedures for investigating the impact of imports on domestic industries provided Congress with a way to assert itself in the policy-making process without compromising the integrity of the Trade Agreements Program. Moreover, these vestiges of the 1920s policy-making experiment enabled Congress not only to renew the president's authority but to extend and replenish this authority in the face of increasing import competition.

Conclusion: Explaining the Success of the New Policy Process for Trade

As established in the Trade Agreements Act, rate adjustment by the president offered a way to insulate the policy process that did not have the drawbacks associated with the previously attempted alternatives. On the one hand, it was not attached to a "scientific" adjustment criterion, and on the other, it did not operate oblivious to the world economy and the foreign economic policies of other states. Unencumbered by a cost-of-production formula, the new rate-adjustment process was designed specifically to lower, not raise, tariffs. It was supposed to ease the United States, once and for all, away from its long-standing policy commitment to protectionism and steer American commercial policy toward liberalism. Furthermore, inherent in this method of rate adjustment was a recognition that unilateral liberalization of trade policy could not guarantee reciprocal moves by trading partners.

The new method for rate adjustment had much to recommend it, but the success of this power-sharing alternative depended on the willingness of Congress (as a body of individuals holding positions of authority) to redefine its role in the commercial policy process. Such willingness was manifested in the succession of trade agreements extension acts passed by both Democratic and Republican majorities. Several factors help explain this phenomenon. First, the original Trade Agreements Act was enacted during a period of profound economic crisis, in response to the collapse of world trade and after a series of acknowledged policy failures in the area of trade (e.g., Fordney-McCumber and Smoot-Hawley). For members of Congress, under these conditions the costs (calculated in terms of their personal positions) of doing nothing or maintaining the status quo were high, while the risks of trying something new were reduced. Second, the organization and procedures that were adopted to administer the program worked to maximize the economic benefits of the agreements and to minimize the potential for domestic economic disruption. This accomplishment was due in part to the Smoot-Hawley tariff schedules, which provided an excessively high negotiating base. As a result, the policy of reciprocity and nondiscrimination generated only sporadic criticism. The policy was renewed and the institutional arrangements that supported it strengthened.

By the time negotiated concessions began to affect adversely greater numbers of domestic producers, the new trade policy process had been institutionalized. Congress adopted ways to respond to the pressures of interest groups without legislating tariffs. Members of Congress discovered that "the power to dole out [tariff] favors to industry is not worth the price of having to beat off and placate the incessant pleas of petitioners" (Bauer, Pool, and Dexter, 1963, p. 37). They preferred to debate and vote on legislation that set the general principles governing trade policy rather than respond directly to the pleas of numerous particularistic interests.

PART III

THE U.S. TRADE POLICY PROCESS AND INTERNATIONAL ECONOMIC COOPERATION

If one country lowers its tariffs against another's exports, it can expect the other country to lower its tariffs in return. This principle [reciprocity] regards a market-opening measure as a concession, for which concessions in return are required. The idea is economic nonsense . . . but it has proved terribly useful all the same.
—*The Economist,* 22 September 1990

[I]n the choice of institutional types and structural arrangements we are making decisions with significant political implications. . . . In the design of any political structure, whether it be the Congress or the executive branch, it is important to build in arrangements that weigh the scale in favor of those advocating the national interest.
—H A R O L D S E I D M A N , *Politics, Position, and Power,* 1980

Reciprocity and the Power-Sharing Alternative: Implications for International Cooperation in Trade

At the turn of the century, American officials confronted a trade policy dilemma. Tariff reform had become a political necessity, but tariff reform within the parameters of the existing policy process remained elusive. The challenge was to create a policy process that removed the compulsion to serve particular constituent groups via the tariff. Equally important was the creation of a policy process that promoted the expansion of foreign trade. Few officials, however, gave serious thought to the implications for international trade inherent in the various strategies and instrumentalities of tariff-making reform. Trade expansion was viewed either as a related but separate issue or as an inevitable by-product of tariff reform.

As the reform efforts of the early decades of this century demonstrate, tariff making through independent commission or disciplined party could insulate the policy process from the pressures of particularistic interests, but neither type of alternative in and of itself could promote trade expansion. Trade expansion necessitated securing increased access for American exports to overseas markets, and neither party nor commission alternatives included provisions designed specifically to foster such access.

Scientific tariff making through commission did not necessarily preclude efforts to access foreign markets through reciprocity agreements or treaties. The integrity of this policy-making alternative did require, however, that tariff concessions negotiated in the context of such agreements/treaties respect "scientifically determined" tariff rates. Due to the political mismanagement of the Canadian reciprocity agreement in 1911, negotiated tariff rate concessions were uncoupled from "scientifically" appropriate rates, a concept widely accepted by Republicans. As a result, reciprocity arrangements became viewed as antithetical to scientific tariff making, and in the pivotal decade of the 1920s scientific tariff making took precedence.

Reciprocity arrangements with trading partners and policy-making through responsible party government were likewise not mutually exclusive. In practice, during the Wilson administration officials nevertheless considered trade agreements/treaties ineffective and indeed superfluous for purposes of trade expansion. No doubt, Wilson administration officials based their assessment on the dismal record of ratification (zero) of the Kasson treaties negotiated under authority of the Dingly Tariff Act (1897) and the ill-fated experience with Canadian reciprocity. But they also dismissed reciprocity arrangements because they believed such arrangements were unnecessary. Unilateral reduction of American tariffs would be sufficient to promote American exports abroad. Thus, advocates of both alternatives came to eschew the negotiation of trade agreements or treaties as a means to promote trade expansion.

Despite the rejection of special trade agreements/treaties, the principle of reciprocity did not disappear from American policy. It had long been a feature of trade policy in the most-favored-nation (MFN) clause of U.S. commercial treaties. Between 1778 and 1922, the United States followed a conditional MFN policy; in 1923 the United States adopted the unconditional variant of this clause.

Under the conditional MFN policy, a third-party MFN did not automatically receive the concessions negotiated between the United States and a trading partner. The third-party MFN could qualify for these concessions only if it granted the United States equivalent concessions. This conditional MFN policy had been enacted at a time when tariffs were of minor importance in the conduct of foreign trade. Of greater concern was the securing through negotiation rights to trade at all and rights to equal treatment for American vessels in foreign ports. When prohibitions against trade and navigation laws ceased to dominate the conduct of international trade, the utility of the conditional variant of the MFN policy waned. As tariffs became the primary instrument of trade policy, it became nearly impossible to determine what might constitute equivalent third-party concessions. The conditional variant of the MFN clause lost all practical utility in American trade policy. Moreover, it became viewed as an endorsement of discrimination among trading partners—precisely the opposite of its original purpose (Culbertson, 1937, pp. 67–68).

Equality of treatment—nondiscrimination—became a critical issue for American business and government officials in the changed economy of the post–World War I period. They wanted to see the level of American exports achieved during the war sustained in the postwar years. American officials feared that in the attempt to reconstruct and stabilize their domestic economies Europeans might establish policies that would discriminate against American exports. Therefore, in 1923 the United States adopted as policy the unconditional variant of the MFN principle. This new policy entitled all MFNs to sell their exports in American markets on the best possible terms. Yet unfortunately, since the United States had rejected the negotiation of any reciprocity agreements or treaties, what constituted the "best possible terms" were the inordinately high tariff rates of the 1922 Fordney-McCumber Act.

Thus, during the 1920s the American commitment to reciprocity once again came to include the principle of nondiscrimination. This proved an essential component of the policy process for trade that was forged in the 1930s. The new process tied nondiscrimination to tariff-rate adjustment by the president in the context of bilateral trade agreements. This new policy process was both insulated from the pressures of particularistic interests and designed to increase international trade.

The American experience demonstrates that international cooperation through reciprocity is the key to trade expansion. In a world of sovereign states, gaining access to international markets generally requires that foreigners be afforded roughly equivalent access to the home market. What is equally clear from the American experience is that reciprocity is a multifaceted concept; it can be manifest in policy in many forms.[1] A more subtle but no less important point is that successful trade expansion requires congruence between the policy *form* reciprocity takes and the primary *instruments* of protectionism used by nation-states. The conditional MFN policy of the United States, for example, no longer served to promote trade expansion once tariffs supplanted prohibition and navigation laws as the primary instrument of trade policy.

This chapter examines these issues associated with the concept and practice of reciprocity in international trade. Such an examination will help to explain the considerable success of the power-sharing alternative for trade policy-making in the United States and the concomitant success of the General Agreement on Tariffs and Trade (GATT) during the postwar period. This examination will also facilitate an assessment of the continued viability of this policy process in the context of the 1990s world economy. Toward these ends, therefore, this chapter first considers the concept of reciprocity as it has been recently analyzed. Second, the issue of reciprocity and American politics is explored. The purpose is to identify the limits of the trade policy process that was forged in the 1930s and institutionalized in subsequent decades. This is critical to an appreciation of the character and scope of GATT. Finally, reciprocity, the American

---

1. For a thoughtful exploration of the various manifestations of reciprocity in American trade policy, see Carolyn Rhodes (1993).

trade policy process, and the trade regime are evaluated with regard to future trends in American policy and international trade.

Understanding International Economic Cooperation

In recent years, there has been considerable interest among scholars of the international political economy about the prospect of sustained economic cooperation in the period "after hegemony" (Keohane, 1984, 1986; Stein, 1984, 1990; Strange, 1985; Lipson, 1982; Gilpin, 1987; Yarbrough and Yarbrough, 1987). The contention of hegemonic stability proponents that international economic cooperation would eventually and inevitably decline as American economic hegemony waned (Kindleberger, 1973, 1981; Gilpin, 1975; Krasner, 1976), prompted a flurry of scholarship. Skeptical scholars sought to contest this prediction by identifying and analyzing the component elements of economic cooperation. Their objective was to demonstrate that continued economic cooperation in the form of trade liberalization was possible without the leadership of a hegemon. Their work sparked renewed interest in the concept of reciprocity.

Structural Impediments to Cooperation

The lack of an international sovereign is the most salient feature of world politics. In anarchy, the leaders of nation-states define national interests, and nothing exists other than the state that can guarantee these interests. International relations, therefore, take place in a "self-help" environment.[2] National leaders determine how to pursue and how to defend state interests. In this environment, force is an acceptable instrument of policy, and cooperation between state actors is difficult to achieve (Greco, 1988).[3]

These characteristics of politics in international anarchy have been

2. Kenneth Waltz (1979) in his now classic *Theory of International Relations* maintained that the self-help environment of international relations is structurally determined—a product of anarchy. More recently, Alexander Wendt (1992) has challenged this characterization. Wendt argues that the characteristics of international anarchy are not structurally determined but rather the creation of states: "[S]elf-help and power politics do not follow either logically or causally from anarchy and that if today we find ourselves in a self-help world, this is due to process, not structure" (p. 394).

3. Two major perspectives dominate scholarship in international relations: realism and liberalism. Both realists and liberals see a world where self-interested actors engage each other in an anarchic environment. For realists this is an environment where conflict abounds and cooperation is difficult to achieve. Liberals, in contrast, see more cooperation than conflict in international relations. Arthur A. Stein (1990) explores the conditions under which nations-states cooperate and those under which they are more likely to engage in conflict. In so doing, he demonstrates that realist assumptions are consistent with international cooperation and that liberal ones are consistent with international conflict.

analyzed in game-theoretic terms via the "stag hunt" and "prisoners' dilemma" models. In both, each actor can choose either to cooperate or to defect from cooperation. The possible combinations of responses in these two-actor models generate four possible rank-ordered outcomes. In the stag hunt scenario, mutual cooperation is the most desired outcome for the players; successful defection (i.e., defecting while the other party continues to cooperate) ranks second. In the stag hunt, therefore, there is only a defensive incentive to defect. When the game is played once, without communication, each actor is compelled to choose the option that will ensure that he does not end up with his least-desired outcome: unreciprocated cooperation. With the prisoners' dilemma game, there is an offensive as well as defensive incentive to defect, as both players rank successful defection as their most desired outcome; mutual cooperation is ranked second.

In both games, when played only once, mutual defection is the likely outcome. Cooperation becomes possible only with repeated plays of the game, when the rewards for cooperation are sufficiently high, and where the players adopt a "tit for tat" strategy (Axelrod, 1981, 1984). One player's willingness to cooperate is contingent upon the other player's demonstrated commitment to cooperate. In other words, the first player's decision to cooperate in the subsequent game depends on the other player's decision in the previous game. "Tit for tat" is a strategy of reciprocity, and inasmuch as international economic relations often resemble these models, reciprocity is revealed as a likely strategy to yield mutual cooperation.[4]

Reciprocity and Its Various Forms

Like other concepts in the lexicon of social science, reciprocity has been used by different people, in a variety of contexts, to mean different things. Like other concepts, reciprocity is fraught with ambiguity. In the domain of international relations scholarship, Robert Keohane (1986) has grappled with these ambiguities. Drawing upon the work of social exchange theorists, Keohane definitionally grounds the concept of reciprocity along two dimensions. The first is contingency. "Reciprocal behavior returns ill for ill and good for good" (p. 6). Conditionality is a fundamental component of a reciprocal relationship; such relationships impose obligations only to the extent that each party responds to benefits conferred or punishments inflicted. Equivalence is the second dimension

4. Beth V. and Robert M. Yarbrough (1987) argue that when there is substantial investment in "transaction-specific assets for trade" by states, the international political economy takes on the characteristics of a prisoners' dilemma. They characterize the postwar world economy in this light.

along which reciprocity is defined. Equivalence can be viewed narrowly or broadly. Strict equivalence would be the exchange of nearly identical benefits/punishments. However, even in the context of arms control negotiations, strict equivalence is difficult to apply. Thus, the range of application of strict equivalence is limited. Most reciprocal relationships involve the exchange of rough equivalents. Rough equivalence is found in reciprocal relationships between both equals and unequals, frequently involving the exchange of incomparable but mutually valued benefits, as in patron-client relationships (Keohane, 1986, p. 6).

Combining the two dimensions, Keohane (1986) offers the following definition of reciprocity: "reciprocity refers to the exchange of roughly equivalent values in which the actions of each party are contingent on the prior actions of the others in such a way that good is returned for good and bad for bad" (p. 8). Reciprocity, therefore, can promote cooperation or its opposite. The focus here is the role of reciprocity in promoting cooperative relations among nation-states.

Economists may dispute the emphasis political analysts place on reciprocity for understanding and explaining trade between states. From the perspective of most economists, the practice of free trade, whether reciprocated or not, leads to the most efficient allocation of resources and the maximization of aggregate income. However, the unit of analysis for the economist is seldom the nation-state. In the calculus of the state, absolute gain matters less than relative gain, issues of adjustment and transaction costs loom large, and reciprocity becomes the vehicle to realize the gains of freer if not free trade.

Reciprocity, even in its positive incarnation, is seldom devoid of power, the sine qua non of international relations. The distribution of power in the international domain can determine what are deemed roughly equivalent values. The distribution of power among nation-states may also contribute to the form reciprocity takes. For example, under the aegis of a hegemon, a highly asymmetrical bargain may emerge (Stein, 1984). In exchange for modest reductions of protectionist barriers, the hegemon provides ready access to its market and acts to maintain stability in the world economy (Kindleberger, 1973).

This exchange of grossly asymmetrical values strains the typical understanding of a reciprocal relationship, in which "specified partners exchange items of equivalent value in a strictly delimited sequence" (Keohane, 1986, p. 4). To distinguish this *specific* reciprocity from that experienced in the postwar world economy in terms of trade, Keohane offers the concept of *diffuse* reciprocity. With diffuse reciprocity, "the definition of equivalence is less precise, one's partners may be viewed as a group rather than as particular actors, and the sequence of events is less narrowly bounded" (ibid.). To further distinguish diffuse from specific reciprocity, Keohane states that "obligations [under diffuse reciprocity] are important. Diffuse reciprocity involves conforming to generally accepted standards of behavior" (ibid.).

These categories demonstrate that reciprocity can take different forms. Several points follow from this observation that are relevant here. First, for reciprocity to serve as a vehicle for trade expansion, domestic policy processes must support, at minimum, specific reciprocity. Second, for trade expansion to occur, there must be congruence, not only between the form of reciprocity and the domestic policy processes but also between the form of reciprocity and the instruments of protectionism utilized by potential trading partners. Finally, in trying to assess the relative importance of hegemony and domestic political process for the success of reciprocity as a means to increase economic cooperation, the opportunities and constraints of domestic political factors should not be underestimated. The remainder of this chapter addresses these points.

Reciprocity and Domestic Politics in the United States

Throughout the nineteenth century, the United States promoted trade expansion through the use of the conditional variant of the MFN clause in its commercial treaties. As tariffs supplanted other instruments of trade policy (e.g., navigation laws, outright prohibition of imports) in the world political economy, the conditional MFN policy became essentially moribund. This occurred for two reasons. First, as *specific* reciprocity,[5] the conditional MFN principle required that a third-party MFN offer equivalent concessions before it could qualify for the concessions granted the second party. Such narrow equivalence was difficult to determine; the conditional MFN and trade policies dominated by complicated tariff schedules were incompatible (Culbertson, 1937, pp. 67–68). Second and equally important, negotiating reciprocity treaties would inevitably prove to be futile once tariffs dominated trade policy because Congress legislated tariffs. Trade treaties offering specific tariff concessions to another nation-state would not, in all likelihood, be ratified by the Senate. In fact, the Senate ratified only three such treaties during the whole of the nineteenth century—one with Canada (1854), another with Hawaii (1875), and a minor one with Spain for Cuba and Puerto Rico (1883–1892) (USTC, 1919, p. 21).

For reciprocity to serve as a vehicle of trade expansion in the United States, therefore, it would have to be squarely in the hands of the president and the executive branch. Furthermore, reciprocity would have to be

5. Keohane (1986) makes this connection (see p. 15).

operationalized by the executive in such a way that it would actually promote trade expansion without inciting Congress to reassert its traditional prerogatives in the trade policy process.

This dilemma was initially tackled in the 1890s by Secretary of State James G. Blaine. In the midst of economic depression, he was among the first to recognize the importance of the government's role in trade expansion. As enacted by Congress in the McKinley (1890) and Dingly (1897) Tariff Acts, Blaine's reciprocity provisions were modest. The reciprocity provision in the McKinley Act enabled the president to impose duties on sugar, molasses, tea, coffee, and hides (otherwise admitted duty-free) if any country exporting these items to the United States imposed tariffs on American commodities that were deemed by the president to be unreasonable (Taussig, 1910, p. 279). The Dingly Act provided for three types of reciprocity arrangements. Under Section 3 of the act, Congress allowed minimal concessions without Congressional approval. The president could also retaliate against discrimination by raising duties on a few select items. In addition, Congress sanctioned the negotiation of reciprocity treaties, the ill-fated Kasson treaties (Terrill, 1973, pp. 200–1; Laughlin and Willus, 1903, chap. 10).

The economic impact of these provisions under the McKinley and Dingly tariff acts was marginal at best. Of the agreements negotiated under provisions of the McKinley Act, only those with Brazil and with Spain for Cuba had any significant impact on American exports (Terrill, 1973, p. 176). None of the agreements negotiated under Section 3 of the Dingly Act had any economic significance, and none of the Kasson treaties was ever ratified by the U.S. Senate (Terrill, 1973, pp. 200–1).

The political significance of these reciprocity measures was far more important. The president had been given the authority to negotiate trade agreements that became law without Senate ratification. Under appropriate circumstances, Congress could be induced to share its tariff-setting responsibilities with the president. Moreover, a case for enhancing the government's role in trade expansion had been made, and a vehicle for this expanded role had been identified and operationalized.

Due in large part to Blaine's efforts, trade expansion became viewed as an important goal of tariff-making reform. Blaine also succeeded in giving the issue of reciprocity a prominent place in all subsequent debates on trade policy and tariff-making reform. This does not mean that Blaine's concept of reciprocity through negotiated agreements was endorsed by policymakers of the early twentieth century. In fact, reciprocity through such agreements was rejected first by the Democrats under Wilson and then in the 1920s by the Republicans. Despite these rejections, however, trade expansion through reciprocity remained a recognized goal of trade policy. The issue in dispute was how to operationalize reciprocity.

President Wilson and the Democrats believed special reciprocity arrangements were unnecessary; once American tariff rates were lowered, a reciprocal response would be forthcoming from American trading partners. In the 1920s, Republicans came to view special reciprocity arrangements as antithetical to scientific tariff making. Instead, they endorsed the adoption in 1923 of an unconditional MFN policy. The adoption of the unconditional MFN clause would later be considered an important breakthrough in the history of American trade policy, but during the 1920s its significance was lost on U.S. trading partners. In exchange for granting the best possible treatment to American goods in their markets, they were entitled to the best possible treatment in American markets—the inordinately high rates of the Fordney-McCumber Act of 1922.

In the 1930s, Secretary of State Cordell Hull resurrected Blaine's idea of reciprocity agreements. Hull viewed negotiation of such agreements not as a supplement to tariff rate setting by Congress but as a substitute for it. In Hull's framework, Congress would delegate to the president tariff rate-setting authority in the context of bilateral negotiations. Hull also envisioned this new policy process as a tremendous impetus to trade expansion.

Reciprocity operationalized through what has been labeled a power-sharing alternative solved the twin dilemmas of American trade policy. It offered tariff-making reform, and, linked to the recently adopted unconditional MFN clause, it provided a vehicle for trade expansion. The power-sharing alternative enabled policymakers to espouse nondiscrimination and liberalization as the pillars of American trade policy; it empowered American officials to spearhead the negotiation of the General Agreement on Tariffs and Trade (GATT) in 1947.

The policy process for trade inaugurated in 1934 had great potential. Indeed, its successful operation and institutionalization permitted the creation of an international trade regime characterized by diffuse reciprocity (Keohane, 1986). In 1934, however, this outcome was hardly a foregone conclusion. Officials of the Roosevelt administration had to administer the Trade Agreements Program in such a way that Congress would renew and extend the president's negotiating authority (the crux of the power-sharing alternative) and would not reassert its traditional rate-setting prerogatives. Congress needed to redefine its role in the process of trade policy-making. However, this would never occur if members perceived their constituents under siege by a flood of imports. Administrators understood that if the program were to survive and eventually become

institutionalized as the cornerstone of a trade policy process, the concessions negotiated in the bilateral trade agreements and generalized via the
unconditional MFN clause could not result in "unacceptable" levels of
import competition for American firms. Therefore, the initial Trade Agreements Program had to be managed to minimize the impact on imports of
the unconditional MFN.

As the previous chapter documents, through the judicious use of techniques such as the chief-supplier principle and reclassification of items
in the tariff schedules, State Department officials were able to negotiate
a series of trade agreements that lowered American tariff rates without
triggering injurious levels of imports. Concessions were generalized to
all MFNs but in such a way that there was a specific beneficiary of each
concession. This meant that potential "free rider" problems were circumvented. The net result was that U.S. negotiators avoided giving significant concessions without getting equivalently significant concessions in
exchange; third-party countries would remain interested in negotiating
their own trade agreement with the United States because the concessions they enjoyed as MFNs were relatively minor. The unconditional
MFN principle was carefully utilized to yield reciprocity that was more
specific than would otherwise have been the case. This was necessary
to assure the long-term success of the power-sharing alternative to trade
policy-making.

The strategy worked. In 1934 the president had been authorized to
reduce any tariff by 50 percent of its Smoot-Hawley level. From 1934
until 1945, bilateral negotiations were concluded with twenty-seven countries. The concessions granted by the United States in these agreements
involved tariff reductions on approximately 64 percent of all dutiable imports. These rates were reduced by an average of 44 percent of their 1930
level (USTC, 1949, pt. 2, pp. 10–14; pt. 3, Table 3).

The strategy worked in yet another way, unintended perhaps but
equally significant. Patterns of behavior characterize relations among
actors in world politics as much as in relations among officials in the
domestic political arena. As these patterns of behavior in an issue area
become regularized, expectations form about future activity. These expectations can develop into norms that prescribe behavior among actors. To
the extent that these norms encourage cooperation, cooperative behavior among the actors is reinforced. Just as astute administration of the
Trade Agreements Program and successive renewals of the president's
negotiating authority helped to institutionalize new patterns of behavior
between the executive and legislature in the United States, the succession
of bilateral negotiations resulting in trade agreements helped to institu-

tionalize cooperative patterns of behavior between the United States and its trading partners.

By the end of World War II there remained only a small portion of the original authority granted to the president in the Trade Agreements Act. Tariffs on 40 percent of U.S. dutiable imports had already been reduced by the full 50 percent permitted under the act, and many other rates had been lowered by less than the maximum amount (USTC, 1949, pt. 2, p. 14). President Roosevelt, therefore, requested and obtained the first authority to reduce tariffs to below the levels authorized in 1934. The Trade Agreements Extension Act of 1945 authorized the president to reduce tariffs by 50 percent of the levels of January 1, 1945. This significant extension of presidential authority was obtained in exchange for the administration's commitment to include a general escape clause in each trade agreement it negotiated (Leddy and Norwood, 1962, p. 125). The new authority was available when, in November 1946, the United States took the first steps toward the creation of an international trade regime and invited other countries to participate in the first multilateral conference for the mutual reduction of tariffs.

The establishment of a postwar trade regime based on nondiscriminatory liberalization was contingent on the institutionalization in the United States of the power-sharing alternative to trade policy-making. The results of this process—the redefined roles of legislature and executive and the establishment of a new pattern of institutional relations—go a long way toward explaining the scope and limitations of the trade regime that emerged in the years after World War II. There were, for example, limits to the liberalization possible within the context of the new policy process. Some of these limits became institutionalized as part of the trade policy process itself and indeed became essential aspects of liberalization even as they delimited its extent (e.g., mechanisms for discretionary or procedural protection—escape clause and peril point). Other limits were not features of the policy process but rather were the product of domestic political factors beyond the scope of the new trade policy process. The failure of the United States to ratify the International Trade Organization (ITO) illustrates this point well.

In 1945 the United States presented a draft charter for the ITO. It was amended from 1945 to 1948 at successive conferences. In the interim, the GATT was drawn up in 1947 to record the results of the multilateral trade negotiations being held in Geneva. It was drawn up "to assure that the tariff concessions it recorded would not be undercut by other trade measures" (Dam, 1970, p. 11). Many of its provisions were incorporated into the Havana Charter (March 1948), the final version of the American proposal to create the ITO (Evans, 1971, p. 9). The final draft included provisions to regulate all aspects of international trade—tariffs, preferences, quantitative restrictions, subsidies, and international commodity agreements (Gardner, 1969, pp. 269–86, 361–68). The Havana Charter was the product of American efforts to obtain commitments to an international organization to promote liberalization and to regulate world trade. However, the international commitment to such an organization evaporated when the United States failed to ratify the Havana Charter.

The trade policy process forged during the 1930s had enabled the United States to resist the demands of particularistic interests for higher tariffs, but it provided no magic formulas that would have permitted the Truman administration to surmount the complex constellation of opponents that ultimately defeated the ITO. The combined opposition of protectionists along with liberals who felt that the Havana Charter did not go far enough toward free trade, and business groups that objected to increased governmental involvement in trade management, convinced the president that the charter had no chance for ratification. After delaying for three years, the Truman administration decided in 1950 not to submit the Havana Charter to Congress (Diebold, 1952).

Originally intended as a temporary agreement to serve until the Havana Charter was implemented, GATT assumed the commercial policy role that had been intended for the ITO. While GATT did not include the provisions of the Havana Charter in such areas as economic development, commodity agreements, and restrictive business practices, it did reflect the prevailing international consensus on trade. It represented the signatories' commitment to international trade liberalization through reciprocity and nondiscrimination.[6]

There have been eight successfully completed rounds of multilateral trade negotiations concluded under GATT auspices. The first Geneva agreement (1947) affected about 54 percent of U.S. dutiable imports. Tariffs on U.S. dutiable imports were reduced by an average of 18.9 percent (calculated from 1945 tariff levels). After 1947, until the Kennedy Round (concluded in 1967), no negotiations produced as successful results. The restrictions placed on the scope of the president's negotiating authority largely explain these lackluster results (Evans, 1971, p. 11).

The Trade Expansion Act (TEA) of 1962 redefined the parameters of possible trade policy, and it set new ground rules for pursuing trade liberalization. For the first time, American negotiators were not bound to item-by-item concessions. Linear reduction represented the first sub-

---

6. The only exceptions to the general rule of equal treatment for all related to existing systems of preference and to future customs unions (see Gardner, 1969, p. 361).

stantive change in the president's negotiating authority since the Trade Agreements Act. The acceptance of linear reduction allowed for subsequent broadening of the president's negotiating authority on issues such as nontariff barriers and trade in services.

The TEA also explored new avenues of safeguarding domestic interests without singling out specific industries or products for special consideration. The provisions for adjustment assistance and the creation of the Special Trade Representative (now the U.S. Trade Representative) are cases in point. These innovations are evidence of a sophisticated and institutionalized policy process that could be adapted to changing world circumstances. The trade legislation that followed the TEA also gave policymakers new opportunities to redefine the parameters of trade policy. These parameters inevitably helped to shape the GATT's agenda.

Operationalized through a power-sharing scheme, reciprocity in the 1930s became more than a concept describing tit-for-tat behavior. It became associated in the United States with a policy process for trade through which Congress delegated its tariff rate-setting authority to the president within specified and changing parameters and in the context of negotiations with trading partners. It also became identified with new patterns of behavior in international trade that promoted nondiscriminatory liberalization. Both aspects, evident in the process whereby the power-sharing alternative became institutionalized and simultaneously fostered the inculcation of nondiscrimination and liberalization as norms of international trade, were crucial to the creation of an international trade regime.

The United States, Reciprocity, and the Trade Regime

As the prospects for the ITO dimmed and eventually disappeared, GATT was transformed from temporary stopgap agreement to trade regime. The creation and evolution of GATT can be explained in very large measure by reference to the United States—its economic power and the range and limitations of its trade policy process. As the world's economic hegemon, American national interests could be enhanced through a liberal economic order (Krasner, 1976; Lake, 1988). The trade policy process that was institutionalized during the 1930s and 1940s could support the creation of such an order. However, as the ITO case demonstrates, American commitment to liberalism was not without limits. These limits were defined by the American trade policy process, and they set the boundaries for the trade regime. This section of the chapter explores how changing U.S. economic power and the evolving American trade policy process shaped the trade regime. It also examines how this trade regime has helped to form the American trade policy agenda. The central question that will drive the discussion is whether a regime founded to promote diffuse reciprocity in trade relations can persist in a posthegemonic era in which the pursuit of reciprocity increasingly implies the exchange of more strictly equivalent values.

The Regime Concept

The concept of regime has been much discussed and much debated among scholars of international cooperation and international political economy. Out of this debate has yet to emerge a consensus with regard to concept definition, and therefore, there is no agreement about the relevance of the concept to our understanding of the dynamics of cooperation among nation-states (Krasner, 1982a, 1982b; Aggarwal, 1985; Haggard and Simmons, 1987, Stein, 1990). Scholarship on regimes, however, has not been wholly disparate. It has focused around three definitions, each one offering a different position on the explanatory power of the concept (Haggard and Simmons, 1987).

In the broadest sense, international regimes can be defined as established patterns of behavior between or among nation-states.[7] The breadth of this conceptualization of regime gives it little weight as an explanatory variable (Puchala and Hopkins, 1982). It may serve as a typology-generating device but little else.

A second definition has been widely supported among scholars of international political economy: "a set of implicit or explicit principles, norms, rules, and decision-making procedures around which actors' expectations converge in a given area of international relations" (Krasner, 1982b, p. 186). Proponents of this definition have meticulously attempted to distinguish the terms one from the other. Principles are "beliefs of fact, causation, and rectitude"; norms are "standards of behavior defined in terms of rights and obligations"; rules are "specific prescriptions or proscriptions for action"; and decision-making procedures are "prevailing practices for making and implementing collective choice" (Krasner, 1982b, p. 186). Proponents, however, concede that these terms and their definitions blend together at the margins (Keohane, 1984, p. 59). Furthermore,

---

7. What distinguishes these patterns from those that define the contours of institutional relations within states is the political setting within which they occur. Institutional change manifested in the establishment of new patterns of institutional relations is typically grounded in law. Identification of patterns of institutional relations that define policy processes, therefore, is far more specific and far less amorphous than a general reference to "patterns of behavior between or among nation-states." In fact, the other definitions that will be discussed try to identify the specific nature of the patterned behavior that typifies an international regime.

as Haggard and Simmons (1987, p. 494) point out in their review essay, disagreements about how to distinguish these terms can lead to strikingly different conclusions about regime stability and change.

A third view defines regimes as "multilateral agreements among states which aim to regulate international actions within an issue area" (Haggard and Simmons, 1987, p. 495). This approach to regimes obviates the need to specify when implicit arrangements have achieved a sufficiently high degree of explicitness to be considered regimes. The basis of this conceptualization is the recognition of regimes' role in facilitating cooperation through joint decision making among self-interested states.[8] Regimes serve to reduce the likelihood that member states will resort to opportunism. They work to keep the benefits of cooperation sufficiently high, and therefore regimes help to offset the potential benefits of defection.

This third, more formal definition of regime is the most appropriate for the purposes of this discussion. GATT is indeed a multilateral agreement, and a broader, less exact definition would not capture a different or significantly greater reality than the more exact and more formal one. Since this is not a study comparing regimes across issue areas, a more encompassing definition of regime is unnecessary, and the problems associated with definitional inexactitude can be avoided.

What cannot be avoided, however, are issues concerning the relevance and utility of the concept. John G. Ruggie (1975) introduced the concept at a time when the implications of declining American economic hegemony were being initially addressed. Ruggie and proponents of what became known as "hegemonic stability theory" used the concept to help explain why international cooperation in a variety of issue areas, including trade, was not collapsing as American hegemony waned. Ruggie (1982) contends that regimes have a normative as well as a power base. The changing distribution of global economic power has eroded the power base of the regimes created under the auspices of American hegemony, but so long as the normative base remains intact, the regime persists and continues to facilitate cooperation in a given issue area. Ruggie labeled the normative base of the postwar economic regimes "embedded liberalism." Robert Keohane (1984) argues along the same line for the sustained relevance of regimes in the posthegemonic era: "[Regimes] create the conditions for orderly multilateral negotiations, legitimate and delegitimate different types of state action, and facilitate linkages among issues within regimes and between regimes" (p. 244).

---

8. Arthur A. Stein (1990) emphasizes the importance of joint decision making to the concept of international regime: "International regimes exist when the patterned behavior of states results from joint rather than independent decision-making" (p. 29).

Regimes persist and continue to promote cooperation only to the extent that the actions and policies of the most important member states conform to the spirit if not the letter of regime agreements. In this regard, the actions and policies of the hegemon or former hegemon are the most relevant. The policies of the hegemon are determinative as regimes are established. Its interests and the repertoire of its domestic policy processes set the parameters for these regimes. As the tremendous power advantage of the hegemon eclipses, its ability to conform its policies to those prescribed by the regime depends on two factors. The first is the adaptability of the regime. Can the regime be transformed to reflect the redefined interests of its member states? The second factor involves domestic politics. Can the policy process in place sustain commitment to the international regime in a given issue area while new agreements are negotiated? These questions will be examined through a discussion of the domestic political determinants of regime creation and regime reconstitution as they pertain to the issue area of trade.

Building the Trade Regime

The power-sharing alternative for policy-making in trade permitted American officials in the 1930s to pursue a policy of reciprocity based on the principles of nondiscrimination and liberalization. This policy process also provided the institutional context for the trade regime. In this regard, therefore, it is not mere curious coincidence that GATT emerged and developed as trade regime at the same time that members of the U.S. Congress were working to redefine the legislature's role in the trade policy-making process. This coincidence of circumstances created an uneasy, ambivalent, and sometimes antagonistic relationship between the nascent trade regime and the American Congress that was mediated by the president and the officials of the executive branch. The awkward but dynamic nature of this troika had a multiplicity of effects. For one, it had a profound impact on the evolution of the trade regime. This impact is evident in the meager quality of GATT's legal and organizational structure, in GATT's truncated procedures for dispute settlement, and in the relatively limited scope of the trade regime.

While the substantive obligations of GATT were nearly identical to those of the ITO charter, there were significant differences between the two documents that made GATT something other than "a pocket edition of the ITO" (Hudec, 1975, p. 44). Specifically, the legal and organizational structure of GATT was substantially different from that of the proposed ITO.

A major concern of American negotiators at Geneva during the first round of multilateral trade talks was the U.S. Congress. Anticipating difficulty obtaining Congressional ratification of the yet to be finalized ITO charter, negotiators wanted to avoid the necessity of seeking Congressional approval of the General Agreement. Therefore, to sidestep Congress, GATT was designed to fit within the framework of the American Trade Agreements Program. This constraint resulted in two major limitations on the legal composition of GATT. First, governments agreed to accept GATT's legal structure provisionally, and except for tariff concessions and the guarantee to accord all contracting parties MFN status, they agreed to bind themselves only "to the fullest extent not inconsistent with existing legislation" (quoted in Hudec, 1975, p. 46). This limitation was executed via a separate protocol called the Protocol of Provisional Application, which expressed the reservations noted above.

Second, GATT's legal structure was limited by the decision not to make it a formal international organization. This decision was necessitated by the need to claim that GATT was but a "trade agreement." Moreover, negotiators wanted to avoid the appearance of having surreptitiously created an international organization for trade. The zealous determination to keep GATT devoid of organizational content, however, resulted in the problem of designating a decision-making apparatus. The negotiators in Geneva maneuvered around this difficulty by identifying the "CONTRACTING PARTIES" as decision-making entity. Their status as a collective, decision-making body was signified only by use of uppercase (Hudec, 1975, p. 46).

The desire to minimize elements of organizational structure also affected the creation of dispute settlement procedures within GATT. The nullification and impairment provision (Article 23) incorporated into the General Agreement provided a substantive definition of nullification and specified rudimentary procedures for resolving potential disputes between contracting parties. The provision made no distinction between disputes arising from violations and nonviolations of GATT obligations; and given the perceived necessity to fit GATT within the rubric of the American Trade Agreements Program, the settlement procedures were understandably inexplicit. In essence, Article 23 stipulates that when adjustment cannot be reached between two disputing parties, the matter may be referred to the contracting parties. The contracting parties are charged with investigating the matter and with making appropriate recommendations for its resolution. If the parties deem the circumstances serious enough, "they may authorize a contracting party or parties to suspend the application to any other contracting party or parties of such concessions or other obligations under the Agreement as they determine to be appropriate in the circumstances" (GATT, 1969, vol. 1, Art. 23, p. 31).

These dispute-settlement procedures were made to function remarkably well during the first decade of GATT operations. This was due to a general consensus about the norms that should guide GATT activity and an "impressionistic" decision-making style that enabled GATT officials to tailor their rulings and recommendations toward exerting subtle influence whenever possible over the commercial policies of the national governments in question (Hudec, 1975). With regard to the United States, this ability to influence was unquestionably limited but nevertheless evident. The wrangling over dairy quotas in the early 1950s illustrates how GATT exercised limited influence over American commercial policy.

In 1951 the U.S. Congress attached provisions (Section 104) for import quotas on dairy products to defense procurement legislation. President Truman signed the bill into law because he deemed its major components too important to risk a veto. He promptly introduced legislation to repeal the offending quotas. Since there was no question that the quotas violated obligations under the General Agreement (the president's swift action to seek repeal acknowledged the violation), GATT's response to Section 104 was aimed at enforcement—the application of sanctions and pressure to secure the removal of the quotas.

In advance of Congressional action on the repeal of Section 104, the contracting parties came down as forcefully as they could against the American action, threatening even the collapse of the General Agreement. The object of the threats was clearly to press for removal of the dairy quotas. The target of the pressure was not so much Congress as it was the president. The other contracting parties wanted to impress upon the president the gravity with which the situation was viewed, and they recognized the probable futility of a direct appeal to Congress. Congress had included a provision in the 1951 extension of the Trade Agreements Act that stated, "The enactment of this Act shall not be construed to determine or indicate the approval or disapproval by the Congress of the Executive Agreement known as the General Agreement on Tariffs and Trade" (Hudec, 1975, p. 356 n). Clearly, Congress wanted to retain a wide latitude for itself in trade policy-making. It was left to the president to package GATT's appeal in a manner most persuasive to members of Congress. The emphasis of the executive's case for repeal was on pocketbook issues, such as potential losses in the export market. In this regard, the threat of GATT retaliation figured prominently. More general international issues, such as the impact of the quotas on European recovery and their impact on American leadership of the world political economy, also were introduced. Equally important in the president's case for repeal was the argument that protection from import competition for American farmers was already available through the escape clause (GATT, 1969, Art. 19) and through Section 22 of the Agriculture Adjustment Act of 1933, which authorized import restrictions whenever necessary to safeguard the price support program (Hudec, 1975, p. 169).

Congress refused to repeal the dairy quotas, but it did liberalize them. GATT tried to keep the pressure on the United States and sanctioned, under the dispute settlement procedure of Article 23, retaliation by the Netherlands. The Netherlands' wheat flour quota is the only example of retaliation authorized under the dispute settlement procedure. Given the manner in which it was administered, the purpose of the wheat quota in retrospect appears to have been designed more as protest than as compensation. (Hudec, 1975, p. 180).

In ongoing efforts to mediate between Congress and GATT, U.S. officials obtained, in 1955, a permanent waiver from GATT obligations for all Section 22 products, including dairy products. This end result of the effort to balance dairy quotas and obligations under GATT was to contribute to the diminution of GATT's relevance and scope in agriculture.[9]

GATT history reveals an interesting tension between efforts to broaden and efforts to narrow its scope. As the dominant partner in GATT, the United States was central in creating and sustaining this tension. Part of an explanation for the failure of the ITO to gain Congressional ratification was its broad scope. The ITO charter contained chapters not only on commercial policy but also on employment policy, economic development, restrictive business practices, and commodity agreements. The American business community objected to many of the provisions of these chapters, and its support for the idea of an international trade organization waned. The narrower focus of GATT was much more amenable to American business interests. Without the support of business groups, the ITO was a dead letter in Congress.

With the waiver for American agricultural products, GATT's limited commercial policy focus was narrowed still further. The trend continued with the evolution of the Orderly Marketing Agreement (OMA) and the Voluntary Restraint Agreement (VRA) or Voluntary Export Restraint (VER). Responding unilaterally to "market disruptions" caused by large quantities of imports, principally from low-wage countries, the United States negotiated a series of VRAs. Except for the first such agreement, the long-term arrangement on cotton textiles (1962), all subsequent agreements of this type were negotiated by the United States outside GATT's legal framework.[10] In addition, these agreements were usually negotiated

---

9. The formation of the European Economic Community (sanctioned under Article 28 of the GATT) and the development of the Common Agricultural Policy (CAP) were even more significant in this process.

10. For an examination of textile trade in the context of international regimes, see Aggarwal, (1985).

after substantial pressure from Congress and under the threat of uni-lateral legislative action. The VRAs on products such as meat, steel, flat-ware, footwear, and automobiles removed a significant portion of world trade from GATT's purview. Attempts to bring VRAs under the rubric of GATT's legal structure during the Tokyo Round of multilateral trade negotiations failed (Krasner, 1979, p. 522).

Simultaneously, American officials worked to expand GATT's scope. Aiming to broaden GATT's geographic range for both economic and politi-cal reasons, the United States was instrumental in gaining membership for Japan in 1955. After Japan's entry, the United States worked to gain its full acceptance by the contracting parties that had invoked Article 35.[11] By the mid-1960s their mutual efforts were wholly successful.

In the 1970s the United States spearheaded a major effort to expand GATT's scope to include codes on nontariff barriers to trade. Authorized by the Trade Act of 1974 and in the context of the Tokyo Round, American officials negotiated codes on technical barriers to trade, import licensing procedures, customs valuation, trade in civil aircraft, and government procurement and subsidies (Krasner, 1979, pp. 511–16).

At its best, the trade regime served to reduce uncertainty and functioned as the hub of decentralized coordination among members (Keohane, 1984, p. 148). GATT could not evolve into an international organization char-acterized by centralized rule enforcement largely because such a body would not fit within the rubric of the American Trade Agreements Pro-gram. Within this rubric the United States forged a new policy process for trade. By 1945 new roles for the executive and legislature had been established, but the parameters of those roles were still in flux. As was discussed above, the efforts of Congress to redefine its role in the trade policy process impacted on the development of the trade regime. Less easy to demonstrate are the effects of the Congress–president–GATT re-lationship on these Congressional efforts to redefine the institution's role in the trade policy process.

It is clear that the presence of GATT and the president's commitment to it gave Congress a certain amount of leverage vis-à-vis the executive. Members of Congress could threaten legislation or could even enact bills that would abrogate GATT rules. Sometimes these actions were directly targeted at specific groups of constituents. But increasingly, in efforts to address constituent concerns, the immediate target of Congressional ac-tions in trade became the president. From this standpoint, Congressional

11. Article 35 entitles a contracting party to refuse to extend the GATT's obligation of nondiscrimination to new members.

actions can be viewed as an elaborate tactic to elicit a desired response from the president in conjunction with U.S. trading partners in GATT. It inevitably had an impact on the nature of GATT. In addition, the tactic became a pattern that characterized legislative-executive relations in trade policy and therefore became an aspect of the redefined role of Congress in trade policy-making. GATT contributed to this development because its existence served to constrain Congress from pursuing a unilateral course in trade policy.

Reconstituting the Trade Regime

In the immediate postwar period, the bedrock of international economic cooperation in trade was the hegemony of the United States. The contours of cooperation, however, were shaped by the twin processes discussed above: the building of the trade regime and the institutionalization of the American trade policy process. Hegemony gave the United States a vested interest in sustained international economic cooperation. American officials pursued such cooperation through policies based on the principles of nondiscrimination and liberalization. These policies were pursued to the limits permitted by the American trade policy process. The United States also sanctioned, even encouraged, its trading partners to abrogate in policy their commitment to nondiscrimination when calculations of economic and political interests justified such practices. The most often cited examples of this are American support for European economic integration and its tolerance of Japanese discriminatory trade practices.

What are the prospects for sustaining economic cooperation in an environment in which the relative economic power of the United States has declined? More specifically, to what extent has the trade regime that was forged at the height of American economic power been transformed to reflect the redefined interests of its member states, particularly the interests of the United States? Answers to both questions depend on the foundation established for such cooperation. A commitment to multilateralism, nondiscrimination, and liberalization provided the mortar for cooperation in the postwar trade regime. There was a consensus among the major trading states of the world economy that these principles should guide policy in trade, and there was a strong commitment by the hegemon to uphold these principles in policy. A willingness to tolerate departures from these principles by the hegemon characterized the "asymmetric bargain" the United States had struck with its trading partners. The likelihood of sustaining cooperation based on multilateralism, nondiscrimination, and liberalization hinges on a restored commitment in practice to these principles on the part of all major world traders.

Certain trends in trade that have emerged in recent years have clouded the prospects of successfully reconstituting the trade regime solely along these three principles. One of these trends is the regionalization of the world economy. European integration and the North American Free Trade Agreement (NAFTA), for example, run counter to the notion that multilateralism and nondiscrimination should guide policy in trade. Moves by the United States such as the Super 301 provisions of the 1988 Trade Act are also troubling to those who envision a reinvigorated regime based unequivocally on these three liberal principles.

Hopes for a reinvigorated trade regime committed anew to multilateralism, nondiscrimination, and liberalization hinged to a significant degree on the successful completion of the Uruguay Round of trade negotiations. American negotiators aimed to have GATT's scope expanded to include, among other things, rules governing trade in services and the handling of intellectual property. They also wanted to reach agreement on a program for the elimination of agricultural subsidies. Given the pivotal role of the Common Agricultural Policy (CAP) in the European Community (now the European Union) and the resistance of some of its member states (viz., France) to compromising on the issue, breakthroughs on the question of agricultural subsidies proved difficult to achieve.

Despite these and other obstacles, successful completion of the Uruguay Round was announced on December 15, 1993. The agreement culminated seven years of negotiations. Its key provisions both deepened and broadened the scope of the trade regime. It continues the process of liberalization through traditional means (e.g., tariff reductions) while it places trade in both services and agriculture under the auspices of the trade regime. The agreement also provides for the phasing out of textile quotas, the protection of intellectual property, and greater enforcement of trade rules through the World Trade Organization (WTO),which it establishes.[12]

With regard to the traditional domain of tariffs, the agreement substantially lowers levies on imports. These reductions affect approximately 85 percent of world trade. Tariffs will be eliminated or significantly reduced on a wide range of products, including pharmaceuticals, steel, paper, equipment for agriculture and construction, beer, and liquor. Tariffs on industrial goods will be reduced from an average of approximately 5 percent to an average of 3 percent. For most products, tariff reductions will be implemented in equal increments over five years. However, in some sensitive industries, like textiles, tariff cuts will be implemented over a ten-year period.

12. The information for this discussion of the major features of the trade agreement was largely drawn from *Congressional Quarterly*, December 18, 1993, pp. 3463–64.

In agriculture, the Uruguay Round achieved considerable success. Most significantly, trade in agricultural commodities was brought into the trade regime. Under provisions of the agreement, governments are to reduce the amount of money they spend on agriculture subsidies by an average of 36 percent, and the total volume of agriculture products exported with the help of subsidies must be reduced by 21 percent. Government-paid income support is to be cut by 20 percent.[13] In addition, nontariff barriers in agricultural trade (including quotas) are to be replaced by tariffs, and countries that have entirely prohibited imports of certain farm commodities will have to guarantee market access equal to 3 percent of domestic consumption (increasing to 5 percent over a six- to ten-year period).

On the textile front, voluntary export restraints are to be phased out over ten years. Under such arrangements, industrial states have been able to shield their textile producers from imports from industrializing states. To protect the U.S. textile industry, tariff reductions on imports of textiles and apparel are considerably less than those for other industrial goods. For textile and clothing imports, tariffs are to be reduced by about 12 percent; for other industrial products, tariffs will be cut approximately 34 percent.

Bringing trade in services under the rubric of the trade regime was one of the major goals of the United States in the 1980s when it pressed for a new round of multilateral trade negotiations. In large measure, the new pact extends regime rules governing trade in goods to trade in services. Nevertheless, achieving multilateral agreements to open specific service sectors such as banking, securities, insurance, and shipping proved unobtainable. The trade pact does, however, offer some protection against piracy for intellectual property such as computer software, semiconductor chip design, books, and films. In addition to success in the areas of trade in services and intellectual property, U.S. negotiators also secured new rules restricting government industrial subsidies. These rules are of particular importance to the U.S. aerospace industry and should result in lower subsidies to the European Airbus consortium, the major competitor of the Boeing Company in civil aeronautics.[14]

The trade agreement also created the WTO, a permanent body with greater authority than GATT to enforce agreements reached in the Uruguay Round. The successful negotiation of enhanced dispute settlement procedures was among the announced goals of U.S. negotiators when

13. The United States has already met this part of the agreement through farm bills enacted in 1985 and 1990.
14. The trade agreement does permit the use of subsidies for new product development.

they sought to undertake a new round of multilateral trade negotiations. The realization of this goal in the form of the establishment of the WTO, however, aroused considerable opposition among conservatives in the United States on the grounds that it compromised American sovereignty. Sufficient Congressional support for the agreement was secured only when the Clinton administration agreed to appoint a commission and to specify procedures whereby the Congress could act to withdraw the United States from the WTO. Comprised of five Federal appellate judges, the commission will review all rulings made against the United States by the WTO to determine whether or not they were fairly reached. If the commission finds three unreasonable rulings within a five-year period, Congress can initiate moves to withdraw the United States from the organization (*New York Times*, November 23, 1994).[15]

The trade pact represents a reaffirmation of member commitment to a rules-oriented trade regime based on liberalization through reciprocity and nondiscrimination. But will the successful completion of the Uruguay Round of trade negotiations and the establishment of the WTO be sufficient to sustain the trade regime into the twenty-first century? The issue has aroused some debate, and alternative visions of a revitalized trade regime have been proposed. These alternatives have generally advocated cooperation in trade through the practice of "managed trade" and a results-oriented trade regime.

The two visions of a reconstituted trade regime—one rules-based, the other results-based—are quite different from each other. Assuming that in order to preserve international cooperation some revitalization of the trade regime is necessary,[16] the issue of political viability looms large. What is the likely impact of the American trade policy process on the present plan for trade regime revitalization? Speculating about the alternative vision of cooperation in trade, could the American trade policy process support a results-oriented, managed-trade-based trade regime? As one of the world's largest markets and as its most accessible, the United

15. Under the terms of the agreement, any country can withdraw with six months notice. Before the Clinton administration's concessions to secure passage of the trade pact, the decision to withdraw was assumed to rest exclusively with the president. The implications of this compromise for the trade policy-making process will be discussed in the next chapter.

16. This assumption is not universally shared among scholars of international political economy. Susan Strange (1985), for one, argues that if GATT suddenly disappeared "world trade would be remarkably little affected" (p. 243). In Strange's view, trade constitutes a "secondary structure" in the international system. It is subsidiary to four primary structures of the international political economy: the security structure, the production structure, the money and credit structure, and the knowledge structure. The trade structure is derivative of the other structures, and the future of world trade depends on their status, not on the existence of a trade regime.

States remains an essential actor in any trade regime, and consequently, these questions are far from insignificant. Therefore, these two different visions of a revitalized trade regime will be juxtaposed.

The label "managed trade" communicates different things to different people. At base, proponents of managed trade advocate the use of quantity instruments to yield specific results in trade. That is why it can be considered a results-oriented approach to trade, as opposed to a rules-oriented one in which quantity targets are not specified and where trade emerges from markets operating under specified rules—like those articulated in the existing trade regime (Bhagwati, 1991, p. 101). Here, managed trade as a basis for international cooperation will be compared with the framework for cooperation endorsed by advocates of a liberal trading order.

Advocates of a more managed system of international trade generally agree that a commitment to liberal values is no longer a sufficient basis for sustaining economic cooperation (e.g., Kuttner, 1990; Thurrow, 1992). Specifically, it cannot sustain cooperation in sectors where supernormal profits or heavy and long-standing subsidization exist (Kuttner, 1991; Tyson, 1992; Thurrow, 1992). This, however, does not preclude cooperation on other bases for such sectors. Kuttner, for example, envisions the creation of a "mixed system" of cooperation in trade. Such a system would not require unconditional allegiance to the principles of nondiscrimination and liberalization. These principles would govern trade whenever and wherever possible and would thus serve as the "default" program for the conduct of international trade. In addition, there would be explicit recognition of conditions that result in an asymmetry of benefits from international trade when strict allegiance to liberal values is applied, and alternative cooperative arrangements would be negotiated to meet the challenge of these conditions.

The starting point for a revitalized trade regime in the managed trade mode is an explicit recognition that, however desirable liberal ideas may be in the abstract, they can no longer serve as the sole goal of international cooperation. The goal of a reconstituted trade regime would be *freer* trade through what has been called a "balance of benefits approach" (Kuttner, 1990, p. 48). Such an approach precludes the adoption of a universal formula to guide the conduct of international trade. Wherever possible, a commitment to multilateralism and liberalism would be sustained, but in addition there would be a complement of subsidiary agreements to cover trade in sectors where adherence to liberalism has proved impossible (e.g., steel, agriculture, and semiconductors).

Applying concepts introduced and discussed earlier in the chapter to this analysis, what is envisioned is something more than a series of discrete agreements rooted in a kind of *specific* reciprocity. The idea would be to draw together these agreements so that some sort of linkage can be achieved. The existing foundation of the postwar trade regime could facilitate the emergence of a third type of reciprocal cooperation. Neither diffuse (with its implicit asymmetries) nor specific (with its tendencies toward blatant discrimination) but rather linked, sector-specific reciprocity would be promoted. This approach would be multilateral, and it would encourage trading partners to pursue, via negotiations, sector-specific trade policy objectives. No participant could or should expect to maximize fully their objectives in every sector but should be willing to compromise by striking deals within and between sectors to achieve an overarching goal—balanced trade accounts.

Economic cooperation under the aegis of American hegemony could be sustained without effective system-wide sanctions because American leaders were willing to tolerate substantial departures from the unifying principles of liberalization and nondiscrimination while keeping U.S. transgressions of these principles at a minimum. However, a revitalized trade regime based on linked-specific reciprocity would require the creation of system-wide sanctions to apply if agreements are abrogated. Without such sanctions, the advantages of linkage would be seriously diminished, if not eliminated altogether.

The question of whether or not effective sanctions can be negotiated and then subsequently enforced presumes a prior question: Can the policy process for trade in the United States support the revitalization of the trade regime along the lines indicated above? One thing is certain. To see this vision of the trade regime realized, the American policy process would have to function without the support of an ideological commitment to liberalism, which has been pervasive among policymakers, particularly those of the executive branch. These policymakers would have to acknowledge that liberalism is not universally applicable and in certain sectors may not offer the best policy prescription for the United States. What sort of impact would such an admission have on the policy process currently in place?

It is true that the policy process instituted in the 1930s and 1940s functioned initially without anywhere near unanimous endorsement for liberalism among the relevant policymakers. Institutionalization of the policy process was facilitated by astute administrators who had a clear vision of what they wanted to accomplish through the Trade Agreements Program and a pragmatic appreciation of the political environment in which they operated. No doubt the context within which they administered this program—severe economic crisis and the very high negotiating base provided by the Smoot-Hawley Tariff Act—aided their efforts, but without a coherent framework for action these contextual opportunities could easily have been lost.

Support for liberalism in trade grew as a result of the experience of the Great Depression and the success of the Trade Agreements Program; it reached its zenith as the United States attained the apex of its power as economic hegemon. Once entrenched, the commitment to liberalism worked to quell the urge to protectionism that arose as U.S. economic predominance waned. The commitment to liberalism, however, has also meant that the significant departures from liberalism have been made for political, not economic, reasons. (From a liberal perspective, there are few economic rationales for such departures.) Therefore, digressions from liberalism typically appear idiosyncratic, and they have seldom achieved their ostensible economic goals. Instead, digressions from liberalism have served, somewhat ironically, as the bulwark of liberalism against a rising tide of protectionist sentiment.

Attempts to instill more systematization into the application of protectionism have come from Congress. Its efforts over the years to relax the criteria under which beleaguered domestic producers could qualify for relief from imports under escape clause, antidumping, or countervailing duty provisions (discretionary or procedural protection) are examples. Members of the executive branch have resisted this trend. What would happen if these same officials were now to abandon their commitment to liberalism? The answer to this question depends on whether or not their departure from strict adherence to liberal principles is packaged into a coherent and consistent framework for action.

Even so equipped, a retreat from liberalism risks policy-making turmoil. First, the announced retreat, presumably couched in the logic of managed trade, would signal lobbyists of beleaguered domestic producers to redouble their efforts to secure legislated protection—a kind of protection that policymakers have successfully resisted for fifty years.[17] For the existing trade policy process to continue, the president would still be compelled to veto any such legislation passed by Congress. The justification for the veto, however, would be made on grounds other than liberal principles. To sustain the integrity of the trade policy process, the president would have to argue effectively that a retreat from liberalism does not herald a return to indiscriminate protectionism. Rather, it marks a new era of commercial policy in service to some developed scheme of

---

17. Congress has passed such bills in the past—quota bills for textiles, for example—but Congress always fails to override the president's veto on these occasions.

managed trade. Whether this would be sufficient to sustain any number of vetoes of crudely protectionist trade bills largely depends on the success of managed trade.

In addition, a retreat from liberalism by the United States could precipitate a movement away from international cooperation by our trading partners. There would certainly be profound skepticism that the foundation for international cooperation in trade could be something other than liberalism supported widely in principle and to varying degrees in practice. Transcending such skepticism would depend largely on the ability of the American policy process to deliver coherent managed trade policy and to provide the executive with sufficiently broad negotiating authority to make the prospect of a more results oriented trade regime a feasible one. The issue of the viability of managed trade in the context of the U.S. policy process is, therefore, central to this discussion.

The concept of managed trade may have more inherent economic soundness than did the cost-of-production equalization formula in the 1920s, but from an administrative standpoint managed trade is very reminiscent of the scientific tariff making of the earlier period. Advocates of managed trade include proponents of strategic trade policy who argue that in industries where abnormal profits (rents) exist or when externalities such as exorbitant research and development costs are an essential feature of production, subsidization or protection by government could yield a better outcome for domestic producers in an international marketplace than free trade can (Krugman, 1984, 1986; Spencer, 1986; Borrus, Tyson, and Zysman, 1986; Tyson, 1992).

The political problems associated with creating and implementing the policy of managed trade are enormous. Among these problems, establishing a criteria under which industries or sectors could be eligible for government subsidies or protection under the rubric of managed trade looms large.

If the lessons of the scientific tariff-making experiment of the 1920s can serve as guide, any set of criteria can be tightened or relaxed by the legislature or manipulated by administrators to yield a politically expedient result. Besides, in the context of the American political system and the trade policy process in particular, the definition and purpose of managed trade could easily become distorted so that the concept becomes nothing more than a rationalization for protectionism or for economic nationalism. This potential development also has a historical antecedent in the 1920s. In its day, the cost-of-production equalization formula worked as a rationalization for supporting a policy of protectionism long after the accepted economic rationale (i.e., the infant industry argument) had any relevance.

Vestiges of the failed scientific tariff-making experiment of the 1920s remain today as fixtures of the American trade policy process. For example, the International Trade Commission (ITC, formerly the Tariff Commission), upon petition, determines which industries qualify for procedural/discretionary protection. The economic benefits of discretionary protection are suspect, but its political benefits cannot be questioned. The ITC, an institutional vestige of a failed policy from the 1920s, contributes to the insulation of the policy process from the pressures for protection from particularistic interests.

Since discretionary protection served a broader goal, enabling the United States to pursue a liberal trade policy, its economic soundness/effectiveness did not matter. However, for managed trade to work as an alternative to liberalism the issue of its economic effectiveness is pivotal. If managed trade is seriously considered as an alternative (or even as a supplement) to liberalism, it matters tremendously whether the policy process in place can produce and administer coherent and effective managed trade policy. And if it cannot, how it can be made to do so? Anyone interested in forging international cooperation through managed trade must come to the task prepared to address these contingencies.

Serious consideration of a results-oriented trade regime has been put on hold by the successful completion of the Uruguay Round. In 1986 the vision for the Uruguay Round put forth in the Punta del Este declaration was to expand the scope of the trade regime by securing an exchange of concessions between the industrial and less developed member states. The industrial countries would liberalize trade in agriculture and textiles, thereby benefiting the less developed countries (LDCs); in return, the LDCs would open their markets to providers of services and capital and establish better protection for intellectual property. In addition, the Uruguay Round aimed to enhance rule enforcement within the trade regime. Despite lengthy delays and serious misgivings that it could be realized, the strategy of the "grand compromise" that the Uruguay Round represented ultimately worked.

In some important respects the trade agreement reached at the culmination of the Uruguay Round aims to resuscitate the trade regime along lines broader than but nevertheless reminiscent of the original GATT. It represents commitment to liberalization through multilateralism and non-discrimination in the trade of services as well as goods. In the context of a broader domain, negotiators were able to commit anew to diffuse reciprocity without the attendant asymmetries that characterized cooperation in trade under the aegis of American hegemony.

Is the American policy process likely to continue to support the de-

sign for cooperation in trade embodied in the Uruguay Round? Precedent weighs in its favor. In terms of American obligations, the agreement
is similar to the original GATT, the contours of which were shaped to
accommodate the exigencies of the trade policy process in the United
States. Precedent, however, also cuts the other way. Early on, the United
States proved unable to abide by the discipline of either the escape clause
or the grievance procedures adopted as part of the original GATT. The
emergence of Voluntary Export Restraints (VERs) or Voluntary Restraint
Agreements (VRAs) and the eventual breakdown of GATT grievance procedures resulted.

These developments helped to safeguard the integrity of the trade
policy process in the United States. Could this same policy process tolerate a return to the discipline of strengthened grievance and enforcement
procedures? Several factors weigh in favor of an affirmative answer to
this question. First, as a result of successfully negotiating the agreement,
policymakers in the executive branch can herald the international resur-
gence of liberalism in trade. This "ideological edge" contributed to the
president's ability to secure the agreement's approval by Congress under
provisions of his "fast track" negotiating authority and should contribute
to his ability to see vetoes sustained if and when Congress attempts to
legislate protection. Second, the policy repertoire permitted by the post-
1930s trade policy process, coupled with the internationalization of the
postwar economy, has changed the nature and composition of constituent
demands on the legislature in this issue area.

A general descriptive comparison of the policy repertoires of the
pre- and post-1930s trade policy processes might characterize the earlier
process as designed to produce legislated protectionism, while the contemporary process is designed to promote liberalization in trade. This fundamental difference means that each elicits distinct responses from constituents. In the contemporary era, therefore, the policy process for trade
no longer predominantly attracts constituents seeking higher levels of
protection, as was the case in the earlier period. Today the policy process
attracts a broad range of beneficiaries of liberalization as well. Moreover,
liberalization of American trade policy contributed significantly to the
internationalization of the economy, which in turn increased the number
of economic actors benefiting from liberalism and continued liberalization
(Milner, 1988).

A recommitment to liberalism and the more diversified policy demands
of an internationalized economy will help to sustain the integrity of the
American trade policy process in the context of the reconstituted trade
regime. Efforts to augment the competitiveness of the American economy would also improve the chances for success. The substance of these

efforts and their point of origin, the government or the private sector, are keenly debated issues that go beyond the scope of this chapter. However, improved competitiveness, regardless of vehicle, would increase the likelihood that the American policy process will continue to support nonhegemonic cooperation in trade.

Conclusion: Reciprocity, International Cooperation, Regimes, and the American Trade Policy Process

The Economist (September 22–28, 1990) has labeled reciprocity to achieve free trade "economic nonsense" but "terribly useful" nevertheless. These comments must be understood in the context of the logic of economic analysis concerning the benefits of free trade coupled with the wry recognition that the economist's unit of analysis is seldom the nation-state. Economic analysis dating back to Adam Smith and David Ricardo demonstrates the economic benefits (in almost every instance) of free trade, even when the policy is practiced unilaterally.[18]

Political calculations about free trade identify risks and short-term costs as well as benefits. Adjusting to free trade can bring economic hardship, social instability, and political repercussions as dislocated voters cast their ballots on election day. Moreover, in an international environment where states remain the dominant, if not exclusive, actors, calculations about political power between or among actors remain important as leaders consider foreign economic policy options. In this political context, the concept and practice of reciprocity allow political leaders to pursue the benefits of a more open global economy while sharing the risks associated with such openness.

Diffuse reciprocity, implemented under GATT via the principles of liberalization, nondiscrimination, and multilateralism, enabled political actors to approximate what economists had long envisioned. What emerged was not the harmony of the "invisible hand" but a regime created for the purpose of promoting international cooperation in trade. This was achieved under the aegis of American leadership but only because the policy process for trade in the United States could support American participation in the trade regime. The scope and dynamic of the trade policy process set the limits of American participation in the trade regime, which in turn shaped the evolution of GATT. Interestingly, GATT exerted its own, albeit subtle, influence on the trade policy process.

As the Uruguay Round demonstrates, the transition from international

---

18. Proponents of strategic trade would insist on putting a few additions on the short list of exceptions, which includes infant industries and optimal tariffs.

cooperation under the auspices of American hegemony to nonhegemonic cooperation is fraught with difficulties, and there are no guarantees of successful transformation of the trade regime. One thing is certain, however: the arrangement for international cooperation hammered out at the Uruguay Round will have to be supported and sustained by the American trade policy process.

CHAPTER EIGHT

American Political Development and Foreign Economic Policy: The Transformation of the Trade Policy Process, Its Impact and Significance

In recent years, the prevailing wisdom among scholars of the international political economy has been that the United States adopted a policy of trade liberalization in the post–World War II period because, as the dominant power in the world economy, it was in the economic and political interest of the United States to do so. This study has not challenged the calculation of state interests put forth by the system-level explanation of trade liberalization. It has challenged, however, the presumption of inevitability inherent in this school of thought. Relying on this explanation alone it is impossible to account satisfactorily for the lag between the emergence of the United States as the preeminent power in the world economy and its adoption of liberal trade policy.

The economic metamorphosis that saw agrarian America transformed into an industrial superpower in the late nineteenth century necessarily altered the relationship between domestic interests and the world economy. Yet the policy that mediated this relationship remained fundamentally unchanged because the existing policy process could not accommodate a policy of trade liberalization. The range of commercial policy options afforded by this process was very narrow. The structural predisposition of Congress to logroll, coupled with the nature of the issue and the resultant interest group pressure, inevitably produced a policy consisting of numerous specific tariffs, high enough to choke off any significant foreign competition. American political institutions unfortunately lacked the insulating mechanisms that would enable policymakers to discriminate among interests and pursue a more liberal trade policy.

Trade liberalization required an alternative trade policy process. Policymakers in the legislative and executive branches of government had to find an effective way (or ways), in the context of the existing constitutional order, to insulate the policy process from the pressures of particularistic interests. Four types of alternatives were available to policymakers and in the first decades of the twentieth century, and three of the four were tried. The dynamics of institutional change (understood as a process of social learning), however, yielded results that only imperfectly reflected the specific policy-making alternatives championed by reform advocates.

This study's focus on organizational interrelationships, patterns of institutional relations, the process of institutional change, and the implications of all the above for international cooperation in trade mark its contribution to the literature on trade and policy-making in the United States. This literature includes the now classic books by E. E. Schattschneider (1935) and Raymond A. Bauer, Ithiel de Sola Pool, and Lewis A. Dexter (1963), as well as the work of Robert A. Pastor (1980), I. M. Destler (1992) and Sharyn O'Halloran (1994).[1]

Schattschneider's *Politics, Pressure, and the Tariff* (1935) captures, like no work before or since, the pattern of institutional relations or modus operandi of the traditional, uninsulated trade policy process of the pre-1934 period, while Pastor (1980) makes interesting and insightful observations about how the post-1934 trade policy process works. Each analysis is circumscribed by the parameters of the policy process it considers. Neither investigates the dynamics of institutional change that so dramatically altered the politics of trade during this century.

In contrast, Bauer, Pool, and Dexter's *American Business and Public Policy* (1963) is about trade politics in transition, and in that sense its concerns more closely parallel those of this study. Their book covers the pivotal decade of the 1950s, when Congress worked to redefine its role in the trade policy process. The authors analyze the influence of interest groups on members of Congress and on policy-making. Although they view their work as in the tradition of Schattschneider, they reach markedly different conclusions about interest group influence on trade policy-making. They speculate that the "change in procedures for the handling of tariff making may account in great part for the difference in the picture painted by us and that painted by so competent a scholar as Schattschneider" (1963, p. 455). They explore the ramifications of the change in procedures, but unlike this study, they do not address how or why the change occurred.

Explicitly addressing the Bauer, Pool, and Dexter case study, Theodore Lowi (1964) attempts to answer the "why" question in his very influential "American Business, Public Policy, Case Studies, and Political Theory." In this article, Lowi introduces his policy typology (distributive, regulatory, and redistributive) and suggests that each policy type elicits a certain

---

1. This list is hardly exhaustive. However, it does include major works on the subject of trade and trade policy-making that have yet to be commented on in this volume.

type of politics. When tariff policy ceased to be infinitely disaggregative (the hallmark of distributive policy), it became regulatory policy. This happened when trade policy attained importance as an instrument of international politics. Lowi posits, moreover, that this evolution in policy called forth one in the politics of trade policy-making: "As the process of redefinition took place, a number of significant shifts in power relations took place as well because it was no longer possible to deal with each dutiable item in isolation" (p. 699).

What this study clearly demonstrates is that Lowi's analysis "puts the cart before the horse," so to speak. The United States undoubtedly needed regulatory policy in trade (i.e., a policy that could discriminate among interests) long before it had the politics to support and sustain such a policy. Institutional change had to precede policy change, not vice versa. Politics, therefore, does not fully derive from the nature of policy.

An appreciation of the role and importance of policy-making processes and institutional arrangements is reflected in the work of Destler (1992) and O'Halloran (1994). Destler's is a comprehensive study of post-1934 trade policy-making. He too notes the shift in policy-making that began with the 1934 Trade Agreements Act. Destler notes that unlike the pre-1934 policy process, the post-1934 process is characterized by Congressional delegation to the president the authority to negotiate agreements with international trading partners. Destler is not particularly interested in how the policy-making shift occurred, but he does credit the post-1934 policy-making process with enabling the United States to escape rampant protectionism and to pursue trade liberalization in the context of an international trade regime.

Destler's central concern is what he sees as the erosion of the post-1934 policy process and the implications of such erosion. He traces the deterioration of the post-1934 trade policy process to, among other things, the very success of the process itself, which can be measured in terms of the near-elimination of tariffs as a trade barrier. The delegation-centered nature of the post-1934 trade policy process is less well equipped to deal with nontariff barriers to trade. Destler also argues that the post-1934 policy process is eroding because of changes in the global economy and the position of the United States in it. In his book, Destler not only considers the causes and effects of erosion, but he also considers the prospects for salvaging the trade system.

In contrast to Destler, O'Halloran (1994) challenges the presidential focus of what she labels the delegation model of trade policy-making. She endorses instead a Congress-centered model for understanding American trade policy over time. From this perspective, Congress has never abdicated its role in trade policy-making. Rather, Congress and Congressional politics determine trade policy. To evince her argument, O'Halloran examines how Congressional organizations and internal operational details of the House and Senate, as well as procedural arrangements designed and delimited by Congress to implement legislation over the years, have shaped policy. In this light, Congressional delegation of negotiating authority to the president does not indicate that Congress had lost or surrendered its control of trade policy to the executive branch. Instead, Congress has never surrendered control of trade policy; even as it delegates, Congress crafts procedures to ensure that legislators' preferences are reflected in policy.

This study represents neither a president-dominant nor a Congress-focused approach to understanding the evolution of American trade policy. It emphasizes patterns of *interorganizational relations* that define the essential character of policy-making and thus delimit a range of policy options. It also focuses on institutional change, the dynamic and nuanced process whereby these patterns are transformed over time.

The Institutional Requisites of Trade Liberalization

Woodrow Wilson, Theodore Roosevelt, Robert La Follette, William Culbertson, and Cordell Hull, among others, recognized the impediments to policy reform posed by existing institutional arrangements for trade policy-making. While each of these policymakers understood the nature of the problem, each promoted a different solution. Woodrow Wilson interpreted the tariff reform problem as symptomatic of a system-wide dearth of responsible government. He envisioned a policy process for trade (and for most issues) whereby party discipline and commitment to a stated platform would replace tariff rate setting via the logroll. This solution would have required members of Congress to give up their traditional prerogative of serving the particularistic interests of localities through the doling out of tariffs. Advocates of the independent commission as solution suggested that Congress surrender its rate setting prerogatives altogether. Robert La Follette and Theodore Roosevelt, for example, sought to establish an independent commission of experts that would determine tariff rates according to some predetermined criteria. Cordell Hull also championed a trade policy process that required Congress to remove itself from the task of rate-setting. Under his power-sharing approach, Congress would delegate rate-setting authority to the president, who would then negotiate tariff rate reductions in the context of international trade agreements.

Each type of alternative (party, commission, power sharing) entailed altering existing patterns of behavior within a setting of organizational interrelationships, and each required officials in positions of authority to surrender cherished prerogatives. The extent to which officials proved willing to surrender these prerogatives in the context of trade policy-making depended, at least in part, on their assessments of the costs and benefits of the proposed change for their personal positions within the institution. These assessments were, in turn, informed by their perceptions of the success or failure of existing policy.

The components of the process of institutional change (individuals armed with solutions derived from cognitive frameworks, organizational interrelationships, and policy success or failure) did not remain constant. The reforms attempted in one period altered the universe of policy options available in the next. They also altered organizational interrelationships. New organizations and new prerogatives figured prominently in subsequent attempts at policy-making reform. Institutional change resulted when new patterns of institutional relations supplanted the old ones and new policy processes were established.

This conceptualization of institutional change sheds light on why policymakers pursued the kind of changes they did. An ardent advocate of free trade, Cordell Hull, for example, understood the limitations of the traditional policy process in this regard. He also understood the inadequacies of the previously attempted alternatives to the traditional trade policy process. His power-sharing alternative was, in a real sense, the product of years of failed attempts to redirect American commercial policy.

Viewing institutional change as a process of "bounded" social learning is critical to understanding why the changes sought were seldom wholly achieved. "Scientific" tariff-making in the 1920s never did "take the tariff out of politics" as anticipated by advocates of the commission alternative. Under the trade policy process established by the Fordney-McCumber Act in 1922, appropriate tariff rates were determined by an independent commission of experts, but the decision to act on the determination was the president's. Under the provisions of Section 315 of the 1922 act, the decision to alter tariff rates by up to 50 percent was ultimately the president's. Although the president's role in rate setting clearly compromised the progressives' vision of a policy process that removed the tariff from the vicissitudes of politics, it was a necessary accommodation to opponents who challenged the constitutionality of the delegation by Congress of its authority to tax. While there was no precedent to support the delegation of this authority to an independent commission, there was precedent for delegating it to the president.

The Trade Agreements Act of 1934 provides another example of changes sought but imperfectly realized. The Roosevelt administration originally sought trade agreements legislation with no specified time limit to the president's rate adjustment authority. The administration bill was amended to include a three-year (renewable) limit to the president's negotiating authority. Periodically renewing the trade agreements program gave Congress the opportunity to explore new legislative options in trade policy-making. These options permitted Congress to respond to the pressures of interest groups without legislating tariffs. Although unanticipated by Secretary Hull and his cohort, the periodic renewals of the president's negotiating authority and the new options thereby afforded Congress worked to facilitate the institutionalization of an insulated trade policy process.

Finally, this view of institutional change as a bounded and accretionary process of social learning serves to flag the impact on policy of the successive and cumulative attempts to alter the trade policy process. The peril point provision, first incorporated into the Trade Agreements Extension Act of 1951, for example, was a direct descendant of the scientific tariff experiment of the 1920s. It worked in the context of the power-sharing alternative to limit the scope of American tariff concessions at multilateral trade negotiations. More generally, the Tariff Commission (now the International Trade Commission), the vestige of the 1920s attempt to insulate the trade policy process, permitted development of discretionary protection that became a cornerstone of Congress's redefined role in the trade policy process. Discretionary protection enabled Congress to delimit the parameters of possible trade liberalization without jeopardizing the integrity of the insulated trade policy process.

Without insulation of the trade policy process, indiscriminate protectionism was the only possible policy option for the United States. In order to pursue any other course in foreign economic policy, the policy process had to afford officials the ability to discriminate among domestic interests and determine which ones would get protection and which ones would not. Insulation, therefore, was a necessary condition for trade liberalization. It was not, however, a sufficient one. An institutional design that provided insulation would not necessarily sustain a policy of trade liberalization.

Intrinsic to each of the alternative policy processes championed by advocates of tariff-making reform was a strategy for insulating the process from pressures of particularistic interests, but inherent in each was also a strategy for foreign economic policy. Institutional arrangements set the parameters of possible policy options. These parameters are not infinitely elastic; not all policy options fall within the purview of the institutions in place. Because this is the case, it follows that the policy repertoire of existing institutions steers policy in a particular and inevitable direction.

This direction or strategy for policy is inherent in institutional design.

The foreign economic policy strategy inherent in Woodrow Wilson's party alternative was unilateral trade liberalization. This alternative provided no instruments to guarantee reciprocal action by trading partners. Despite historical precedent to the contrary, advocates of this alternative simply assumed that American actions to liberalize its commercial policy would be matched abroad.[2]

The trade policy process of the 1920s was insulated, but unfortunately the commission alternative could not accommodate a foreign economic policy based on negotiation and reciprocity. Embedded in this insulation alternative was an inordinately protectionist policy. What officials like William Culbertson first failed to realize and then later understood was that insulation was useless without instruments to pursue trade liberalization. The power-sharing alternative showcased in the provisions of the Trade Agreements Act (1934) offered both insulation and instruments for trade liberalization. It insulated the trade policy process by relieving Congress of its tariff rate-setting duties, and it delimited a range of foreign economic policy options that accommodated a policy of liberalization through negotiation and reciprocity. The result has been eight completed rounds of multilateral trade negotiations conducted under the auspices of the General Agreement on Tariffs and Trade (GATT, also a by-product of the post-1934 trade policy process). The power-sharing instrumentality that defines the trade policy process provided the vehicle for participating in the Uruguay Round of multilateral trade talks and for negotiating the North American Free Trade Agreement (NAFTA).

NAFTA, the WTO, the American Trade Policy Process, and Prospects for the Future

In many respects NAFTA and the newly established World Trade Organization (WTO) reflect the power-sharing alternative at its evolutionary peak. Congress delegates sweeping authority to the president to negotiate a new multilateral trade agreement, under GATT auspices, that aims to broaden and deepen the rules of the international trade regime. It also authorizes negotiations with Mexico and Canada to determine the terms of an agreement (NAFTA) that will create a continent-wide free trade zone. The negotiations take place under "fast track" authority, a variation

---

2. History has demonstrated that the unilateral actions taken by Great Britain in the 1840s to lower its barriers to trade (e.g., repeal of the Corn Laws) were not reciprocated. The nineteenth century's "Golden Era of Free Trade" began only after Britain negotiated with France to conclude the Cobden-Chevalier Treaty (1860). (See Stein, 1984.)

on the institutional pattern of the power-sharing policy process introduced in 1974.[3] Since their inception, fast-track procedures have yielded
broad-based coalitions in favor of the negotiated agreements. Members
of Congress (although seldom totally satisfied) have found far more in
the agreements—considered "package deals"—to support than to reject,
and trade agreements have been approved by overwhelming majorities.
As it has turned out, however, easy approval proved hardly a foregone
conclusion for either NAFTA or the most recent GATT agreement.

   The coalitions that support NAFTA and GATT—coalitions that included big business and exporters of high-tech and capital goods as
well as agricultural products—were significantly challenged by broad-
based coalitions of detractors. NAFTA, specifically, was opposed by labor
unions, along with environmental organizations, church groups, supporters of Ross Perot ("United We Stand"), and even influential Hispanic
groups. A similarly constituted coalition challenged GATT and its provision to establish the WTO. Not since the charter for the ITO was tabled
during the Truman administration had such coalitions formed in opposition to trade liberalization. But while the fate of the ITO was due largely
to the fact that it exceeded the institutional boundaries of the trade agreements program of the era, the same cannot be said of NAFTA and GATT.
In contrast, both NAFTA and GATT reflected the institutional design that
gave rise to them. Difficulties securing their approval had more to do with
a transformed world economy and the United States' position within it.

   For one thing, the world economy no longer consists simply of trade
flows (namely, trade in goods) between nation-states. It has become far
more integrated and interdependent. Multinational corporations have become truly *trans*national actors who make production and marketing decisions based on internally generated global strategies. The competitive
position of the United States in a number of sectors has declined. With regard to its labor force, the United States, while home to a tier of the most
highly skilled workers in the world, is also home to a growing number of
inadequately skilled and poorly trained individuals.[4] Inevitably, it is the
inadequately skilled who bear a disproportionate share of the adjustment
costs that are a natural consequence of an open economy. In this context,

----

   3. Fast track indeed represents a variation on the power-sharing trade policy process. According to the provisions of the 1934 Trade Agreements Act, Congress specified
a time frame for negotiations and specified the limits of the president's tariff-cutting
authority. The agreements went into force without a vote by Congress. With fast track,
Congress grants largely unspecified authority, but reserves the right to accept or reject
the completed agreement by simple majority.
   4. The scope of this problem was recently underscored by a study revealing that 80
million American adults are functionally illiterate and lack basic computational skills
(see *New York Times*, September 9, 1993.)

it is hardly surprising to find in the United States a substantial number of people and their representatives who believed their interests would not be served by either NAFTA or GATT.

Certain premises about the United States in the world economy guided the early advocates of the power-sharing alternative in their efforts to redesign the American trade policy process. The American trade policy process came to embody these premises, which current economic realities may now challenge. Included among these were: (1) the idea that the United States, with the largest, most technologically advanced economy and the most highly skilled, well-educated labor force in the world, would benefit tremendously from trade liberalization; (2) the recognition that the benefits of liberalization, however great and however widely diffused throughout the economy, would not accrue equally to all economic actors; and (3) the expectation that if (and only if) a policy process could be crafted that prevented the dissatisfied (and presumably small) minority from sabotaging the interests of the overwhelming majority, the benefits of liberalization could be realized. The fact of the matter is that the dissatisfied minority has grown considerably. People in significant numbers are becoming convinced that increased liberalization will deliver more in terms of job loss and economic disruption (i.e., adjustment costs) than job creation and new markets. Hence, we begin to understand why securing approval for NAFTA proved so difficult and why GATT became such a lightning rod for popular debate.

It might be argued that the problems associated with NAFTA specifically had more to do with the specifics of the agreement and the very divergent economic profiles of its signatories than with a growing reluctance to pursue increased liberalization. It is true that the disparate levels of economic development of the United States and Canada, on the one hand, and Mexico on the other fueled claims that NAFTA would precipitate massive job flight to Mexico. Other issues peculiar to NAFTA (e.g., environmental protection) also galvanized opposition to it. Nevertheless, the fact of the matter is that NAFTA was not the only major trade liberalization initiative since the successful completion of the Tokyo Round to encounter serious opposition.

Despite annual exhortations of support by the leaders of the G-7, the Uruguay Round of multilateral trade negotiations remained stalled for years. American negotiators had taken unwavering positions on agricultural subsidies and on issues relating to trade in services. The steadfast position of American negotiators underscores their understanding that Congressional approval would ultimately hinge on securing broad-based support for the agreement. Such support would have been a sure bet a few decades ago. It isn't any longer. The opposition to NAFTA and the

Uruguay Round trade agreement (finally concluded in December 1993 and approved by the U.S. Congress a year later) may indicate that, given the transformed status of the United States in the world economy, the bent toward liberalization that has characterized American trade policy for over fifty years can no longer suffice. The United States may require a policy process for trade that can deliver more.

Indeed, integral to the institutional design of the power-sharing alternative for trade policy-making is a strategy of trade liberalization.[5] Over the years, Congress has tried to regulate and to modify this strategy. In fact, it is around these tasks that Congress has redefined its role in the trade policy process.[6] The issue for the future is whether the strategy inherent in the existing institutional design can be sufficiently modified to meet the economic policy needs of the United States in a changed international economic environment.

The history of American foreign economic policy offers lessons for modern policymakers. In the 1890s, for example, Secretary of State James G. Blaine tried to modify (through reciprocity agreements) the indiscriminate and inevitably protectionist policy of the uninsulated policy process. He was minimally successful at first with the reciprocity provisions of the McKinley Act (1890). The denouement of his efforts, however, was ostensible failure. None of the reciprocity treaties (Kasson treaties) negotiated under provisions of the Dingly Act (1897) were ratified. The uninsulated policy process could not accommodate a trade policy based on reciprocity; the need for altering the pattern of institutional relationships was clearly manifest.

The current situation is reminiscent of but more complicated than that faced by policymakers in the 1890s. The policy-making question is the same: Can the institutional arrangements for foreign economic policy-making be modified to meet new demands? As noted above, however, the context is drastically different—American economic power has declined relative to some of its major trading partners. In addition, world trade

5. This has once again been made evident by the announced intention to seek a free trade pact with the countries of the Pacific Rim and to extend NAFTA to include the countries of Latin America.

6. It is in this context that the deal struck between President Bill Clinton and Senator Robert Dole (R., Kansas) in order to secure Dole's endorsement for the trade agreement can best be understood. President Clinton agreed to appoint a five-member commission, made up of appellate judges, to review unfavorable rulings of the WTO. If within a five-year period, this commission finds three of these rulings to be unfair or otherwise unjustified, the Congress can initiate U.S. withdrawal from the WTO. Although the trade agreement contains a provision that any member can withdraw with six-months notice, the presumption had been that the decision to withdraw was exclusively the president's. With this arrangement, Congress secures a role in trade regime exit procedures.

has been conducted under a trade regime (GATT) largely the product of American postwar economic preeminence. The challenge a hundred years ago was to dismantle protectionism and to promote trade expansion through trade policy liberalization. The challenge today is to recast foreign economic policy into a larger policy context in which seemingly unrelated issues like trade, education, defense conversion, export promotion, and research/development are woven together to form a comprehensive strategy for promoting American interests in an increasingly competitive and interdependent global economy. The old debate pitting protectionists against free traders has lost much of its salience in the new world economy. This larger context clearly extends beyond what has been traditionally defined as trade policy, and it would probably require serious pursuit of industrial policy.[7]

American policymakers are only beginning to think about the meaning and implications of industrial policy. For most, their ideas have yet to congeal into coherent frameworks for action. While the work of scholars (turned policymakers) Robert Reich (1991) and Laura D'Andrea Tyson (1992)[8] may help to clarify the issues and to identify goals regarding industrial policy, policymakers in both the executive and legislative branches need to appreciate the institutional context within which policy is made. Policymakers need to couch their ideas about desirable policy into pragmatic assessments of the interorganizational dynamics of policy-making. With regard to trade specifically, they must modify the liberal strategy inherent in the power-sharing policy process without destroying the prospects for sustained international cooperation.

Liberalism Waning? Reconsidering Business-Government Relations in the United States

It is impossible to predict how the economic challenges of the next century will be met. This study does, however, enable the analyst to understand the dynamics and appreciate the complexities of the situation. Modifying the existing policy process is problematic. Ostensibly, one would attribute tremendous flexibility to the power-sharing process. Congress can tinker in any number of ways with the criteria for discretionary protection. Some suggest (e.g., Kuttner, 1990, 1991) however,

---

7. Because it means different things to different people, "industrial policy" is difficult to define precisely. Advocates of industrial policy, however, are united in their belief that direct government intervention in specific industries could improve their economic performance in a highly competitive global economy.

8. Reich serves as President Clinton's secretary of labor, and Tyson chaired the Council of Economic Advisers.

that such protection has been ineffective because of the pervasiveness of laissez-faire thinking among policymakers. This could very well be part of the problem. But it may be the case that liberalism, endemic to the power-sharing design, is immutable.

This may explain, at least in part, why the United States came to rely on voluntary export restraint agreements to modify its liberal trade policy. It also may explain the evolution of the Congressional technique of signaling the president and America's trading partners of its discontent with trade policy by threatening protectionist legislation (Pastor, 1980). These represent adaptive variations on the pattern of institutional relations that has defined the policy process in trade since the 1930s. This process has worked to forge and then, more or less, to sustain the essentially liberal character of American commercial policy.

But it may be the case that the key to sustaining the viability of the power-sharing alternative in the twenty-first century is to reconceptualize its role. In the broader and more complex economic policy context of the next century, the delegation of authority to the president to negotiate the terms for international economic cooperation (the essence of the post-1934 trade policy process) may no longer be considered the central feature— the core—of the policy process. In service to new conceptual frameworks that incorporate trade policy into the larger context of integrated policies for competitiveness in a global economy, the power-sharing alternative could become but one aspect (and perhaps not the defining one) of the interorganizational patterns that would come to characterize the complex of policy processes at work. This vision of future economic policy and policy-making would necessarily entail reassessment of the nature of business-government relations in the United States. Instead of conceptualizing this relationship in adversarial terms, successful economic policy-making of the future may require that a partnership mentality between government and business be forged. Conceptual frameworks that would recast business-government relationships in this way would be very much in the tradition of modern corporatism. Historically, Americans have not thought about politics in corporatist terms. Only during times of war or grave economic crisis (the Great Depression) have Americans entertained the notion that a coordinated business-labor-government partnership might offer a useful approach to policy-making. This negative predisposition toward corporatism may be changing. Increased fascination with industrial policy is leading some to reconsider the benefits of such a partnership. A case in point is the announced collaboration of the Big Three auto makers with the federal government to develop a super-energy-efficient "dream car" (*New York Times*, September 30, 1993).

How might "new thinking" about economic policy and business-

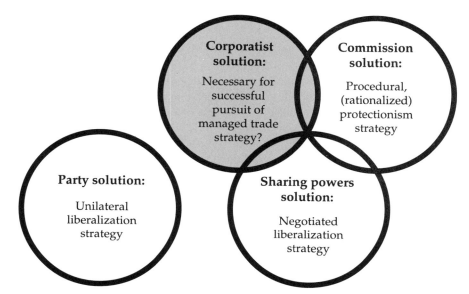

Figure 8.1 The cumulative and reinforcing policy-making reform alternatives and their inherent strategies for foreign economic policy.

government relations affect policy-making? In pondering this question, it is important to remember that the pattern of institutional relations whereby Congress delegates authority to the president to pursue global trade liberalization (power-sharing alternative) has not operated in an institutional or historical vacuum. Vestigial patterns of scientific tariff making have been adapted over time to supplement ongoing liberalization efforts—most recently evident in the agreement struck between President Bill Clinton and Senator Robert Dole (R., Kansas) to appoint a five-judge commission to review WTO rulings. Obviously, the commission alternative did not disappear with the failure of the 1920s policy-making experiment. Studying institutions and institutional change in terms of patterns of interorganizational relations makes clear the implications of this observation. These patterns are not mutually exclusive; overlapping, reinforcing, redundant, and even contradictory patterns can exist and operate simultaneously. One might envision, therefore, the development of other institutions, so conceived, to supplement the power-sharing alternative. In the scenario being postulated here, new patterns of interorganizational relations could be created that would enable the instrumentality of the power-sharing alternative to serve other visions of economic policy and international economic cooperation (Fig. 8.1).

Institutional Change as an Ongoing Process

This study has demonstrated the importance of institutional design to the process of trade liberalization. It is the institutional dimension of trade liberalization that explains why it took the United States, a state of unprecedented economic power, so long to move toward liberalization. Institutional design also helps explain why the United States has not abandoned liberalism in the face of a decline in its relative economic status. Economic power of whatever proportion does not automatically translate into commercial policy. The political institutions must be capable of producing the "appropriate" policy. Moreover, once the political process is producing "appropriate" policies, the distribution of power may shift, leaving the process to produce now-anachronistic policies.

This study, with its focus on institutional arrangements, policy processes, and institutional change, provides a particularly useful vantage point from which to consider the recent interest in "reinventing government."[9] The notion challenges Americans to rethink the role or mission of government and to reconceptualize how government goes about fulfilling this mission. And it is in this context that the idea of reinventing government is quite germane. In a very real sense, this is a study about the process of reinventing government—creating new patterns of inter-organizational relationships in order to produce new policies. What this study does, in effect, is to deepen appreciation for what it really means to reinvent government.

Popularized versions of the notion have underscored the importance of new thinking about government and its role vis-à-vis the society it serves. What is less clear from the popular assessments and their recommendations is how new ideas become manifest in government and in policy-making. The problem does not go unrecognized by those who endorse new thinking about government: "The lessons are there. . . . Yet few of our leaders are listening. . . . This is perhaps our greatest stumbling block: the power of outdated ideas" (Osborne and Gaebler, 1992, p. 23). In this regard, John Maynard Keynes once observed, "the difficulty lies not so much in developing new ideas as in escaping from old ones" (quoted in Osborne and Gaebler, 1992, p. 23). What advocates of reinventing government seldom explore is the process of escape. As the present study demonstrates, this process is particularly problematic when the ideas are embedded in the institutional arrangements of established policy processes.

9. The book that popularized the notion is *Reinventing Government: How the Entrepreneurial Spirit Is Transforming the Public Sector* by David Osborne and Ted Gaebler (1992).

Reinvention in the context of a stable institutional framework does not presume "starting from scratch." It presumes that existing patterns of interorganizational relationships can be altered to accommodate, to make room for, to superimpose, or otherwise to inject these new ideas into or onto the established framework. Because institutions structure a "universe of opportunities, risks, incentives, and constraints"[10] for actors in the political system, they circumscribe individual and group actions by determining their political resources and by influencing their conception of their own self-interest. Policy outcomes are therefore inextricably linked to institutional design. Consequently, if government is to be reinvented, if new ideas are to be manifested in policy, institutional change is usually required.

With regard to American foreign economic policy, the old commitment to protectionism could not be rooted out of American policy unless and until the institutional arrangements for trade policy-making were altered. The process of reinvention, here understood as a process of institutional change, witnessed the old instrumentality of tariff rate setting by Congress replaced by the new one of presidential rate setting in the context of international negotiations. Over time, the institutionalized instrumentality of the post-1934 trade policy process evolved beyond negotiating tariff rates. Today, as NAFTA and the latest GATT agreement demonstrate, the president has considerable latitude to negotiate terms of access to the American market.

Interestingly, however, for all of its significance for American trade policy and for post–World War II international economic cooperation, the power-sharing alternative did not fundamentally alter government's role vis-à-vis the economy. Power sharing in foreign economic policy-making is very much in keeping with the "arms-length" approach to economic management that has generally prevailed in the United States. Viewed at this basic level, the power-sharing alternative is not all that different from its nineteenth-century predecessor. Both policy processes placed the government in essentially a gatekeeper role. Granted, the nineteenth-century policy process kept the gate that controlled access to the American market effectively closed, and the power-sharing alternative has worked to keep the gate open. Still, American policymakers have yet to move beyond this gatekeeper mentality when they debate foreign economic policy and the appropriate role of government in this regard.

The challenge for the next century may be to reconceptualize the role of government relative to the world economy beyond the gatekeeper notion. Indeed, such reconceptualization may have already begun. As has been

10. A phrase coined by Stephen Skowronek.

noted, business-government partnerships are now being cultivated. More generally, there is a growing appreciation that government can affect the ability of private actors to compete in the world economy in positive ways. But whatever new thinking emerges, whatever new ideas are generated, reinventing government in this or any other policy context will inevitably involve institutional change.

It is impossible to predict how such a process of reinvention would unfold. All that can be said with certainty is that policymakers today, like their counterparts of a hundred years ago, must confront new economic realities; and, also like their nineteenth-century counterparts, they will assess these realties in the context of established institutional arrangements. Meanwhile, as long as protectionist legislation is rejected, episodes of Congressional posturing in this regard will simply be deemed additional demonstrations of established practice under the existing policy process. If, however, blatantly protectionist bills are enacted or if efforts to promote trade liberalization languish, one thing is certain—international cooperation in trade would be seriously strained. Policy failures of the magnitude of the defeat of NAFTA or Congressional rejection of the GATT agreement of the Uruguay round have been averted. But even defeats of this magnitude or legislated protection would probably not herald the demise of the post-1934 trade policy process. However, they would certainly usher in a period of uncertainty in which the institutional arrangements for trade policy-making would be challenged and redefined.

Adams, Brooks. 1900. *America's Economic Supremacy*. New York: Macmillan.

Aggarwal, Vinod K. 1985. *Liberal Protectionism: The International Politics of Organized Textile Trade*. Berkeley: University of California Press.

Anderson, Donald F. 1973. *William Howard Taft: A Conservative's Conception of the Presidency*. Ithaca, N.Y.: Cornell University Press.

Anderson, J. 1980. *Cognitive Psychology and Its Implications*. San Francisco: Freeman.

Ashworth, William A. 1952. *A Short History of the International Economy*. London: Longmans, Green.

Avery, William P., and David P. Rapkin, eds. 1982. *America in a Changing World Political Economy*. New York: Longman.

Axelrod, Robert. 1981. "The Emergence of Cooperation among Egoists." *American Political Science Review* 75:306–18.

———. 1984. *The Economics of Cooperation*. New York: Basic Books.

Bailey, Stephen K. 1966. *The New Congress*. New York: St. Martin's Press.

Baker, Ray Stannard. 1937. *Woodrow Wilson: Life and Letters*. Vol. 6. Garden City, N.Y.: Doubleday, Doran.

———. 1946. *Woodrow Wilson: Life and Letters*. Vol. 3. New York: Charles Scribner's Sons.

Balasa, Bela, ed. 1967. *Studies in Trade Liberalization: Problems and Prospects for the Industrialized Countries*. Baltimore: Johns Hopkins University Press.

Ball, George W. 1982. *The Past Has Another Pattern: Memoirs*. New York: W. W. Norton.

Bartlett, C. J., ed. 1969. *Britain Pre-Eminent: Studies of British World Influence in the Nineteenth Century*. London: Macmillan.

Bartlett, Randall. 1973. *Economic Foundations of Political Power*. London: The Free Press.

Bauer, Raymond A., Ithiel de Sola Pool, and Lewis A. Dexter. 1963. *American Business and Public Policy: The Politics of Foreign Trade*. New York: Atherton Press.

Beard, Charles A. 1935. *The Open Door at Home: A Trial Philosophy of National Interest*. New York: Macmillan.

Becker, William H. 1982. *The Dynamics of Business-Government Relations: Industry and Exports, 1893–1921.* Chicago: University of Chicago Press.

Becker, William H., and Samuel F. Wells, Jr., eds. 1984. *Economics and World Power: An Assessment of American Diplomacy since 1789.* New York: Columbia University Press.

Beckett, Grace. 1941. *The Reciprocal Trade Agreements Program.* New York: Columbia University Press.

Benoit, Emile. 1961. *Europe at Sixes and Sevens: The Common Market, the Free Trade Association, and the United States.* New York: Columbia University Press.

Bergsten, C. Fred. 1971. "Crisis in U.S. Trade Policy." *Foreign Affairs* 49:619–35.

———. 1980. *The International Economic Policy of the United States: Selected Papers of C. Fred Bergsten, 1977–1979.* Lexington, Mass.: D. C. Heath.

———, ed. 1973. *The Future of the International Economic Order: An Agenda for Research.* Lexington, Mass.: D. C. Heath.

Bhagwati, Jagdish. 1991. *The World Trading System at Risk.* Princeton, N.J.: Princeton University Press.

Bidwell, Percy W. 1933. "Tariff Policy of the United States: A Study of Recent Experience." Paper presented at the Second International Studies Conference on the State and Economic Life, London, May 29–June 2.

———. 1938. *Our Trade with Britain: Bases for a Reciprocal Trade Agreement.* New York: Council on Foreign Relations.

———. 1939. *The Invincible Tariff.* New York: Council on Foreign Relations.

Binkley, Wilfred E. 1962. *President and Congress.* New York: Vintage Books.

Blum, John Morton. 1956. *Woodrow Wilson and the Politics of Morality.* Boston: Little, Brown.

———. 1977. *The Republican Roosevelt.* 2nd ed. Cambridge, Mass.: Harvard University Press.

Borrus, Michael, Laura D'Andrea Tyson, and John Zysman. 1986. "Creating Advantage: How Government Policies Shape International Trade in the Semiconductor Industry." In *Strategic Trade Policy and the New International Economics,* edited by Paul Krugman. Cambridge, Mass.: MIT Press.

Bowers, Claude G. 1932. *Beveridge and the Progressive Era.* Cambridge, Mass.: Houghton Mifflin.

Brandes, Joseph. 1962. *Herbert Hoover and Economic Diplomacy.* Pittsburgh, Pa.: University of Pittsburgh Press.

Brownlee, W. Elliot, Jr. 1974. *Progressivism and Economic Growth: The Wilsonian Income Tax, 1911–1929.* New York: Kennicott Press.

Buell, Raymond Leslie. 1932. "A New Commercial Policy for the United States." Paper presented before the New York Federation of Women's Clubs, New York, September 26.

Bullock, Charles J., John H. Williams, and Rufus S. Tucker. 1919. "Balance of Trade of the United States." *Review of Economic Statistics* 1:215–66.

Calleo, David P. 1982. *The Imperious Economy.* Cambridge, Mass.: Harvard University Press.

Calleo, David P., and Benjamin J. Rowland. 1973. *America and the World Political Economy.* Bloomington: Indiana University Press.

Chalmers, Henry. 1953. *World Trade Policies.* Berkeley: University of California Press.

Chamber of Commerce. 1921. *Referendum, No. 37.* Washington, D.C.: Chamber of Commerce.

Chambers, William N. 1963. *Political Parties in a New Nation; The American Experience 1776–1809.* New York: Oxford University Press.

Chambers, William N., and Walter Dean Burnham, eds. 1967. *The American Party Systems.* New York: Oxford University Press.

Chandler, Alfred D., Jr. 1962. *Strategy and Structure: Chapters in the History of the Industrial Enterprise.* Cambridge, Mass.: MIT Press.

Cheh, John H. 1974. "United States Concessions in the Kennedy Round and Short-Run Labor Adjustment Costs." *Journal of International Economics* 4:323–40.

Cobden, W. M. 1971. *The Theory of Protection.* Oxford: Oxford University Press.

Cohen, Benjamin J., ed. 1968. *American Foreign Economic Policy.* New York: Harper and Row.

Cohen, Stephen D. 1971. *The Making of U.S. International Economic Policy: Principles, Problems, and Proposals for Reform.* New York: Praeger.

Cohen, Stephen D., and Ronald I. Meltzer. 1982. *United States International Economic Policy in Action: Diversity of Decision-Making.* New York: Praeger.

Congressional Record. 1883–. Washington, D.C.

Conybeare, John A. C. 1984. "Public Goods, Prisoners' Dilemmas, and the International Political Economy." *International Studies Quarterly* 28:5–22.

Cooper, Richard, ed. 1973. *A Reordered World: Emerging International Economic Problems.* Washington, D.C.: Potomac Associates.

Croly, Herbert. 1909. *The Promise of American Life.* New York: Macmillan.

———. 1915. *Progressive Democracy.* New York: Macmillan.

Cuff, Robert D. 1973. *The War Industries Board: Business-Government Relations during World War I.* Baltimore: Johns Hopkins University Press.

Culbertson, William S. 1919. *Commercial Policy in War Time and After.* New York: Appleton and Co.

———. 1937. *Reciprocity: A National Policy for Foreign Trade.* New York: McGraw-Hill.

Curtis, Thomas B., and John Robert Vastine, Jr. 1971. *The Kennedy Round and the Future of American Trade.* New York: Praeger.

Curzon, Gerard, 1974. *Multilateral Commercial Diplomacy: The General Agreement on Tariffs and Trade and Its Impact on National Commercial Policies and Techniques.* New York: Praeger.

Curzon, Gerard, and Victoria Curzon. 1968. *After the Kennedy Round: What Trade Policies Now?* London: Dirching Press.

Cushman, Robert E. 1941. *The Independent Regulatory Commissions.* New York: Oxford University Press.

Dam, Kenneth W. 1970. *The GATT: Law and International Economic Organization.* Chicago: University of Chicago Press.

Davidson, John Wells, ed. 1956. *A Crossroads of Freedom: The 1912 Campaign Speeches of Woodrow Wilson.* New Haven, Conn.: Yale University Press.

Davis, Hugh O. 1942. *America's Trade Equality Policy.* Washington, D.C.: American Council on Public Affairs.

Degler, Carl N. 1977. *The Age of Economic Revolution, 1876–1900.* 2nd ed. Glenview, Ill.: Scott Foresman.

Destler, I. M. 1980. *Making Foreign Economic Policy.* Washington, D.C.: Brookings Institution.

———. 1992. *American Trade Politics*. 2nd ed. Washington, D.C.: Institute for International Economics.

Destler, I. M., and Hideo Sato. 1982. *Coping with U.S.-Japanese Economic Conflicts*. Lexington, Mass.: D. C. Heath.

Destler, I. M., Hideo Sato, Priscilla Clapp, and Haruhiro Fukui. 1976. *Managing an Alliance: The Politics of U.S.-Japanese Relations*. Washington, D.C.: Brookings Institution.

DeWitt, Benjamin Parke. 1915. *The Progressive Movement*. New York: Macmillan.

Diebold, William, Jr. 1952. *The End of the ITO*. Essays in International Finance, no. 16. Princeton, N.J.: Princeton University Press.

———. 1972. *The United States and the Industrial World: American Foreign Economic Policy in the 1970s*. New York: Praeger.

Dobson, John M. 1976. *Two Centuries of Tariffs*. Washington, D.C.: Government Printing Office.

———. 1978. *America's Ascent: The United States Becomes a Great Power, 1880–1914*. DeKalb, Ill.: Northern Illinois University Press.

Dorfman, Joseph. 1949. *The Economic Mind in American Civilization, 1865–1918*. Vol. 3. New York: Viking Press.

Downs, Anthony. 1957. *An Economic Theory of Democracy*. New York: Harper and Row.

Eaton, Amasa M. 1913. *Free Trade versus Protection*. Chicago: A. C. Maclurg.

Eckstein, Harry. 1979. "On the 'Science' of the State." *Daedalus* 108:1–20.

———. 1982. "The Idea of Development: From Dignity to Efficiency." *World Politics* 34:451–86.

Edwards, Richard C. 1970. "Economic Sophistication in Nineteenth Century Congressional Tariff Debates." *Journal of Economic History* 30:802–38.

Elchardus, Mark. 1988. "The Rediscovery of Chronos: The New Role of Time in Sociological Theory." *International Sociology* 3:35–59.

Elster, Jon. 1979. *Ulysses and the Sirens: Studies in Rationality and Irrationality*. New York: Cambridge University Press.

Evans, John W. 1971. *The Kennedy Round in American Trade Policy*. Cambridge, Mass.: Harvard University Press.

Faulkner, Harold V. 1951. *The Decline of Laissez-faire, 1897–1914*. New York: Rinehart.

Feis, Herbert. 1966. *1933: Characters in Crisis*. Boston: Little, Brown.

Fenno, Richard F., Jr. 1973. *Congressmen in Committees*. Boston: Little, Brown.

Ferrell, Robert H. 1957. *American Diplomacy in the Great Depression*. New Haven, Conn.: Yale University Press.

Festinger, L. 1957. *A Theory of Cognitive Dissonance*. Stanford, CA: Stanford University Press.

Fisher, Louis. 1972. *President and Congress: Power and Policy*. New York: The Free Press.

Forsythe, Dall W. 1977. *Taxation and Political Change in the Young Nation, 1781–1833*. New York: Columbia University Press.

Frank, Charles R. Jr. 1979. *Foreign Trade and Domestic Aid*. Washington, D.C.: Brookings Institution.

Freidel, Frank B. 1970. *America in the Twentieth Century*. 2nd ed. New York: Alfred A. Knopf.

Friendly, Henry J. 1962. *The Federal Administrative Agencies*. Cambridge, Mass.: Harvard University Press.

Gardner, Lloyd C. 1964. *Economic Aspects of New Deal Diplomacy*. Madison, Wis.: University of Wisconsin Press.

——, ed. 1966. *A Different Frontier: Selected Readings in the Foundations of American Economic Expansion*. Chicago: Quadrangle Books.

Gardner, Richard N. 1969. *Sterling-Dollar Diplomacy: The Origins and the Prospects of Our International Economic Order*. Expanded ed. New York: McGraw-Hill.

Garraty, John A., ed. 1968. *The Transformation of American Society, 1870–1890*. Columbia: University of South Carolina Press.

Garson, G. David. 1978. *Group Theories of Politics*. Sage Library of Social Research, no. 61. Beverly Hills, Calif.: Sage.

Gawthrop, Louis C. 1970. *The Administrative Process and Democratic Theory*. Boston: Houghton Mifflin.

Gayer, Arthur D., and Carl T. Schmidt. 1929. *American Economic Foreign Policy*. New York: American Coordinating Committee for International Studies.

General Agreement on Tariffs and Trade. 1969. *Basic Instruments and Selected Documents* 4. Geneva: GATT.

George, Alexander L., and Richard Smoke. 1974. *Deterrence in American Foreign Policy: Theory and Practice*. New York: Columbia University Press.

Gerschenkron, Alexander. 1943. *Bread and Democracy in Germany*. Berkeley: University of California Press.

Gersting, J. Marshall. 1932. *The Flexible Provisions in the United States Tariff, 1922–1930*. Philadelphia: University of Pennsylvania Press.

Giddens, Anthony. 1979. *Central Problems in Social Theory: Action, Structure, and Contradiction in Social Analysis*. London: Macmillan.

——. 1981. *A Contemporary Critique of Historical Materialism*. Vol. 1. Berkeley: University of California Press.

——. 1984. *Constitution of Society: Outline of the Theory of Structuration*. Berkeley: University of California Press.

Gilpin, Robert. 1975. *U.S. Power and the Multinational Corporation*. New York: Basic Books.

——. 1987. *The Political Economy of International Relations*. Princeton, N.J.: Princeton University Press.

Ginger, Ray. 1965. *Age of Excess: The United States from 1876 to 1914*. New York: Macmillan.

Glassie, H. T. 1925. "The Tariff Commission and the Flexible Tariff." *Virginia Law Review* 11:329–435, 442–466.

Goldstein, Judith. 1993. *Ideas, Interests, and American Trade Policy*. Ithaca, N.Y.: Cornell University Press.

Gourevitch, Peter Alexis. 1977. "International Trade, Domestic Coalitions, and Liberty: Comparative Responses to the Crisis of 1873–1896." *Journal of Interdisciplinary History* 8:281–313.

——. 1984. "Breaking with Orthodoxy: The Politics of Economic Policy Responses to the Depression of the 1930s." *International Organization* 38:95–129.

Graebner, Norman A., ed. 1961. *An Uncertain Tradition: American Secretaries of State in the Twentieth Century*. New York: McGraw-Hill.

Graham, Otis L., Jr., ed. 1971. *The New Deal: The Critical Issues.* Boston: Little, Brown.

Greco, Joseph. 1988. "Anarchy and the Limits of Cooperation: A Realist Critique of the Newest Liberal Institutionalism." *International Organization* 42:485–507.

———. 1990. *Cooperation among Nations: Europe, America, and Non-Tariff Barriers to Trade.* Ithaca, N.Y.: Cornell University Press.

Gregory, T. E. 1921. *Tariffs: A Study in Method.* London: Charles Griffin and Co.

———. 1923. *Recent Tariff Changes and Their Probable Influence on British Trade.* London: Executive Committee of London and Cambridge Economic Service.

Hagan, Everett E. 1958. "An Economic Justification of Protectionism." *Quarterly Journal of Economics* 72:496–514.

Haggard, Stephan, and Beth A. Simmons. 1987. "Theories of International Regimes." *International Organization* 41:491–517.

Hamilton, Alexander. [1791] 1928. "Report on the Subject of Manufactures." In *Industrial and Commercial Correspondence of Alexander Hamilton, Anticipating His Report on Manufacturing,* edited by Arthur Harrison Cole. Chicago: A. W. Shaw.

Harris, Seymour E. 1948. *Foreign Economic Policy for the United States.* Cambridge, Mass.: Harvard University Press.

Hawke, G. R. 1975. "The United States Tariff and Industrial Protection in the Late Nineteenth Century." *Economic History Review,* 2nd ser., 28: 84–99.

Hawkins, Harry C., and Janet L. Norwood. 1962. "The Legislative Basis of United States Commercial Policy." In *Studies in United States Commercial Policy,* edited by William B. Kelly, Jr. Chapel Hill: University of North Carolina Press.

Hawkins, Robert G., and Ingo Walter. 1972. *The United States and International Markets: Commercial Policy Options in an Age of Controls.* Lexington, Mass.: D. C. Heath.

Hayes, Michael T. 1981. *Lobbyists and Legislators: A Theory of Political Markets.* New Brunswick, N.J.: Rutgers University Press.

Heclo, Hugh. 1974. *Modern Social Politics in Britain and Sweden.* New Haven, Conn.: Yale University Press.

Hicks, John D. 1960a. *Normalcy and Reaction, 1921–1933: An Age of Disillusionment.* Washington, D.C.: American History Association.

———. 1960b. *Republican Ascendancy, 1921–1933.* New York: Harper and Brothers.

Hirschman, Albert O. 1980. *National Power and the Structure of Foreign Trade.* Expanded ed. Berkeley: University of California Press.

Hogan, Michael J. 1977. *Informal Entente: The Private Structure of Cooperation in Anglo-American Economic Diplomacy, 1918–1928.* Columbia: University of Missouri Press.

Houston, David F. 1926. *Eight Years with Wilson's Cabinet.* Vol. 1. Garden City, N.Y.: Doubleday, Page.

Hudec, Robert E. 1975. *The GATT Legal System and World Trade Diplomacy.* New York: Praeger.

Hughes, Kent H. 1979. *Trade, Taxes, and Transnationals: International Economic Decision Making in Congress.* New York: Praeger.

Hull, Cordell. 1948. *Memoirs.* 2 vols. New York: Macmillan.

Humphrey, Don D. 1955. *American Imports*. New York: Twentieth Century Fund.

Huntington, Samuel P. 1962. "Congressional Responses to the Twentieth Century." In *The Congress and America's Future*, edited by David Truman. Englewood Cliffs, N.J.: Prentice-Hall.

————. 1968. *Political Order in Changing Societies*. New Haven, Conn.: Yale University Press.

————. 1982. "American Ideals versus American Institutions." *Political Science Quarterly* 97:1–37.

Hurst, James Willard. 1956. *Law and the Conditions of Freedom in the Late Nineteenth Century*. Madison: University of Wisconsin Press.

Hutcheson, John. 1978. *Dominance and Dependency: Liberalism and National Policies in the North Atlantic Triangle*. Toronto: McClenand and Stewart.

Ickes, Harold L. 1953. *The Secret Diary of Harold L. Ickes: The First Thousand Days, 1933–1936*. New York: Simon and Schuster.

International Monetary Fund. 1972, 1981. *International Financial Statistics, September 1972 and December 1981*. Washington, D.C.: Author.

Israel, Fred L., ed. 1966. *The State of the Union Messages of the Presidents, 1790–1966*. Vol. 3. New York: Chelsea House, Robert Hector Publishers.

Johnson, Harry G. 1958. *International Trade and Economic Growth*. London: George Allen and Unwin.

Jones, Charles O., and Randall B. Ripley. 1966. *The Role of Political Parties in Congress: A Bibliography and Research Guide*. Tuscon: University of Arizona Press.

Jones, Joseph M. 1934. *Tariff Retaliation: Repercussion of the Hawley-Smoot Bill*. Philadelphia: University of Pennsylvania Press.

Josephson, Matthew W. 1938. *The Politicos*. New York: Harcourt, Brace and World.

Katzenstein, Peter J., ed. 1978. *Between Power and Plenty: Foreign Economic Policies of Advanced Industrial States*. Madison: University of Wisconsin Press.

Kaufman, Burton L. 1974. *Efficiency and Expansion: Foreign Trade Organization in the Wilson Administration, 1913–1921*. Westport, Conn.: Greenwood Press.

————. 1982. *Trade and Aid: Eisenhower's Foreign Economic Policy, 1953–1961*. Baltimore: Johns Hopkins University Press.

Kelly, William B., Jr., ed. 1963. *Studies in U.S. Commercial Policy*. Chapel Hill: University of North Carolina Press.

Kenkel, Joseph F. 1983. *Progressives and Protection: The Search for a Tariff Policy, 1866–1936*. New York: University Press of America.

Keohane, Robert O. 1980. "The Theory of Hegemonic Stability and Changes in International Economic Regimes, 1967–1977." In *Change in the International System*, edited by Ole Holst, Randolph M. Siverson, and Alexander L. George. Boulder, Colo.: Westview.

————. 1984. *After Hegemony*. Cambridge, Mass.: Harvard University Press.

————. 1986. "Reciprocity in International Relations." *International Organization* 40:1–27.

Kindleberger, Charles P. 1962. *Foreign Trade and the National Economy*. New Haven, Conn.: Yale University Press.

————. 1973. *The World in Depression, 1919–1939*. Berkeley: University of California Press.

————. 1975. "The Rise of Free Trade in Western Europe, 1820–1875." *Journal of Economic History* 35:20–55.

————. 1976. "Systems of International Economic Organization." In *Money and the Coming World Order*, edited by David P. Calleo. New York: New York University Press.

————. 1981. "Dominance and Leadership in the International Economy." *International Studies Quarterly* 25:242–54.

————. 1986. "International Public Goods without International Government." *American Economic Review* 76:1–13.

Kindleberger, Charles P., and Peter H. Lindert. 1978. *International Economics*. 6th ed. Homewood, Ill.: Richard D. Irwin.

Kirkland, Edward C. 1961. *Industry Comes of Age: Business, Labor, and Public Policy, 1860–1897*. Vol. 6 of *The Economic History of the United States*. New York: Holt, Rinehart, and Winston.

Kolko, Gabriel. 1965. *Railroads and Regulation, 1877–1916*. Princeton, N.J.: Princeton University Press.

Kottman, Richard N. 1968. *Reciprocity and the North Atlantic Triangle, 1932–1938*. Ithaca, N.Y.: Cornell University Press.

Krasner, Stephen D. 1976. "State Power and the Structure of International Trade." *World Politics* 28:317–47.

————. 1978. *Defending the National Interest: Raw Materials Investments and U.S. Foreign Policy*. Princeton, N.J.: Princeton University Press.

————. 1979. "The Tokyo Round: Particularistic Interests and Prospects for Stability in the Global Trading System." *International Studies Quarterly* 23:491–531.

————. 1982a. "Regimes and the Limits of Realism: Regimes as Autonomous Variables." *International Organization* 36:497–510.

————. 1982b. "Structural Causes and Regime Consequences: Regimes as Intervening Variables." *International Organization* 36:185–205.

————. 1984. "Approaches to the State: Alternative Conceptions and Historical Dynamics." *Comparative Politics* 16:223–46.

————, ed. 1983. *International Regimes*. Ithaca, N.Y.: Cornell University Press.

Kraus, Melvyn B. 1978. *The New Protectionism: The Welfare State and International Trade*. New York: New York University Press.

Kreider, Carl. 1943. *The Anglo-American Trade Agreement: A Study of British and American Commercial Policies, 1934–1939*. Princeton, N.J.: Princeton University Press.

Krugman, Paul R. 1984. "Import Protection as Export Promotion." In *Monopolistic Competition and International Trade*, edited by H. Kierzkowski. Oxford: Oxford University Press.

————, ed. 1986. *Strategic Trade Policy and the New International Economics*. Cambridge, Mass.: MIT Press.

Kurth, James R. 1979. "The Political Consequences of the Product Cycle: Industrial History and Political Outcomes." *International Organization* 33:1–34.

Kuttner, Robert. 1990. "Managed Trade and Economic Sovereignty." In *International Trade: The Changing Role of the United States*, edited by Frank J. Macchiarola. New York: Academy of Political Science.

————. 1991. *The End of Laissez-faire*. New York: Alfred A. Knopf.

Kuznets, Simon. 1966. *Modern Economic Growth: Rate, Structure, and Spread*. New Haven, Conn.: Yale University Press.

La Follette, Robert M. 1953. *Autobiography*. Vol. 1. New York: Macmillan.

LaFeber, Walter. 1963. *The New Empire*. Ithaca, N.Y.: Cornell University Press.

Lake, David A. 1983. "International Economic Structures and American Foreign Economic Policy: 1897–1934." *World Politics* 35:517–43.

———. 1984. "Beneath the Commerce of Nations: A Theory of International Economic Structures." *International Studies Quarterly* 28:143–70.

———. 1988. *Power, Protection, and Free Trade: International Sources of U.S. Commercial Strategy, 1887–1939*. Ithaca, N.Y.: Cornell University Press.

Landis, James M. 1938. *The Administrative Process*. New Haven, Conn.: Yale University Press.

Larkin, John Day. 1936. *The President's Control of the Tariff*. Cambridge, Mass.: Harvard University Press.

Laughlin, J. Laurence, and Willus H. Parker. 1903. *Reciprocity*. New York: Baker and Taylor.

LaVergne, Real P. 1983. *The Political Economy of U.S. Tariffs*. Toronto: Academic Press.

Leddy, John M., and Janet L. Norwood. 1962. "The Escape Clause and Peril Points Under the Trade Agreements Program." In *Studies in United States Commercial Policy*, edited by William B. Kelly, Jr. Chapel Hill: University of North Carolina Press.

Leschier, Don D., and Elizabeth Brandeis. 1935. *History of Labor in the United States, 1896–1932*. New York: Macmillan.

Levitt, Barbara, and James G. March. 1988. "Organizational Learning." In *Annual Review of Sociology*, edited by W. Richard Scott and Judith Blake. Vol. 14. Palo Alto, Calif.: Annual Reviews Inc.

Levy, Jack S. 1994. "Learning and Foreign Policy: Sweeping a Conceptual Minefield." *International Organization* 48:279–312.

Lewin, K. 1947. "Group Decision and Social Change." In *Readings in Social Psychology*, edited by T. Newcomb and E. Hartley. New York: Henry Holt.

Lindblom, Charles E. 1977. *Politics and Markets: The World's Political-Economic Systems*. New York: Basic Books.

Link, Arthur S. 1947. *Wilson: The Road to the White House*. Princeton, N.J.: Princeton University Press.

———. 1954. *Woodrow Wilson and the Progressive Era: 1910–1917*. New York: Harper and Brothers.

———. 1956. *Wilson: The New Freedom*. Princeton, N.J.: Princeton University Press.

———. 1971. *The Higher Realism of Woodrow Wilson*. Nashville, Tenn.: Vanderbilt University Press.

Lippmann, Walter. 1914. *Drift and Mastery*. New York: Mitchell Kennerly.

Lipsey, Robert E. 1983. *Price and Quantity Trends in the Foreign Trade of the United States*. Princeton, N.J.: Princeton University Press.

Lipson, Charles. 1982. "The Transformation of Trade: The Sources and Effects of Regime Change." *International Organization* 36:417–55.

Lowi, Theodore J. 1964. "American Business, Public Policy, Case Studies, and Political Theory." *World Politics* 16:677–715.

———. 1967. "Party, Policy, and Constitution in America." In *The American Party Systems*, edited by William N. Chambers and Walter Dean Burnham. New York: Oxford University Press.

———. 1972. "Four Systems of Policy, Politics, and Choice." *Public Administration Review* 32:298–310.

————. 1979. *The End of Liberalism*. 2nd ed. New York: W. W. Norton.

Madison, James. [1788] 1981. "Federalist 51." In *The Federalist Papers* by Alexander Hamilton, James Madison, and John Jay. New York: New American Library of American Literature.

Malmgren, Harold B. 1972. *International Peacekeeping in Phase II*. New York: Quadrangle Books.

Manley, John F. 1970. *The Politics of Finance: The House Committee on Ways and Means*. Boston: Little, Brown.

Mathias, Peter. 1969. *The First Industrial Nation: An Economic History of Britain, 1700–1914*. London: Methuen.

Mayhew, David R. 1974. *Congress: The Electoral Connection*. New Haven, Conn.: Yale University Press.

McClure, Wallace A. 1924. *A New American Commercial Policy*. Studies in History, Economics, and Public Law, no. 255. New York: Longmans, Green.

————. 1941. *International Executive Agreements: Democratic Problems under the Constitution of the United States*. New York: Columbia University Press.

McKeown, Timothy J. 1986. "The Limitations of 'Structural' Theories of Commercial Policy." *International Organization* 40:43–64.

Meier, Gerald M. 1973. *Problems of Trade Policy*. New York: Oxford University Press.

Metzger, Stanley D. 1964. *Trade Agreements and the Kennedy Round*. Fairfax, Va.: Corner Publications.

————. 1974. *Lowering Nontariff Barriers: U.S. Laws, Practice, and Negotiating Objectives*. Washington, D.C.: Brookings Institution.

Milner, Helen V. 1988. *Resisting Protectionism: Global Industries and the Politics of International Trade*. Princeton, N.J.: Princeton University Press.

Moe, Terry. 1987. "Institutions, Interests, and Positive Theory: The Politics of the NLRB." *Studies in American Political Development* 2:236–99.

Mohr, Lawrence B. 1969. "Determinants of Innovation in Organization." *American Political Science Review* 63:111–26.

Moley, Raymond. 1939. *After Seven Years*. New York: Harper and Brothers.

Moore, James R. 1974. "Sources of New Deal Economic Policy: The International Dimension." *Journal of American History* 61:728–44.

Moore, John Bassett. 1905. "Treaties and Executive Agreements." *Political Science Quarterly* 20:388–420.

Mowry, George E. 1946. *Theodore Roosevelt and the Progressive Movement*. Madison: University of Wisconsin Press.

————. 1958. *The Era of Theodore Roosevelt*. New York: Harper and Row.

National Association of Manufacturers. 1909. *Proceedings of the Fourteenth Annual Convention of the National Association of Manufacturers of the United States of America*. New York: Secretary's Office (NAM).

Nordlinger, Eric A. 1981. *On the Autonomy of the Democratic State*. Cambridge, Mass.: Harvard University Press.

O'Halloran, Sharyn. 1994. *Politics, Process, and American Trade Policy*. Ann Arbor: University of Michigan Press.

Olson, Mancur. 1965. *The Logic of Collective Action*. Cambridge, Mass.: Harvard University Press.

————. 1982. *The Rise and Decline of Nations: Economic Growth, Stagnation, and Social Rigidities*. New Haven, Conn.: Yale University Press.

Orfield, Gary. 1975. *Congressional Power: Congress and Social Change*. New York: Harcourt, Brace, Jovanovich.

Orren, Karen. 1991. *Belated Feudalism: Labor, the Law, and Liberal Development in the United States*. New York: Cambridge University Press.

Orren, Karen, and Stephen Skowronek. 1991. "Beyond the Iconography of Order: Notes for a 'New' Institutionalism." Paper presented at the Annual Meetings of the American Political Science Association, Washington, D.C., August 30.

Osborne, David, and Ted Gaebler. 1992. *Reinventing Government: How the Entrepreneurial Spirit Is Transforming the Public Sector*. Reading, Mass.: Addison-Wesley.

Page, Thomas Walker. 1924. *Making the Tariff in the United States*. New York: McGraw-Hill.

Parker, George F., ed. 1892. *The Writings and Speeches of Grover Cleveland*. New York: Cassell.

Parkinson, J. F., N. A. M. MacKenzie, and T. W. I. MacDermot. 1944. *Canada in World Affairs; The Prewar Years*. Toronto: Oxford University Press.

Partini, Carl P. 1969. *Heir to Empire: United States Economic Diplomacy, 1916–1923*. Pittsburgh, Pa.: University of Pittsburgh Press.

Pastor, Robert A. 1980. *Congress and the Politics of U.S. Foreign Economic Policy, 1929–1976*. Berkeley: University of California Press.

Peck, George N., and Sanford Crowther. 1936. *Why Quit Our Own?* New York: Van Nostrand.

Penrose, F. I. 1953. *Economic Planning for the Peace*. Princeton, N.J.: Princeton University Press.

Peterson, S. A. 1985. "Neurophysiology, Cognition, and Political Thinking." *Political Psychology* 6:495–518.

Pincus, Jonathan J. 1977. *Pressure Groups and Politics in Antebellum Tariffs*. New York: Columbia University Press.

Piquet, Howard S. 1958. *The Trade Agreements Act and the National Interest*. Washington, D.C.: Brookings Institution.

Polsby, Nelson W. 1968. "The Institutionalization of the U.S. House of Representatives." *American Political Science Review* 62:144–68.

Preeg, Ernest H. 1970. *Traders and Diplomats*. Washington, D.C.: Brookings Institution.

Pringle, Henry F. 1964. *The Life and Times of William Howard Taft*. 2 vols. Hamden, Conn.: Archon Books.

Puchala, Donald J., and Raymond F. Hopkins. 1982. "International Regimes: Lessons from Inductive Analysis." *International Organization* 36:245–76.

Putnam, Robert D. 1988. "Diplomacy and Domestic Politics: The Logic of Two-Level Games." *International Organization* 42:428–60.

Ratner, Sidney. 1972. *The Tariff in American History*. New York: Van Nostrand.

Reich, Robert B. 1991. *The Work of Nations*. New York: Alfred A. Knopf.

Reichard, Gary W. 1975. *The Reaffirmation of Republicanism: Eisenhower and the Eighty-Third Congress*. Knoxville, Tenn.: University of Tennessee Press.

Rhodes, Carolyn. 1993. *Reciprocity, U.S. Trade Policy, and the GATT Regime*. Ithaca, N.Y.: Cornell University Press.

Richardson, J. David. 1990. "The Political Economy of Strategic Trade Policy." *International Organization* 44:107–35.

Richardson, James D., ed. 1897–1914. *A Compilation of Messages and Papers of the Presidents*. 18 vols. New York: Bureau of National Literature.

Robinson, James A. 1967. *Congressional Foreign Policymaking: A Study in Legislative Influence*. Rev. ed. Homewood, Ill.: Dorsey Press.

Roosevelt, Theodore. 1910. *The New Nationalism*. New York: Outlook Co.

Rosenau, James N. 1968. "National Interest." *International Encyclopedia of the Social Sciences*. Vol. 2. New York: Macmillan.

Rothman, David J. 1966. *Politics and Power: The United States Senate, 1869–1901*. Cambridge, Mass.: Harvard University Press.

Ruggie, John Gerard. 1975. "International Responses to Technology: Concepts and Trends." *International Organization* 29:557–83.

———. 1982. "International Regimes, Transactions, and Change: Embedded Liberalism in the Postwar Economic Order." *International Organization* 36: 379–415.

Russett, Bruce M. 1963. *Community and Contention: Britain and America in the Twentieth Century*. Cambridge, Mass.: MIT Press.

Sayre, Francis Bowes. 1939. *The Way Forward: The American Trade Agreements Program*. New York: Macmillan.

Schattschneider, E. E. 1935. *Politics, Pressures, and the Tariff*. New York: Prentice-Hall.

———. 1942. *Party Government*. New York: Rinehart.

———. 1960. *The Semi-Sovereign People: A Realist's View of Democracy in America*. New York: Holt, Rinehart, and Winston.

Schlesinger, Arthur M., Jr. 1958. *The Age of Roosevelt: The Coming of the New Deal*. Boston: Houghton Mifflin.

Schmitter, Philippe. 1977. "Modes of Interest Intermediation and Modes of Societal Change in Western Europe." *Comparative Political Study* 10:7–38.

Schriftgiesoer, Karl. 1951. *The Lobbyists: The Art and Business of Influencing Lawmakers*. Boston: Little, Brown.

Schuyler, Eugene. 1886. *American Diplomacy and the Furtherance of Commerce*. New York: Charles Scribner's Sons.

Semmel, Bernard. 1970. *The Rise of Free Trade Imperialism: Classical Political Economy, the Empire of Free Trade and Imperialism, 1750–1850*. Cambridge: Cambridge University Press.

Shefter, Martin. 1978. "Party, Bureaucracy, and Political Change in the United States." In *Political Parties: Development and Decay*, edited by Louis Maisel and Joseph Cooper. Beverly Hills, Calif.: Sage.

Shepsle, Kenneth A. 1988. "Representation and Governance: The Great Legislative Trade-Off." *Political Science Quarterly* 103:401–84.

Shepsle, Kenneth A., and Barry R. Weingast. 1984. "When Do Rules of Procedure Matter?" *Journal of Politics* 46:206–21.

———. 1985. "Policy Consequences of Government by Congressional Subcommittees." *Proceedings of the Academy of Political Science* 35:114–31.

———. 1987. "The Institutional Foundations of Committee Power." *American Political Science Review* 81:85–104.

Shonfield, Andrew. 1965. *Modern Capitalism: The Changing Balance of Public and Private Power*. London: Oxford University Press.

Sinclair, Andrew. 1966. *Available Man: The Life Behind the Mask of Warren G. Harding*. New York: Macmillan.

Skocpol, Theda, and Kenneth Finegold. 1982. "Economic Intervention and the Early New Deal." *Political Science Quarterly* 97:255–78.

Skowronek, Stephen L. 1982. *Building a New American State: The Expansion of National Administrative Capacities*. New York: Cambridge University Press.

———. 1984. "Presidential Leadership in Political Time." In *The Presidency and the Political System*, edited by Michael Nelson. Washington, D.C.: Congressional Quarterly Press.

————. 1993. *The Politics Presidents Make: Leadership from John Adams to George Bush*. Cambridge, Mass.: Belknap.

Slemp, C. Beacon, ed. 1926. *Mind of the President*. Garden City, N.Y.: Doubleday, Page.

Soward, F. H., J. F. Parkinson, N. A. M. MacKenzie, and T. W. L. MacDermot. 1941. *Canada in World Affairs: The Prewar Years*. Toronto: Oxford University Press.

Spencer, Barbara J. 1986. "What Should Trade Policy Target?" In *Strategic Trade Policy and the New International Economics*, edited by Paul Krugman. Cambridge, Mass.: MIT Press.

Stanwood Edward. 1903. *American Tariff Controversies in the Nineteenth Century*. 2 vols. Boston: Houghton Mifflin.

Stebbins, Richard, ed. 1964. *Documents on American Foreign Relations, 1961*. New York: Harper and Row.

Stein, Arthur A. 1984. "The Hegemon's Dilemma: Great Britain, the United States, and the International Economic Order." *International Organization* 38:355–86.

————. 1990. *Why Nations Cooperate: Circumstance and Choice in International Relations*. Ithaca, N.Y.: Cornell University Press.

Stewart, Gordon T. 1982. "A Special Contiguous Country Economic Regime: An Overview of America's Commercial Policy." *Diplomatic History* 6:339–57.

Stone, N. I. 1952. *One Man's Crusade for an Honest Tariff: The Story of Herbert E. Miles, Father of the Tariff Commission*. Appleton, Wis.: Lawrence College Press.

Strange, Susan. 1985. "Protectionism and World Politics." *International Organization* 39:233–59.

Summers, Festus P. 1953. *William L. Wilson and Tariff Reform*. New Brunswick, N.J.: Rutgers University Press.

Tarbell, Ida M. 1911. *The Tariff of Our Times*. New York: Macmillan.

Tasca, Henry J. 1938. *The Reciprocal Trade Policy of the United States*. Philadelphia: University of Pennsylvania Press.

Taussig, F. W. 1888. *The Tariff History of the United States*. New York: G. P. Putnam's Sons.

————. 1910. *The Tariff History of the United States*. 5th edition. New York: G. P. Putnam's Sons.

————. 1915. *Some Aspects of the Tariff Question*. Cambridge, Mass.: Harvard University Press.

————. 1920. *Free Trade, the Tariff, and Reciprocity*. New York: Macmillan.

————. 1931. *The Tariff History of the United States*. 8th edition. New York: G. P. Putnam's Sons.

————. 1933. "Necessary Changes in Our Commercial Policy." *Foreign Affairs* 11:397–405.

Terrill, Tom E. 1973. *The Tariff, Politics, and American Foreign Policy, 1874–1901*. Westport, Conn.: Greenwood Press.

Thurrow, Lester C. 1992. *Head to Head: The Coming Economic Battle among Japan, Europe, and America*. New York: William Morrow.

Tilly, Charles, ed. 1975. *The Formation of National States in Western Europe*. Princeton, N.J.: Princeton University Press.

Truman, David B. 1951. *The Governmental Process.* New York: Alfred Knopf.
Tugwell, Rexford G. 1957. *The Democratic Roosevelt.* Garden City, N.Y.: Double-day.
Tyson, Laura D. 1992. *Who's Beating Whom? Trade Conflict in High Technology Industries.* Washington, D.C.: Institute for International Economics.
United Nations Economic Commission of Europe. 1949. *A Survey of the Economic Situation and Prospects of Europe, 1948.* Geneva: United Nations.
U.S. Bureau of the Census. 1960. *Historical Statistics of the United States: Colonial Times to 1957.* Washington, D.C.: Government Printing Office.
U.S. Commission on Foreign Economic Policy. 1954. *Report to the President and the Congress.* Washington, D.C.: Government Printing Office.
U.S. Commission on International Trade and Investment Policy. 1971. *United States International Economic Policy in an Interdependent World.* Vol. 1. Washington, D.C.: Government Printing Office.
U.S. Congress. 1961. Joint Economic Committee, Subcommittee on Foreign Economic Policy. *Hearings.* 87th Cong., 1st sess.
U.S. House. 1937. *Report to Accompany H.J. Res. 90,* Rep. no 166. 75th Cong., 1st sess.
U.S. House, Committee on Ways and Means. 1934. *Reciprocal Trade Agreements: Hearings on H.R. 8420.* 73rd Cong., 2nd sess.
———. 1948. *Report to Accompany H.R. 6556.* 80th Cong., 2nd sess.
———. 1962. *Hearings on the Trade Expansion Act.* 87th Cong., 2nd sess.
U.S. Industrial Commission. 1900–1902. *Reports of the U.S. Industrial Commission.* 19 vols. Washington, D.C.: Government Printing Office.
U.S. Senate. 1922. *Senate Report, no 595.* 67th Cong., 2nd sess.
———. 1937. *Report to Accompany H.J. Res. 90,* Rep. no. 111. 75th Cong., 1st sess.
U.S. Senate, Committee on Finance. 1951. *Hearings on H.R. 1612.* 82nd Cong., 1st sess.
———. 1962. *Hearings on the Trade Expansion Act.* 87th Cong., 2nd sess.
U.S. Tariff Commission. 1882. *Report of the Tariff Commission Appointed Under Act of Congress Approved May 15, 1882.* 2 vols. Washington, D.C.: Government Printing Office.
———. 1917–1929. *First Annual Report through Thirteenth Annual Report.* Washington, D.C.: Government Printing Office.
———. 1919. *Reciprocity and Commercial Treaties.* Washington, D.C.: Government Printing Office.
———. 1921. *American Valuation.* Washington, D.C.: Government Printing Office.
———. 1922. *Report on the Emergency Tariff Act of May 27, 1921.* Rev. ed. Washington, D.C.: Government Printing Office.
———. 1923a. *Dictionary of Tariff Information.* Washington, D.C.: Government Printing Office.
———. 1923b. *Handbook of Commercial Treaties.* Washington, D.C.: Government Printing Office.
———. 1924. *Wheat and Wheat Products.* Washington, D.C.: Government Printing Office.
———. 1926. *Sugar.* Washington, D.C.: Government Printing Office.
———. 1933. *Tariff Bargaining under the Most-Favored-Nation Treaties.* Washington, D.C.: Government Printing Office.

————. 1937. *Reciprocal Trade: A Current Bibliography.* 3rd ed. Washington, D.C.: Government Printing Office.

————. 1949. *Operation of the Trade Agreements Program, June 1934–April 1948.* Washington, D.C.: Government Printing Office.

————. 1962. *Operation of the Trade Agreements Programs.* 4th Report. Washington, D.C.: Government Printing Office.

Viner, Jacob. 1966. *Dumping: A Problem in International Trade.* New York: Augustus M. Kelley.

Waltz, Kenneth N. 1979. *Theory of International Politics.* Reading, Mass.: Addison-Wesley.

Warren, Harris Gaylord. 1967. *Herbert Hoover and the Great Depression.* New York: W. W. Norton.

Wayne, Stephen J. 1978. *The Legislative Presidency.* New York: Harper and Row.

Well, Gordon L. 1975. *American Trade Policy: New Round.* New York: Twentieth Century Fund.

Wendt, Alexander. 1992. "Anarchy Is What States Make of It: The Social Construction of Power Politics." *International Organization* 46:392–425.

White, William A. 1938. *A Puritan in Babylon: The Story of Calvin Coolidge.* New York: Macmillan.

Wiebe, Robert H. 1962. *Businessmen and Reform.* Cambridge, Mass.: Harvard University Press.

Wilcox, Clair. 1949. *A Charter for World Trade.* New York: Macmillan.

Wildavsky, Aaron B. 1986. *Budgeting: A Comparative Theory of Budgeting Processes.* 2nd rev. ed. New Brunswick, N.J.: Transaction Books.

Wilensky, Norman M. 1965. *Conservatives in the Progressive Era.* Gainsville: University of Florida Press.

Williams, Benjamin H. 1967. *Economic Foreign Policy of the United States.* New York: Howard Fertig.

Williams, William Appleman. 1969. *The Roots of the Modern American Empire.* New York: Random House.

Wilson, James Q. 1966. "Innovation in Organization: Notes toward a Theory." In *Approaches to Organizational Design,* edited by J. D. Thompson. Pittsburgh, Pa.: University of Pittsburgh Press.

————, ed. 1980. *The Politics of Regulation.* New York: Basic Books.

Wilson, Joan Hoff. 1971. *American Business and Foreign Policy, 1920–1933.* Lexington: University Press of Kentucky.

————. 1975. *Herbert Hoover: Forgotten Progressive.* Boston: Little, Brown.

Wilson, Woodrow. 1916. *The New Freedom.* London: J. M. Dent.

————. 1921. *Constitutional Government in the United States.* New York: Columbia University Press.

————. 1924. *The Messages and Papers of Woodrow Wilson.* Vol. 1. New York: Review of Reviews.

————. 1925. *Public Papers of Woodrow Wilson.* 6 vols. New York: Harper and Brothers.

Wood, Gordon S. 1969. *The Creation of the American Republic, 1776–1787.* Chapel Hill: University of North Carolina Press.

Woody, Carroll H. 1934. *The Growth of the Federal Government.* New York: McGraw-Hill.

Yarbrough, Beth V., and Robert M. Yarbrough. 1987. "Cooperation in the Liberalization of International Trade: After Hegemony, What?" *International Organization* 41:1–26.

Yeager, Mary. 1980. "Trade Protection as an International Commodity: The Case of Steel." *Journal of Economic History* 40:33–42.

Young, James Sterling. 1966. *The Washington Community*. New York: Columbia University Press.

Zysman, John. 1983. *Governments, Markets, and Growth: Financial Systems and the Politics of Industrial Change*. Ithaca, N.Y.: Cornell University Press.

Zysman, John, and Laura Tyson, eds. 1983. *American Industry in International Competition*. Ithaca, N.Y.: Cornell University Press.

UNIVERSITY PRESS OF NEW ENGLAND publishes books under its own imprint and is the publisher for Brandeis University Press, Dartmouth College, Middlebury College Press, University of New Hampshire, University of Rhode Island, Tufts University, University of Vermont, Wesleyan University Press, and Salzburg Seminar.

Library of Congress Cataloging-in-Publication Data
Hody, Cynthia Ann, 1955–
    The politics of trade : American political development and foreign economic policy / by Cynthia A. Hody.
        p.   cm. — (The Nelson A. Rockefeller series in social science and public policy)
    Includes bibliographical references and index.
    ISBN 0-87451-729-x (alk. paper)
        1. Free trade—United States—History—20th century.   2. United States—Commercial policy—History—20th century.   3. United States—Foreign economic relations—History—20th century.
    4. International trade—History—20th century.   5. United States—Politics and government—20th century—Decision making.   I. Title.
    II. Series.
    HF1716.H63   1996
    382'.71'0973—dc20   95–8765
    ⊗